CREATURE COMFORT

From a veterinarian's journal

People caring for pets –
pets caring for people

James D. Stowe, D.V.M.

CREATURE COMFORT

From a veterinarian's journal

People caring for pets –
pets caring for people

James D. Stowe, D.V.M.

Illustrations by Darren James Stowe

Published by
Veredus Inc. Canada

Canadian Cataloguing in Publication Data

Stowe, James D.
Creature Comfort: from a veterinarian's journal
Includes bibliographical references and index.

ISBN 0-9682388-0-7

1. Pet medicine - Popular works.
I. Stowe, Darren James.
II. Title.
SF613.S77A3 1997   636.089   C97-931580-8

Credits
Book Production by **Culture Concepts Inc.**
Front & Back Cover Photography by **The Silver Parrot**, Port Dover, Ontario Canada.
Graphic Animation by **Rebecca Brebner**, Lifelearn Inc., Guelph, Ontario Canada.

Printed and Bound in Canada.

Dedication

To Bill and Mom
Your laughter and compassion fill these pages

Acknowledgments

A book like this is a personal symphony that blends the lyric of the written word with the melody of life's experience. I would never have been able to compose this score had I not met several of the instrumentalists in my concerto. The list includes friends and clients who have enjoyed and suffered with me the tunes and dirges of their animals' lives. I am particularly grateful to a client who became a good friend, a storyteller and a true lover of nature and its beasts -- Chuck Powell. Chuck had helped immensely with both moral support and sharing of stories to help make this album sing with laughter. And in the wings, the counsel, encouragement and hours of editorial review by Thelma Barer-Stein helped to bring this to your hands.

I take great pride in the veterinary profession, having met thousands of practitioners, scores of dedicated hospital staff and visited hundreds of practices. There is harmony with this earth when it is peopled with 'musicians' who love animals, the so-called lower orders. I am especially grateful to Dr. Brian Wicks for his review of this material and Dr. Wayne Bagnell for sharing experiences.

My family has always been my string section, giving comfort and stability whenever life gets out of tune. This is evidenced tangibly in the sketches by my son, Darren.

The choir of this piece has been the chorus of animals I have met and treated. The divas and tenors have been my own pets that have laid their heads under my hand as my personal friends and companions, from Rusty my first dog when I was six years of age, to current pals, Cody and Pud.

It is the unconditional love of pets, friends and family that can instill empathy into the heart and soul. Nothing but music can result.

James D. Stowe, D.V.M.
Simcoe, Ontario

CREATURE COMFORT
Contents
Preface

Dr. Larry Patrick Tilley, the 1989 American Animal Hospital Association 'Veterinarian of the Year', and one of the most prolific authors of textbooks on Internal Medicine and Cardiology for the veterinary profession — internationally renowned as an educator - confers applause for the author and his offering.

Prelude...

...The search for creature comfort

The human animal is constantly seeking the 'meaning of life'. Every other species lives day to day, moment to moment perhaps oblivious to justified existence. Bridging the chasm between humankind's rush to the edge of the cliff and the serenity of understanding this hectic world, is the warm nose of a dog or cat nuzzled close to your side. Your pet is seeking creature comfort from you, and offering a truckload of unconditional love in return.

Chapter One

February 15:   At The Ark and Bark.

Unique to this book, each chapter follows appointments taken from the daily schedule of the Ark and Bark Animal Clinic. Set in Heron Point, a small fictional town on the north shore of Lake Ontario, Dr. Jonathan Runcibal recounts the days events, specific ones highlighted on the day sheet. Unforgettable characters and animal stories, like Dr. Dave 'Trip' Tripper; and the Muscovy duck and his 'famous phallus', bring the clinic to life.

Chapter Two

March 10:   Love is a four-legged word.

An important puppy comes to the hospital to be put to sleep. He and his mother had been struck by a train. Dr. Runcibal cannot bring himself to close such a tragic, compelling pair of eyes. Puppy and kitten care is established as the first of many lessons to follow on responsible pet ownership. Anecdotes from the appointment pad highlight the joys and stresses of a busy day in an animal hospital. We meet the loquacious Nathan Biddle and are tripped up by another Trip misadventure.

Chapter Three

May 23:   Tighter, titer.

Boz Budgie's tale comes to a dramatic ending and we follow the clinicians through the hectic day that ensues. Canine characters today include a Spooky German Shepherd and Ruby the Red Setter. The mystery of the mynah bird that won't stop talking is solved. The pet owner is given a synopsis of vaccinations needed by dogs and cats.

Chapter Four

June 5 :   Tempest in a teacup.

A determined Canada goose, broken wing or not, is determined to walk north. Samaritans on the road and in the hospital revise his destiny. Brush a dog's teeth? You've got to be kidding! In addition to fundamentals of dental care we are also advised of the basic training needed by dogs — and your cat is taught how to train a human! A teacup Chihuahua is brought in by a mutable Major and we meet the pony who thought he was a dog. Mrs. Flitz, introduced in an earlier chapter, returns with more problems, not all of them pet related and a 'smiling dog' stops a robbery.

Preface
by Dr. Larry Patrick Tilley.

As an educator and specialist in canine and feline internal medicine, I am particularly pleased to write the introduction to this book, Creature Comfort, by James D. Stowe. Drawing on his background as a veterinary practitioner and well-recognized for innovations in veterinary continuing education, he has introduced an inventive book for the pet owner that is both authoritative and practical. Both his extensive experience as a practitioner and his expertise in adult education come across clearly and provide a comprehensive review of the most important aspects of canine and feline veterinary care.

Dr. Stowe's consistent, pragmatic approach to pet owner edification in the care of their pets is emphasized throughout the book to provide a continuity that will be appreciated by all pet owners. The format of the book is unique, giving the reader some understanding of the workings of a veterinary hospital. Further, the humorous, touching and sometimes tragic stories illustrate important points in responsible pet care. These engaging anecdotes help readers learn what they need to know as pet owners. There is especially useful advice on just when to call the local veterinarian.

I have many pet care books on my bookshelf — but now I have one that finally meets the needs of the pet owner.

I had a difficult time putting this book down, as the lifelike stories from a typical veterinary practice are most entertaining. The added bonuses are the principles of preventive pet care on puppy and kitten health, vaccination requirements, care of the young, adult, middle-aged, and geriatric dog and cat — and then that very difficult time when a pet has to be put to sleep. Chapters seven and eight illustrate Dr. Stowe's love of pets and his evident empathy for the pet owner.

His principles are always drawn from actual clinical experience, keeping the focus of the book throughout where it should be — on the pet owner and the pet which may be suffering. One of my own major educational objectives in veterinary medicine has been to foster an understanding of medicine as a profession and as a personal human experience. Dr. Stowe has successfully reached this goal in this brilliant book.

This book also provides some excellent general beliefs as a guide and an inspiration to veterinarians in practice as they pursue the healing of their patients. Dr. Stowe has written a book filled with compassion and insight, not only for the pet owner but also for a broad scope of people involved in veterinary care. With this book, he has helped pet owners make their experience with medicine both joyous and a way to demonstrate the harmonious relationship of the healing interaction between humans and their pets. Need I say more?

Editor's Note:

Dr. Larry Tilley is a Diplomate of the American College of Veterinary Internal Medicine (Internal Medicine). He is author of over 200 papers and nine textbooks. His latest, The Five Minute Consult, is published by Williams and Wilkins. Internationally known, Dr. Tilley's books have been translated into several languages including Japanese, Italian, Spanish, German and Iranian. In 1992, Dr. Tilley hosted "Attitudes" a Lifetime television series of weekly programs on veterinary medicine. Currently he is President of VetMedFax Consultation Service in Sante Fe, New Mexico. A teacher, educator and leader in veterinary diagnostics through transtelephonic technology, Dr. Tilley is one of the profession's most respected alumni.

A puppy's love...

Prelude...
The search for creature comfort

My first best friend

Rusty. He was my first dog. My first best friend. I can still see his deep brown penetrating eyes looking up at me. A look that I can only translate as love and companionship. Rusty was a blonde Cocker Spaniel with soft fur and long ears and a tail that
started as a ripple in a pond to eventually become a total body tidal wave of wagging
dog. I was only five years old.

I can still see the accident. Before my eyes Rusty was struck by a hit and run driver
and killed instantly. The shock, pain, tears, anger, disbelief and emptiness are still
within me forty nine years later. I'm certain that Rusty was one of the reasons that I
became a veterinarian. The helplessness that I felt as I saw my best friend lifted from
the road by my father was unbearable. I thought that I would never be able to have
a dog again.

Certainly I could never replace that special bond that I had with Rusty. But as the
years went by I found that I could indeed find the friendship, love and companionship of several furry creatures. What followed as I grew older were Mr. Chips, Lucky,
Jiggs, Hobo, Lollipop, Spook, Cody and Pud. They all helped shape my respect for
animals and the desire to become an animal doctor. I enjoyed 18 years of practice
and eight years consulting with my colleagues and developing educational programs
for the profession.

If we adapt to the world, it will befriend us.

This too can best be described as the new age answer to finding spirituality through
Rover and Felix (or rather our modern-day Arnold and Sly). I say this in seriousness
though my tongue is deeply imbedded in cheek. It seems that we have evolved in
the developed world to the stage indigent peoples had achieved eons before us.
Humans now seek self-fulfillment through diet, crystals and tarot. Veterinarians can
tell you that many pet owners worship their pets. Why that's not new! Ancient
Egyptians worshipped cats centuries before.

Native Americans were one with nature until so-called civilized man came here and
ravaged it. Contemporary humans though, seem to be getting the message. If we
adapt to the world it will befriend us. If we destroy the environment we destroy our
own home. Rather than worship animals, it makes more sense to take care of them

well. We will subsequently benefit from their companionship.

Why are we afflicted with this affection for the lower species? Could it be that we relish the dominance over the four-legged? Perhaps so for a few. In my view we have evolved to a state closer to equilibrium with the earth — at least those of us who love animals. (At least those of us who love animals as we love mankind, not those who love animals to the exclusion of mankind.) Mind you, we have not reached equilibrium with the universe. That's going to take one heck of a lot more evolution.

Comfort and unconditional love.

Animal lovers have been seeking the comfort that animals provide to shield them from the barrage of modern consequence. That stabilizing force is the pat along the crown of a dog's head or the stroke under the chin of a purring cat. We can truly express 'love' for these beasts. Even better, they love us back regardless of our imperfections! This is the true descriptor for unconditional love. We can scold Cody for digging up the flower garden. He'll be back nonetheless to nuzzle his nose towards our previous-pointing-fingers for a pat. We can shout at Panther for scream-ing at the moon in the middle of the night but he will be playfully tapping the cov-ers fluttering by our snoring breath in the morning.

To care for these precious companions we take them to the veterinarian. This is a relatively modern phenomenon. Cats and dogs used to be expendable. They used to be kept outside. Now they are not only invited across the hearth, they are wel-comed at the table. Mother still has words to say about this though. Many veterinary clinics see the same pets two or three times a year. Is this really necessary? You bet your boots! By seeking out the best care in the world for these new found friends we achieve comfort for ourselves.

Creature Comfort has been written to provide a link between a James Herriot world where the pace of life was slower, idyllic and not fraught with information overload. The coming millennium will generate a library of volumes relative to the care of pets. This book will not provide you with encyclopedic solutions for everything about pets. It will provide you with what you need to know as a pet owner. It will also give you a guide for working with your veterinarian towards responsible preventive medicine.

Three egos and two themes

In this book, I decided to divide my persona into three alter egos: the experienced owner of a veterinary practice, the younger ambitious associate, and my 'feminine side'. Each of the three characters allows me to cover feelings and experiences that I have had in veterinary practice over the years. By thrusting my mind into a feminine image I can attempt to understand some of the issues that have confronted my female colleagues, although I realize that this may never be accurate given the bias of the male psyche.

This book has two themes. One is a romp through dozens of anecdotes from experiences in veterinary practice. The other is a rationalization of how and why we must care for these creatures. I have created a composite veterinary practice, complete with composite veterinarians. The stories are real. Characters have been fabricated so as to embarrass no one. Animals do not get embarrassed so their character is intact.

This text comes with the required caveat. Veterinary science is not only a dynamic, ever-changing entity but one that encompasses simply too much information for any one person to comprehend, remember, understand, relate. What I write is my opinion based on 18 years of practice and eight years developing educational programs for practitioners. Disagreement is not only inevitable, it is desirable. I propose a course of care that I would provide to my own pets. Colleagues may have other insights or biases that preclude offering the same advice. Neither is wrong, only different, based on opinions and experience. Put ten experts of any profession in a room and ask the same question and you'll get ten differing (not different) responses. It is the mode of teaching the fundamentals of what you need to know as a pet owner that I hope is effective in this book.

"Stay away from animals"

Allergies. On a bitter cold December day in a Respiratory Clinic in Toronto a specialist with less than a modicum of compassion explained that I was to "Stay away from animals!" He either didn't read my chart or it wasn't entered that my career was the care of animals. That was 20 years ago. I stayed in practice despite the warning, for as long as possible. I found other opportunities within my chosen profession to keep me involved with my love of animals. I pursued the axiom that when one door closes, others open and found it to be true. I've met some of the best clinicians, teachers and business professionals along this circuitous veterinary career. Yet my most memorable experiences remain with those pets, cows, horses, birds, wildlife, and the loving people who cared for them. Creature Comfort is a testament to the bond between human and animal. A bond that started with me years ago. With Rusty.

James D. Stowe, D.V.M.
Simcoe, Ontario

WELCOME

Come and meet our staff

Welcome to The Ark and Bark Clinic ...come and meet the staff...

"Ark and Bark Animal Clinic, May I help you?"....

"Arrrooowrrroorrrooo" ...thwack, thwack, thwack...

"Baaarrrnnn..."...thwack, thwack, thwack, thwack...

I am greeted with strange, familiar sounds as I stomp clumps of snow from knee-length farm boots at the side entrance to the veterinary hospital. The phone conversation registers to my mind, the commotion begs investigation. To seek out the source of the peculiar moans and thumps, I follow the noise to the front of the clinic. Peering over the counter into the waiting room I still hear the clamor, but see no one.

Until I lean well over the ledge. There in the corner of the waiting room sits Gerald and Barney. There's Gerald Shelby, a six-foot-four retired consulting engineer, squatting Hindu style in the far corner with Barney, his abbreviate-legged Basset climbing happily all over him, licking his face and chewing his ears. Mr. Shelby, standing, would stoop to get through most doorways. He looks much like the geriatric Jimmy Stewart, but with a much more robust voice that booms...

"Baaarrney, oh yeah, Baarrnn," he continues as Barney's tail thwacked the chairs beside them. Mr. Shelby noticed me staring. "Oh, sorry, Doctor. Don't mind me. I'm a little early for Barney's appointment. We took our morning constitutional by walking to the clinic. Claire is going to be here by ten, she went downtown for a few groceries." Claire was his wife, smaller in stature, tolerant of the devotion between her two pets.

Here was an archetypal consequence of affection for an animal. This was a man who had executives around the world groveling at his every command. Now he is reduced — no, aggrandized — to an uninhibited, contented and fulfilled human being.

Just watching people truly enjoying their pets keeps those in a veterinary hospital gratified. I smiled and nodded my approval of their frolic, quietly wishing that I could join their joyous romp. But duty forces a return to the appointment scheduler to peruse the stories that would be played out today.

Leslie, the receptionist slash book-keeper, slash animal health technician, is the anchor of this modern-day ark, who keeps it from drifting into oblivion. She's the only one who remembers client names, pet names, directions to the farms, and where I left my stethoscope ("It's still around your neck Jonathan!").

Jonathan Runcibal was my name before entering the Veterinary College in Guelph. It's been twenty years since I first heard the salutation for which I had worked so diligently, 'Doctor Runcibal.' After spending a couple of years scraping the green-ness from my professional persona, I started this clinic in Heron Point. It was summer of 1972. The town of 12,400 people and 34,700 animals, sits on a promontory into the North Shore of Lake Ontario just across from Rochester, New York. Eighteen years ago my wife, Mary, and I came to town looking for an inexpensive property suitable for my humble shingle.

Dilapidation transformed to clinic

What we settled for was a long neglected red brick house set back on an expansive lot along a well-traveled side street. Windows were cracked and shattered and the untrimmed trees along the north side of the lot spread their branches across the roof to give it a haunted demeanor. The foundation gave way under zigzag clefts in both front corners. Yet this 70- year old dilapidation was the only real estate with commercial zoning in poverty pricing. So we rolled up our sleeves and started a one-time renovation business. With a new roof, siding, paint, paved parking lot, sweat and ingenuity, we transformed an ugly duckling into a charming veterinary clinic.

Kitchen became waiting room; the living room a reception area; the dining room gave birth to an examination room; and the surgery replaced a downstairs bedroom. Kennels went into the refurbished back porch. We lived upstairs until there was enough income to look for a home of our own. It took more than five years of prolonged days and nights before there were enough clients to cover expenses and a salary. But we desperately wanted to make a go of it here in the Cumbersome Hills of Eastern Ontario. We chose to settle here in Heron Point for its aesthetics. Along side roads, lanes and highways, enchanting tangible paintings stretch for miles across the lake or down tree-lined valleys. In time we came to love the people as much as the panorama. No, even more.

Over the years, The Ark and Bark has treated just about everything in the animal world except for Homo sapiens. That care occurs vicariously though. Our routine cases are dogs, cats, horses and cows, and there are also pig farms in the area, a couple of goatherds, several sheep farms, and a small zoo down on Highway Two. Any day we could be presented with a pocket pet such as a hamster or rabbit, or an exotic creature like a snake or iguana. We could have an injured wild animal or bird brought in by a benevolent Samaritan.

Introducing 'Trip'

I'm not the only veterinarian here. About the time Mary and I moved out of the clinic, I realized that there could be enough work for about one-and-a-half vets. I thought if I hired another veterinarian, the new clinician would generate more business to help pay for the new salary. Mary was soon to give birth to our second child, and I wanted time with my kids before they flew from our nest.

That's how I hired Dr. David Tripper, a graduate from Ohio State University. First he crossed the Erie pond to work for a year in Southern Ontario. In reality, he was following a pretty young nurse he had met, and eventually married. He and I met at a Veterinary Conference and hit it off immediately. We both seemed to have the same passion for practice, and the same ethic — work and professional. Dave's an excellent practitioner. We call him 'Trip'.

We call him that for more than the diminution of his name. Although he always means well, somehow he manages to come out the loser in a crisis that shouldn't have been one. He's been chased by more animals than I can remember. Not that he deserves their wrath, far from it. He just paints himself into too many corners.

If ever there was a 'typical' mixed practice veterinarian, Trip suits the portrait. Mind you, I was that model ten years ago, but I've noticed my...features...sagging lately. Dave Tripper is just a hair over 5 foot 11 inches (same as my height although my thinning hair is making me shorter). He's a solid 190 pounds, (I'm a flabbier 180...give or take...OK give), has a dark mustache and brown wavy hair, (I still have hair.... most of it).

Since he came from an army family his upbringing exposed him to over ten US bases and states resulting in a drawl with a San Antonio twang on a New England dialect. He scratches his left ear as he ponders cases. When the train of thought comes to the station, he starts with "Ah'm wondrin"...You can always tell when he's made a diagnosis by the glimmer in his pale-green eyes. Trip's passion is to beat the devil (to him, animal disease) in a fair fight.

And here's Dr. 'Sam'...and Leslie

We have sort of a third veterinarian now. She's Dr. Samantha Skeen-Wilson. Sam works in the clinic about three days a week. She and her husband, Jim, have a swine operation east of town, where they raise Yorkshires — pigs and terriers. Trip and I reached a point two years ago when the practice could support two-and-a-half veterinarians. Samantha had just graduated from Guelph University and married Jim Skeen who had inherited his dad's farm. Necessity brought us all together. Samantha was raised knowing that women were simply superior to men. No 'women's libber' was ever going to lower her to the level of a man!

Leslie Salk, as receptionist-technician, volunteered as soon as we opened the kitchen/clinic door. She loves animals and always wanted to work in a veterinary clinic. I had no income for personal salary, let alone money to pay a full-time receptionist. But Mary was then pregnant with our first child and could no longer fill in as secretary, so I accepted Leslie's overture to help. Thankfully, I now offer her a reasonable paycheck.

Leslie's an Animal Health Technician. She graduated from a two year course that could be compared to a veterinary nursing school. Unfortunately, regulations that dictate what a technician can do, haven't caught up to their training. She is understandably frustrated to spend most of her time on secretarial duties.

Like most clinics, this one is piloted by the appointment book. It's the only way to time-manage routine health care with daily crises. Sometimes I don't see how we can get everything done when I look at a page full of calls and appointments. We labor through though, by great traffic control from Leslie, and sheer love of what we do.

I won't talk about every case in the appointment book today or for those in the months to come, just a few out-takes to give you the flavor of a typical veterinary practice. You've heard Barney already. We'll meet Smokey and Mark Haley, Jake and Rambo Burtle, Boz Budgie and you'll never forget Fred, the Muscovy duck.

It seems that clients coming to this clinic have put their faith in us. Have you wondered how to choose a veterinarian and a veterinary hospital? Perhaps some of these cases can shed some light on the question.

CHAPTER ONE

CHAPTER ONE

Ark & Bark Animal Clinic
Wednesday February 15, 1989

Morning Emergencies:
Jeremy Dickson - calving
Blake Snider - downer cow

Morning Farm Calls:
Tony Viscusso - cow off feed
Beth Rocklin - horse is lame
Henry de Vost - herd health call

Morning Surgeries:
Mrs. Tuttle - cat spay
Bill Stewart - cat neuter
Jill Judd - dog spay
Angela Dunn - hematoma

Morning Appointments:
10:00 *Mr. and Mrs. Shelby - Barney's nails clipped*
10:15 Rose Walton - 2 kittens for first vaccination
10:30 John Archer - litter of pups, tails docked
10:45 *Mark Haley - Smokey*
11:00 Mrs. West - dog with ear infection
11:15 Bud Mclean - dog vomiting and coughing
11:30 Mrs. Giddings - bringing cat in, not eating
11:45
12:00 Mrs. Coles - dog dragging its bum

Afternoon Farm Calls:
Steve Beech - herd health check
Mrs. Osborne - check goat
Hunter Brothers - sow off feed
Drop by Bud Mullit's to check duck

Afternoon Appointments:
2:00 Mrs. Kasper - cat's hair is falling out
2:15 Ken Johns - dog, swollen body
2:30 Mrs. Bolton - cat ears and vaccinate
2:45 *Jake Burtle - Rambo shots*
3:00 Mrs. Furrow - first distemper for dog
3:15 Jack Peterson - Bovair, annual vaccination
3:30 Kate Healey - shots
3:45 *Mrs. Redding - parakeet with a lump*
4:00

Evening Emergencies:

Wednesday February 15, 1989, 9:45 AM...

"Mornin' Leslie. Man...that's a frigid wind out there! They say it's cold up in space where the Americans took a walk outside their ship last September. I swear, people outside today bundled up in parkas and coveralls look like astronauts waddling slow-motion against the storm in space-suits."

"Good Morning Dr. Runcibal. Yeah...my car just about didn't start."

"That brings us back to earth, doesn't it? How was Trip's on-call?"

"Right now Dr. Tripper is out at Blake Snider's checking that Downer Cow. The answering service said that he had a calving at about two this morning."

"Two! I'm glad it was him." I winced. "I never get back to sleep when I wake up in the middle of the night. See if Trip can check Tony's cow this morning and then go to Rocklin's to see that horse. I've already done Henry de Vost's herd health call. Sam is doing the surgery for the morning. I'll start the appointments." I paused as my finger reached a familiar name in the daybook. "I see that Mark is coming in with Smokey," I muttered more to myself although Leslie heard me and read my non-verbal message as well.

"I'm not looking forward to seeing Smokey put to sleep," Leslie joined in my thoughts, as she sorted through the files for the cases that were to be seen today. Then she smiled and whispered, "Did you see Mr. Shelby sitting in the corner?"

10:00 AM Mr. and Mrs. Shelby, nails clipped...

....Baaaarrrnnney and the Shelbys

Claire and Gerald Shelby were both waiting in the examination room at ten o'clock. Barney, their 17 year old Basset Hound was lying on his belly on the stainless steel table. Leslie had helped to lift him. I would guess that Mr. Shelby would be about 84 and his wife Claire close behind him. Yet they both wore their years well. Gerald had been an engineer, working overseas on pipeline projects in the Middle East. He and his wife had traveled the world. They had no children.

Mr. Shelby's career laid the world's treasures at their feet. Now that they were too feeble to travel, they opted for the mundane of a lakeside property in Heron Point. To fill their quiet days, they bought a Basset puppy in 1972. I was Barney the

Basset's first and only Doctor.

The Shelbys would bring the love of their life in to see me, at least three times a year: every spring for his annual vaccinations, in the summer for a check-up and flea bath, and at least once or twice to have his nails trimmed, or for any other minor concern. Although Gerald was several inches taller than me, I never had to look up at him.

He would always be bent over Barney, scratching the hound's domed head and pulling at the loose folds of skin to the point where the dog's wrinkled face could contort to a dozen different images. Mr. Shelby would nuzzle Barney nose-to-nose, and kiss the delighted dog who clearly relished the attention.

The most endearing show of affection was Gerald's constant repetition of Barney's name. Shelby's voice was as generous as his measurement and he would snuggle up to his precious friend booming, "Barney, Barney, yes my old Baarrrney pal, aren't you Barney, old boy?" Barney would cock his head in the direction of his moniker maker, roll his huge affectionate brown eyes to his master, showing the white below his pupils and the red bulging conjunctiva below. Maintaining this buoyant glare he would thwack his tail to emphasize his affection.

"I've never had kids till now, Doctor Runcibal. Suddenly, I've got two of them!" murmered Claire as she watched with laughing eyes. Barney let out his Basset howl of enjoyment. "Owhooo Whoooerrr...Whrrr!" ...thwack thwack thwack went the tail on the steel table.

"Here to trim our nails today?" I asked as I smiled at this picture of faultless enjoyment. I gave Barney a quick examination with my stethoscope before clipping his toenails. Seventeen years was getting along considerably, especially for a Basset. Today he seemed in great shape, but then why wouldn't he be, with such loving parents.

"There," I said as I finished Barney's nails, checked his pendulous ear flaps and wrinkles in his face folds for any sign of infection. "Barney's still doing fine. But keep in touch with me. He's at an age when things can and will start to happen."

"He's almost as old as me now I guess," said Mr. Shelby. "I must look a fool making such a fuss over this old dog. But he's all we have now, other than our memories. And I can tell you that a lot of them go missing every day! I can't help but act like a blithering idiot. Claire's not quite right, she's got two old dilapidated geriatrics to look after."

"No one's a fool who loves their dog," I said, not just in reply, but I'm sure I was thinking out loud, admiring this family of friends.

Baaarrney...

Claire, Gerald and Barney left the examination room and headed out the door. The three of them walking down the street leaving an indelible image — Claire and Gerald arm-in-arm, diminishing their years with their youthful affection for one another, Barney hopping around their feet, stumbling onto his broad flapping ears, almost tripping the Shelbys as he wrapped the leash around their legs. "Oh Barney!" they would say as the three twirled, laughing, to unravel.

Finding the right chemistry...

Gerald and Claire have come to this clinic for over 17 years. There were three hospitals in driving distance from which to choose. Mine could be classified as a risky choice for my shingle was still quite green. Gerald dropped into the office as my wife and I were painting trim in the waiting room. He looked briefly at our paint-stained clothes and faces and glanced around the room to see the amenities we had added. Now there was a picture of a child smothering its face into the fur of a Sheepdog, and sitting on the coffee table an enamel cat licking its paws. Over in the corner, a bookcase with animal classics, Lassie Come Home, Beautiful Joe, and so many other favorites, also an encyclopedia of cats and a handbook for the bird watchers.

"I've just bought a Basset pup," he said. "I heard there was a new vet in town. My wife and I are new to the area too. I see you're busy, but could you tell me what to do with a new puppy. I can come back later if you..."

"No no!" I said wiping more paint onto my jeans, anxious to generate new clients. "If you've got him with you and don't mind our disarray, I'd be happy to look at him now." Shelby cocked his head and winced one eye to study me. Then for whatever reason, he made the decision that I was to be his vet despite the unprofessional outward appearance of this first impression. He must have seen past my naiveté, my lack of funds to hire someone to do the painting and my evidence of not being very busy since I obviously had the time to paint.

But Gerald and several thousand others chose to use my services. How do they decide? Gerald found the chemistry he was looking for. He wanted a young veterinarian with new ideas and freshly trained in current medicine to look after his new-found pride. That was all I could offer at that point.

*L*et's talk... It takes an average of eight years to complete a veterinary education. A few students are able to do so in the requisite six years (two years pre-vet and four years of veterinary medicine). But since the competition to get into veterinary school is enormous, it often takes several tries and one or two additional degrees to finally qualify just for entrance. As a result the academic quality of the veterinarian today is exemplary.

A key though, to your veterinarian's credentials is whether he or she keeps up-to-date. As with any professional, this is evidenced more by the Continuing Education Certificates hung on the wall than by the heavy medical books on the shelf.

Only rarely would one find a practitioner who felt that once they graduated they knew all there was to know. Such an individual may have textbooks that they don't read, journals that they haven't opened and brochures describing conferences and seminars that they won't attend. It may seem frightening to think that there may be such medical doctors or veterinarians out there with such an attitude. Fortunately, survival in any profession in this age of information makes it almost impossible for any practitioner to ignore the need for lifelong learning. Clients are becoming better informed, sophisticated consumers so that the deficient doctor should be spotted immediately.

...and the right veterinarian

How to choose a veterinarian? Do you phone each clinic to compare the costs of spaying, neutering and vaccinating? This won't really work. It may allow you to get those procedures done at a cheaper rate. Some clinics feel forced to lower some general procedures like vaccinations, spays and neuters. Other hospitals feel it is morally wrong to charge inadequate fees for major surgery or to minimize the value of the health examination. In either case the hospital likely has the most competent people and currently equipped veterinary facility.

The means to finding your family veterinarian is the personal rapport that you are able to establish with him or her. Your pet will receive dedicated care from almost any animal doctor provided the lines of communication are connected and understood.

There is a high cost to establishing a veterinary practice. This includes not only the usual mortgage or lease payments for the building, but also costly renovations to comply to the professional regulations requiring strict standards of practice. Each clinic must be a fully-equipped hospital with anesthetic machine, autoclave, x-ray machine, surgery table, surgical instruments. Not only is a veterinary clinic a full hospital, it is a complete veterinary pharmacy. The cost of drug inventory is staggering —- I know because I've had to stock the shelves!

Choose your veterinarian as you would choose your plumber. Call friends and neighbors. If you are new to town ask local merchants and people you meet. You did this when you bought or moved into your first home didn't you, in order to find a reliable plumber?

> Local wisdom goes a long way to providing market intelligence on acquiring the services of a plumber, doctor, dentist, veterinarian and septic tank guy.

That's how Gerald Shelby found me. He met Mark Haley who manages the local hardware store. They got to talking about dogs because they both had young pups. Mark had just been to see me with his Black Lab, Smokey. She had sniffed a little too close to his fishing tackles and became entangled with several hooks in her mouth. Mark was pleased with the way that I handled the puppy and case. "Why don't you give Runcibal a try? He seems to know what he's doing." Mark and Smokey are both my friends now.

10:55 AM ... Mark Haley, check Smokey...

It's hard to say good-bye.

"Hi Mark! Hi there Smokey old girl!" I said as I crouched down to nuzzle with this beautiful black Labrador Retriever now more than 17 human years in age, but geriatric in real terms. Smokey wagged her tail as best she could. It hurt her to even move, she was so decrepit with arthritis. But she was such a loving and strong personality that she wouldn't let a little pain get in the way of a friendly greeting.

"Hi Jon!" was all that Mark could say. He was having a tough time deciding what to do about Smokey. She was aging rapidly. And age was one of the diseases for which we haven't yet found a cure. Fortunately for animals, we have decided that it is more

Smokey nudges for a pat...

humane to perform euthanasia as an alternative to prolonged suffering. Yet the decision as to when suffering reaches the 'put to sleep' button, is never consistent or easy to determine. And it's always a tough button to push.

"How's Smokey now, Mark?" I asked as I checked her over. Her heart was weak, pulse thready, and breathing labored. She was severely arthritic and she wavered on her feet. She could only navigate a few steps before needing to sit down.

"She seemed a bit better with all the medicine you gave me last time. And she's eating that special diet you gave me. But she's steadily going downhill. I know I need to do something, but I can't bring myself to do it." Smokey sat with dark, friendly, searching eyes, looking from me to Mark and back again. She moved herself closer to Mark's dangling arm and forced her head under his hand for a pat. You could see Mark slump as he felt this familiar friend cuddle for attention. His eyes glistened. Smokey sat there contented as we discussed her fate.

"You know what we will have to do sooner or later, Mark," I said finally. "We've taken all the tests possible to everything but her age. We're treating her arthritis, kidney failure and dying heart. But I know how much she means to you. You aren't ready for this today. To be honest, neither am I. And you know, Smokey is still not suffering unduly. She's still the dog we know. I'll give her a shot of B-Vitamins and we'll keep her on the medication."

Mark seemed immediately heartened to think that the pardon had been called in for now. Smokey felt his renewed energy and creaked to her feet to start out the door. "Whoa, Smoker, I want to give you this first," I said as I gave her the injection. I looked into those black knowing eyes that showed nothing but affection, and patted her head. I put my hand onto Mark's shoulder as he left the exam room, this time at least, with his friend still on her leash.

Veterinarians inevitably become immersed within patient and client lives, at least as it relates to the care of the pet. We are admitted into veterinary school because of academic credentials. Somehow compassion is an innate precept. It is this empathy, in my view, that tells you whether you have the right veterinarian. It gives him or her that element of good cage-side manner to assure you of a dedicated clinician.

More clues for a good practitioner...

Let's Talk...After you've gone the plumbing route there are a few

caveats to add to the mix. If you are satisfied with evident empathy and the chemistry is right between you, look for the following clues for a good practitioner:

* evidence that the hospital has the latest equipment. Most veterinarians are proud to give clients a tour of their hospital. Be cognizant though, that the clinic would only be able to do so when the commotion of visitors would not bother patients. You will be pleasantly surprised to see the human-hospital comparisons. A fully equipped animal hospital today is likely to have one or more examination rooms with several instruments such as ophthalmoscopes, Woods lesions), various test kits and reagents; a treatment room which may also be the dental suite with companion animal dentistry equipment; a laboratory with blood, urine and fecal analysis instruments; an x-ray with lead lined walls, door or screen and a dark room that may even have an automatic processor; a surgical suite with state-of-the-art anesthetic machine, oxygen supply and monitoring instruments. Finally, the patient wards include very expensive kennels, often stainless steel, where creatures of all types can be safely comforted and monitored. In addition, mixed animal practice has likely invested in one or more mobile units that effectively take medical and surgical supplies to the farm.

* evidence that the clinic promotes the latest treatments. The pet owner is bombarded with information from the radio, television, acquaintances, magazines, newspapers and the Internet. It is difficult in this era of data overload to be unaware of new developments in medicine. One cannot absorb or understand every novel discovery however. Using your veterinary practitioner as the filter for any innovation that you feel is relevant to the care of your pet, you will help to determine or to develop a sense of trust with your vet.

* evidence that your veterinarian(s) attend continuing education seminars. Don't go by the books on the shelf. Most practitioners barely have enough time in a busy practice to catch their breath let alone read every page of every new textbook. Veterinarians consume an inordinate number of books, primarily for reference to help analyze a difficult case. Your best indicator may be the certificates on the wall depicting courses attended or certificates achieved. Rather than exhibiting frustration with your vet if he or she happens to be away at a conference just when it was convenient for you to get Gizmo vaccinated —- rejoice that you have a family veterinarian who takes the time to get away to keep up to date.

* evidence that they care for the clinic. Is it clean? Are the staff happy or do they seem upset or grumpy? Are there repairs obvious that remain undone from one visit to the next? Don't be too hard on them though.

It could be that this hospital is one of the most popular in the region and they are so over-worked that the clinic is always in disarray. If they're that busy though, they can afford to get someone in to clean up. Tell them gently, if you observe disturbing patterns of neglect.

Summary of a good veterinary practitioner:

The hospital has the latest equipment.

The clinic promotes the latest treatments.

Your veterinarian(s) attend continuing education seminars.

The whole staff promote a caring and cheerful ambience despite the routine workload.

Hospital staff should be cheerful despite routine workload. There is always the next case, like the Muskovy duck, to break the monotony...

2:25 PM –- drop by Bud Mullit's...

...The Muscovy duck.

Bud Mullit coming through a doorway leaves scarcely an inch on either side. Adding to the imposing girth is a bushy head of straw-colored hair with bangs streaming down his face making him look as though he's peering through vertical venetian blinds. Heads turn as soon as he speaks in a voice with a sonic boom and a hand that slaps his foreleg like a clap of lightning whenever he gets to a punch line. It's the reverberation of his laughter coupled with the shaking of his belly, effectively hiding his belt and then some, that mollifies his dominating presence.

Betty Mullit is his antithesis. She's just shy of five foot two and must be a mere 90 pounds. You stop to listen when she speaks too, not to hear an abrupt and thunderous voice, but to listen carefully lest you miss what is coming from a barely audible whisper. Betty's hair is raven black, straight and neatly clipped short to her cherub-like face. Rather than carry an immutable grin like Bud's, she constantly nods her head and crinkles her cheek, first the left, then the right, as a visual apology for Bud's obstreperous nature.

When Bud and Betty moved to their farm five years ago they realized that they knew little about rural life. Bud had been an auto mechanic with Betty as his book-keeper in a body shop that they operated in Willstown. They loved animals and there was always a junk-yard dog lying across the doorway to trip customers, and a litter of kittens mewing every three months or so from a discarded tire in the corner. But they had always dreamed of moving to the country where they could raise ducks and chickens, horses and cows.

There is a riotous adventure with every call to the Mullit estate, due partly to the joy with which Bud bumps life full in the face — largely due to the innocence of novice hobby farmers. Their homestead covered 48 acres, ten of which was thorn bushes, five acres of aged orchard, 12 acres of tree covered ravine and the rest needing a lot of work in order to become productive land. The soil was good enough to plant young apple trees to expand the Mullit orchard. The barn was decrepit when they moved in but not as ragged as the farmhouse. Never fearing toil or adversity, Bud and Betty turned this lump of coal into a Town and Country showcase.

I had rarely heard Bud with a loss for words but today was an exception as evidenced by the perplexing phone request that would lead me to an unforgettable house call...

"Dr. Runcibal, Bud Mullit wants to speak to you. He won't tell me what he wants. I'm sure that something serious is wrong but he can't seem to come out with it to me," Leslie said as she handed me the phone.

"Hi Bud, What's up?" I asked innocently.

"Now Doc, I don't want you to think that this is an obscene phone call or anythin' but I've got a duck here with a frozen dick!" Bud blurted immediately, his voice less boisterous and obviously nervous.

"What?" His statement was clear enough but I couldn't quite grasp whether this was one of Bud's knee-slapping jokes or if the quiver in his voice really spoke to an urgent problem. My mind quickly reflected on the slew of ducks that populated the Mullit barnyard. Of course they had to have ducks on their ranch since it boasted a large muddy pond just back of the barn. So Bud bought a pair of Muscovy ducks.

These are the typical barnyard ducks that waddle across country roads from streams to ponds. Often plain white ducks with combs like wattles on a rooster, they can also sport black racing stripes along their head, neck or back feathers. With a beak similar to a wood duck that curves down at the sides, they wear a perpetual frown.

Reaching up to 15 pounds, ten or so roastable, they are able to fly reasonably well for short distances.

I've driven by the Mullit place enchanted by the row of Muscovys lined up on the barn roof like overweight albino crows. With every year that passed, I kept seeing more and more ducks. I remembered now when Bud was at the Heron Point Public School open house last fall, his thigh slapping discourse on Fred the Muscovy duck.

Fred and Della were the pair of fowl that started populating the Mullit property. Fred was exceptionally prolific. By the end of the first year Bud could count 30 ducks that had hatched from this one male, his first mate, and the incest to follow. Fred was the hottest beast in the barnyard. Bud had bellowed for all the prim and proper teachers and parents to hear at that open house, 'Fred's so horny, he would ride anything! Why he was right out of a porno movie!"

Within a couple of years they must have had 200 ducks. There were black and white, gray and white, and just plain white Muscovy ducks ambling freely around Mullit Acres. There was one slight problem, not considered when livestock was purchased for this farm operation, that allowed for this over-population. Betty would not allow any animal to be killed. "My god, kill them? We can't do that Bud!" Betty would whisper as loud as she could.

So Fred was allowed to proliferate progeny. They hatched month after month, duck after duck after duck. Till this cold February afternoon with the fateful call about Fred's dilemma.

"What?" I said again, realizing that perhaps there was fruit to this story.

He repeated. "I've got a duck here with a frozen dick!"

Silence at my end was due to my own inability to rationalize this condition.

"I know, I know, it doesn't sound right or nothin' but old Fred here, our Muscovy, has got his....'thing'....frozen to the ground!" cried Bud with considerable difficulty. "I guess you'd call it 'duck dick'. I don't know how else to explain it."

Bud went on to account that he had been noticing late in the fall, that Fred was dragging his 'most precious piece' but he never thought much of it. "If you've made as many little ones as Fred," he guessed, "You'd be proud to leave it out." Bud later came to realize that old Fred had, in his words, "broken his re-wind". As the credentials for Fred's conquests became more and more pendulous it finally

Fred's dilemma...

started dragging through the first snows.

When winter hit its peak, with permanent freezing days and nights, Bud went out to feed the ducks on this fateful February morning. He knew exactly where to find Fred by this time, because of the obvious trace in the snow of two flat duck feet and a drag in the middle.

This morning Bud had followed Fred's steps-and-drag to the pond. There stood an unfortunate duck anchored to what had previously been his winterized domain, now only a quickly-frozen-over pond.

The edges of Fred's beak drooped more than usual as he stood, stuck. Looking up at Bud's mountainous build then down between his legs , Fred quacked miserably for salvation. His 'precious piece' was frozen to the pond. After feeble attempts to remedy the predicament Bud finally called the clinic.

"I've never heard of such a thing," I confessed.

"I never have neither, but I've got one!"

"Well, for now, why don't you get some warm water to thaw him out and free him from his present situation," I offered as a suggestion. "I've got a call that will take me right by your place this afternoon. I'll stop in to have a look."

Now, I don't often make house calls for ducks, but this was a case in a million that I just had to see for myself.

Sure enough, when I stopped by later that day, there was Fred, frozen to the pond.. "I keep runnin' out here with the kettle to unfreeze 'im, and he just turns around and seizes up again!" explained an exasperated Bud Mullit. Betty was back at the kitchen door, chewing her nails and crimping her cheeks.

"As soon as he stops at any one spot he's stuck there! I even took him into the house to put 'im in the bathtub. I figgered his re-wind might get better swimmin' in the water. Enough anyways, that he'd be able to pull it up to clear the ground," Bud went on. "But no dice. As soon as I took 'im back outside, he's froze up again!"

"What can we do Doc?" asked Bud. "Please don't tell me we have to kill'im. He's the pride of the farm! Why he's the main duck!"

"The only thing I can suggest," I said feeling the withered and blackened tissue. "Is to amputate."

Bud crossed his legs. "Don't you think that's kind of drastic?" he said in a rather high pitched voice.

"I know, I know," I agreed. "But as you can see the penis is already shriveled up and most of the tissue is dead. At least if I amputate he has a chance." Clearly it was the only recourse for old Fred. Bud carried him to the house so we could operate over the kitchen sink. A baleful quack emanated from the turned-down bill like a horn fading with a dying battery. Bud held the wings close to the bird's body as I cleaned his underside with antiseptic. I snipped off the dangling appendage as close to fresh looking flesh as I could. Fred felt absolutely nothing given that the famous phallus was already anesthetized. After applying a smear of topical antibiotic, I left Fred and Bud, now both with legs crossed, but at least with ground clearance and relief from kettle duties respectively.

Fred survived for some time afterwards. Bud said later though, "I had to do poor old Fred in. His heart just wasn't in the barnyard anymore."

The solution to Fred's dilemma

Let's talk...Fred's dilemma highlights a clear need to understand the power and the consequence of the sex drive. Left unchecked we become populated with ducks, puppies, kittens. It is the overburden of dogs and cats that troubles animal caregivers. One of the most unpleasant tasks I have ever had to perform has been the weekly visit to the local Humane shelter to euthanize. Cage after cage of trusting eyes stare up at the last person they will ever see. Years of training and practice become meaningless as you prepare the row of syringes. You are not here to save. You are here to kill.

You must make your heart cold and your mind blank in order to tighten the tourniquet onto each puppy and kitten's forearm. You cannot look into their eyes. A final pat and kind farewell is the least and only comfort you can give them, "Go to sleep little guy..."

The Humane Associations do all they can to find homes for thousands of animals. Many thousand more are put to sleep because there is simply not enough demand for the over-produced supply.

The spay and castration provide solutions. Stop production! The sex drive will not go away unless we dismantle the equipment. I must debunk those old wives who have spread tales of error. So many pet owners think that it's best for their female dog or cat to have at least one litter before they are spayed. Men tend to jump to the conclusion that it is therefore a right for their male dog to sow his oats before he's fixed.

Neither is valid thinking.

> The dog or cat that is spayed or neutered, ignorant of the act of procreation, is just as happy, likely happier, without the experience.

2:45 PM —- *Jake Burtle, Rambo's Shots*

The story of a man and a woman...and half a dog...

Samantha Skeen-Wilson is a skilled clinician and surgeon. Having her work in the clinic for just a few days a week is a godsend. There is more work for Dave and I to handle, but not enough income to provide three full-time salaries (such as they are, veterinarians still tend to be one of the lowest paid professionals.)

But Sam still encounters chauvinism from time to time, being a female professional in what has been a significantly patriarchal fraternity for many years. This afternoon, she tests her mettle during an appointment with Jake Burtle. Jake is the local 'truck drivin man'. He's six foot three, and 210 pounds of serious labor.

If you need someone to backhoe, bulldoze, snowplow, or tow you, Jake's the man. His complexion almost matches his radish-red hair. The outdoors has weathered deep lines in his face that are exacerbated by his constant smile. His solution for just about any difficulty or disease, man or animal, is, " Shoot it!" Today, after plough-ing snow out of our lane and parking lot, Jake has brought Rambo, his new Boxer, in for 'shots'. "Hello, Mr. Burtle," Samantha said as she came into the examining room, head down in the medical chart she was starting for Rambo. Sam, on first glance, especially with stereotypical vision, could be mistaken for a model rather than a doctor. Her blonde hair bounces off her shoulders and slightly covers her blue eyes and genial face.

"G'day Miss. Is the Doc in?"

"I'm Doctor Skeen," said Samantha, abruptly stern, cold and deliberate. Jake froze. This was an alien situation for him. Sam moved deliberately to the table glaring carefully at Jake. "Rambo looks to be in pretty good shape," she said as she

Rambo, something's missing...

began her examination. "I see that you have only asked for Rabies. I recommend that we give Rambo the first puppy vaccination as well as Rabies on this visit, then give him a booster when you bring him in to be neutered." Jake's smirk withered. This otherwise gregarious talker was speechless, or dumbfounded, by Sam's assertiveness.

"Oh oh, what have we here?" Sam muttered to herself, as she was palpating Rambo. Jake, who was leaning against the wall, looking skeptically at the procedure till now, edged towards Rambo with concern.

"What's wrong?...Doc?" questioned Jake. His ruddy face was getting more flushed as he cocked his head to see that Sam had her hand around Rambo's scrotum. He stepped back a pace.

"I'm afraid Rambo has a cryptorchid testicle," Sam explained matter-of-factly.

"A crypto' what?" asked Jake, wincing.

"One of his testicles has refused to come down to the scrotum, from it's place in the abdomen where it normally is while inside the womb. If Rambo was a little younger I would rather we wait, but since he's just over six months now, I suggest we go after it when we neuter him."

Jake stood stunned for a moment, till he found himself. "I wasn't even thinkin' about gettin'im fixed," he said. He thought for a minute. " This damn dog is useless with just one nut. I'd be better off to shoot 'im." Clearly, a Boxer named Rambo, with only one evidence of masculinity was not in Jake's world.

Now Samantha was stunned. It was hard enough for Jake to accept her as a female veterinarian, now she had to convince this macho guy that it's okay to have a virile dog with no testicles. Jake's the kind of man who had been terribly insulted that the professional deregulation hearing last week in New Jersey declared the sport of wrestling a fake. Dr. Skeen-Wilson recovered carefully. "Uhm, well, yes, in the old days, I guess you'd be right. If a dog was not up to snuff, it would be better to shoot him. But current research has told us an awful lot about these things."

Jake rubbed a grizzled hand across his scruffy chin and shifted his feet, looking down to the floor. His eyes glanced anxiously towards the door. He was clearly planning his escape, perhaps even loading the shotgun in his mind. Sam realized by his body language that this needed 'red neck' to 'red neck' talk. "Y'know, Jake, if we don't remove that nut from the belly there is a greater risk of cancer of the balls. We now know that fixin' a dog extends their life expectancy. That cuts down the number of times we have to get a new dog."

Jake startled and pleased by this down-to-earth talk, was starting to reconsider his bullet prescription, so Samantha went in for her kill. "And to tell you the truth, this is one of the most muscular and powerful dogs I've seen in a long time, balls or no. If we do the surgery you will be able to train him to be much more responsive to your commands."

There was just one more obstacle on Jake's mind, "I er, I, I thought he.... Wouldn't a little, uh, foolin' around...wouldn't he be happier, if he could 'get it' once in a while?" Jake finally blurted, his face now as red as his hair.

"Actually, no," said Samantha firmly. "In fact, he could become more of a problem for you, if he were an intact male. He would run away all the time to follow the scent of females." Jake smiled wryly. This was just what he thought best for a male dog. "We get more dogs hit by cars or cut up from dog fights, that are intact males. Really Mr. Burtle, you will have a great dog here, a healthy one who will live longer, if we do the right thing for him." That was the clincher. No matter what Jake ever thought about a subject he always supported doing the right thing.

"Okay, Doctor Skeen," he said with distinct respect. "Give 'im what shots you want, and set up a time to cut 'im." Jake shuffled his feet a bit and looked up at Sam with a friendly smile. "I 'spect you'll do the operation yourself?"

3:45 –- Mrs. Redding, Boz Budgie's Bump...

The saga of the reluctant surgeon.

Later that afternoon a worried Faith Redding came into the examination room with a shoe box tucked under her arm. She was concerned about a lump that had appeared on her bird's side. Mrs. Redding was in her early 80s, a kindly old lady, slightly bent as she walked. She wore a knee length overcoat and a scarf over her head. On her eyes a pair of appropriate granny glasses dangled precariously. Behind those glasses was a pair of anxious eyes. She shuffled into the room as Sam came in from the laboratory on the opposite side of the examination room. "Hello, Mrs. Redding, is little Boz' in the box?" asked Samantha as Mrs. Redding handed the treasure over to her.

"Yes, he's in there. I'm sorry, but I didn't know how else to bring him, on such a

Beautiful Boz' with a bump...

cold day. He would freeze to death if I carried him in his cage," Mrs. Redding apologized."Oh, this box is perfect," assured Sam, as she opened it up to find a cerulean Budgerigar crouching into a soft and comforting face towel. It was clearly frightened and confused to be carried away in this dark coffin, then exposed to light of day in the face of a stranger in foreign surroundings. "Look at those deep blue feathers!" Sam exclaimed as she gently wrapped her hand around the cringing budgie. "Ah," she said as she brought Boz over to the exam light, "He does have a little growth here."

"Yes," added Mrs. Redding. "And, I just noticed it. I'm really worried that it might be cancer. Little Boz is 15 years old now and I'm concerned that I might lose him."

"Do you mind if I ask Dr. Runcibal to have a look?" Sam asked. Mrs. Redding agreed.

Sam brought the handful back to the treatment room where Trip and I were having coffee. "I'd like to see what you think about this lump on Mrs. Redding's budgie. It's a Gray-Winged, Sky-Blue Budgie," Sam said, as she turned the little bird over to show us the otherwise healthy, beautifully blue feathered bird with an almond-sized growth on the left brisket. We each palpated the bump and asked the usual questions.

"Yes, it's the first she's seen it and the bird is eating well, singing and happy otherwise. Have either of you operated on a bird before?" None of us had. And we knew Mrs. Redding couldn't afford the time or effort to refer this case to a specialist.

"Let's keep an eye on it for a while," I suggested. "If the bird is not affected by the growth, there's no need to risk an anesthetic on such a frail creature." We all concurred and Mrs. Redding was happy with our decision. She carried Boz back home with instructions to bring him in again should the growth change in size or nature...

Humans make mistakes

Let's talk...Veterinarians treat every animal species but one. At least they can, legally. In reality it is impossible today to be an expert on every species of animal. It is difficult enough keeping up to date in disciplines within one animal like the dog or cat.

> Despite the best intentions, veterinarians suffer from the same ailment that afflicts your doctor, nurse and plumber —- they're human. Humans make mistakes.

Just as the most scrutinized surgical procedure during an appendectomy for a human can still result in an unwelcome sponge in the abdomen, so can the veterinarian be in error. Learning from each foible is just one side of the wisdom of experience. The other margin is the positive reinforcement one gains from the majority of successes. Both are glued together with continued education.

Education doesn't stop with the granting of the degree. Research and technology is adding to veterinary knowledge exponentially. Maintaining skills as an animal doctor demands a lifetime of learning.

Choose a veterinarian who is dedicated to more than today's medicine. Find out what he or she thinks about tomorrow's hopes. One can only talk about what is around the corner if one takes a peek through the periscope of current knowledge.....

CHAPTER TWO

Ark and Bark

Animal Clinic

CHAPTER TWO

Ark & Bark Animal Clinic
Friday March 10, 1989

Morning Emergencies:
Milk Fever at Eber Smale's
Norty Glip - horse with colic

Morning Farm Calls:
Nathan Biddle - worm horses
Dan Tunney - trim feet, 3 cows
Maggie Flint - cow off feed

Morning Surgeries:
John Archer - dog spay
Jake Burtle - castrate dog (cryptorchid)
Rose Walton - cat abscess

Morning Appointments:
10:00 *Discuss breeding with Mrs. Traney*
10:15 John Doyle - Sparky's arthritis
10:30 G. Reynolds - first puppy shot and deworm
10:45 Caroline Rose - euthanize 10 year old Chihuahua
11:00 *Mrs. Flitz - vaccinate Pershing and Calicat*
11:15 Agnes Huskins - Shadow, annual vaccination
11:30 Kate Healey - remove stitches
11:45 Dog with ear mites
12:00 Call Cindy Tipple about mice

Afternoon Farm Calls:
Steve Beech - herd health check
Elmer Lodge - dehorn calves

Afternoon Appointments:
2:00 Mrs. Roman - check if poodle is pregnant - spay? vaccinate?
2:15 *Mrs. Redding - budgie growth, recheck*
2:30 Knowlton Brice - yearly shots for 3 dogs
2:45 *Julie Baldwin - check cat and kittens*
3:00 Joyce Walsh - dog penis looks bad
3:15 Allanis Scriven - old dog has nose bleeds
3:30 Mrs. Witteveen - poodle eating its toes
3:45
4:00 Mrs. Jubb - dog won't eat

Evening Emergencies:
Mrs. Crockett - cat blocked
Al Latimer - dogs hit by a train

Love is a four-legged word.

Friday March 10, 1989

9:00 AM Nathan Biddle, worm horses...

"You don't say?"

My first call for the day, was to worm Nathan Biddle's horses.

Nathan Biddle is a talker. He doesn't just pass the time with conversation. He simply won't stop talking. I'm certain that some of the calls he's made to me on the pretence of checking one of his horses, or times he's brought pets to the office, were merely excuses to resume discussion. He knows exactly where he left off last, as though his verbose audiotape has been put on 'pause' and at our next meeting he pushes 'play'.

Nathan is a retired University Professor. He taught History and Literature at Queens University. When given the gold watch he decided to make a clean break from the collegiate environment rather than degenerate into a shuffling campus relic. So he revitalized himself and became a country gentleman.

He and his wife renovated a fieldstone farmhouse nestled in a clearing on a hillside that overlooks the lake. At the back of the barn were 40 or 50 acres of hilly pasture for his horses, Winston, Dickens and Thackery. He was not a farmer in any sense of the word, so he hired back Garth Kitchens, who sold Nathan the farm. It was a perfect arrangement. Garth was able to stay on the land that nurtured him — Nathan and his wife had a knowledgeable advocate to care for their property and animals.

Most importantly, Nathan could spend his time refining his repertoire of lectures on any unsuspecting visitor. He's diminutive in stature, the top of his head reaching my shoulders and he has a paunch that makes him roly-poly. His disposition heightens him. He has gray, thinning hair and a perpetual smile. The twinkle in his eye makes you look twice, to see if this is man or elf. He lets Garth do all the work while he stands off to the side, hands behind his back, rocking back and forth on squeaking shoes, his high pitched voice spewing a litany of facts.

I had finished passing stomach tubes into each of the horses, syringing creamy doses of anti-verminous medication down each tube. Wiping the nostrils of the residue of the liquid medication, I bent down to check Winston's hind leg. It appeared that a piece of a barbed wire had imbedded into the base of the horse's hoof. Nathan, at first concerned for Winston's welfare, eventually relished the additional labor as it gave him time to refine his oration to me.

Years of teaching allowed him to weave in and out of any ensuing conversation. His musings began with the wire that I was removing from Winston's hoof . For him, this was a perfect segue to the evolution in the manufacture of barbed wire, then onward to the use of barbed wire in the first world war. This in turn piqued a discourse, speaking of World War I, into Gavrilo Princip, the wayward student whose assassination of the Archduke Franz Ferdinand pushed the dominoes towards the start of the war.... Well, you get the idea.

In my attempt to get the conversation back to the care and well-being of Winston, he explained that he named the pony after Winston Churchill, (obviously) but went on to talk about Churchill's role in the first world war. "Of course everyone knew about Churchill during World War II, but did you know about his politics prior to that?" I found out. We progressed to the family tree of Winston the pony, then off on a tangent to cover the discovery of antibiotics as I gave Winston an injection of penicillin. Conversation jumped back to the first Great War and the events at it's conclusion, that set wheels in motion for an inevitable second World War.

My part of the discussion was very much like phone calls to mother, "Yup, nope, uh uh, really! Really? Yeah, okay". Occasionally, I would break in to give medical instructions, but I learned from earlier encounters with Nathan that if you took an active role in the discussion, you were truly adding fuel to the fire. The pyre swelled with each topic offered to the monologue.

Packing up my medical bag, I inched my way towards the barn door. If Nathan could back his audience up against any wall or corner, he had till who knows when. I side-stepped gradually towards daylight, as Nathan expounded on the similarities of the ethnic differences at the turn of the century, and the difficulties today in Sarajevo. He was saying, "Mark my words, the trouble isn't over for those people!"

"There are no real changes in life," I offered. "Only variations."

What a dumb time to get philosophical! That little observation led to an hour and a half on the topic of change in general, then on to peoples' need to grow, and the natural resistance we have to real change...and more.

No hint could end the soliloquy. I looked at my watch every three to five minutes,

Nathan's barnyard lecture...

at one time showing a surprised expression, the next a look of panic, then an added gesture of pointing apologetically to the wrist. Shifting my heavy case from one hand to the other made no difference. In fact it made matters worse. Rather than seeing this as a need to leave, Mr. Biddle offered to take the grip from me if it was getting heavy. "No bloody way," I thought. "If you get your hands on this bag, I'm here for a week!"

Finally, I reached the door and walked briskly to the truck with Nathan Biddle right on my heels, talking now about how agriculture in North America has changed — speaking of change. And how that has led to 'hobby farms' where people just like him, loving animals and nature, could move from the city to the wonders of country life.

Whoa! I knew that topic well. Nathan loved to talk about how he came to move to the country, find his house and renovate. From Garth, he even knew the genealogy of the family that farmed this land well before the Kitchens, and I'd heard descriptions of remodeling of every room more than once. It wasn't necessarily the same story each time either. Nathan remembered what he had told you before. He simply added embellishments that he had left out the first (or second) time.

I squeezed into the truck. I mean truly *squeezed* in, because one of Nathan's techniques to keep his audience, was to stand close to the front of your car door to keep you from getting it open. I started the engine as Nathan got to the part about making the outhouse into a sauna. Once behind the wheel, I shifted into 'drive' and moved my foot from the brake to the gas. Nathan prattled on.

I put ever increasing pressure on the pedal to move the truck out of the barnyard to the lane. Nathan was still at my window, talking, walking in pace with the truck. I slowly rolled up the window saying, "Really? Uh uh, really! Well I gotta go now!" Nathan was walking faster to keep up with me, still talking through the diminishing crack in the window.

He started to fade and I saw my chance, so I pressed down on the gas. Nathan was running now, his topic somehow shifting to the 'foods of France'. But he was losing ground. He was now at my back bumper, panting and talking, running after my truck. "Give me a call in a week to let me know how Winston is coming along," I called back as I floored it and sped away.

Fool! Why did I say that? One week later I received a one-hour call from Mr. Biddle. "Winston was fine, thank you very much, and did you know how it happened that Napoleon had a dessert named after him?"

The true parasites —- worms.

${Let's\ talk}$...Part of my time spent at Nathan Biddle's farm was dedicated to eradicating worms from his horses' innards. Most of my time was spent planning my escape. I don't see Nathan as a parasite. I would enjoy my time spent with him if I too was retired. Rather, he simply adds a time constraint to an otherwise busy day. Worms are true parasites. They suck the blood and nutrients from their host.

Animals are plagued with dozens of species of worms. From tiny threads wiggling and swimming through the fluids of the bowels to long chained tapeworms replicating new segments to consume the animals devoured ingesta.

Only a fraction of the stool sample kits that we send out from the clinic return with desired content. Clients avoid the stoop to scoop a spoonful of poop. We can't necessarily blame them. Putting a wad of feces into a plastic cup is not the most pleasant of tasks.

But these worms must be eradicated. Otherwise they sap the vitality out of the animal. Hair coat becomes dull, dry and lack-luster; energy wanes; and appetite becomes ravenous just to feed the worms.

By examining a fecal (stool) sample mixed in salt solution we can determine exactly what worm or worms are infesting the animal from which the stool had come. What we see are the microscopic eggs of the worms which float to the surface. By placing the uppermost liquid portion onto a microscope slide we can not only identify the species of worms but usually get an idea as to the severity of the infestation.

Just as you can differentiate bird species by the color and size of the eggs in their nests, we can determine whether the dog or cat is infested with roundworms, whip worms, hookworms, tapeworms or more exotic species of pests by the shape and size of eggs in the sample. Knowing precisely which egg of which worm is present allows us to prescribe the exact medicant to rid them.

Worming blindly (giving worm medicine without knowing which parasite is present) is a dangerous game of roulette. Giving roundworm medication when hookworms are present can only lead to debility. But most current medications available from your veterinarian cover the gamut of internal parasites.

Hookworms are the Captain Hook of the realm of the bowel. Their hook-like mouth parts grab a piece of the intestinal wall. While one hookworm may only be three millimeters long, it is the aggregate that cause disaster. Enough of a population sucking blood from their clasps to the bowel lining can lead to anemia, especially in puppies and kittens. Dogs are also affected by the larvae of hookworms burrowing into their skin causing localized itchiness and discomfort.

Roundworms, reaching up to eight centimeters in length, look like slender white earthworms. Rather than feed off of blood they consume nutrients in the intestine as they surge in and through the partly digested food. Infested puppies and kittens especially, will suffer from loss of appetite, vomiting, diarrhea, even death if the number of worms is great enough to steal nutrition at critical stages of growth. Adult dogs and cats may be less prone to illness but if they have these worms they are a source of infection for others.

How do dogs and cats get worms?

An infested bitch or queen can send these parasites to their incubating embryos through the uterine blood supply. It is paramount then, for female dogs and cats that are raised for breeding, to be checked for worms. Otherwise the newborn can become infested further through nursing. Puppies and kittens get worms like roundworms through suckling mothers milk. The eggs are in the milk of infected bitches or queens so infestation of the litter is inevitable.

Hookworm eggs are present in the soil after being deposited by an infected animal's feces, and can be ingested by the puppy or kitten as they nose around the dirt in the environment. Even adults become infected in this way. In addition, hookworm larvae are able to infest a host by migrating through the skin.

Tapeworm eggs are carried to the dog or cat by flea larvae. In the jungle of carpet strands of the rugs beneath your feet, these squiggly larvae, newly hatched from flea eggs, eat the tapeworm eggs that have dropped from the rectum of the animal. Each larva becomes an adult flea, still carrying the tapeworm eggs. When the dog or cat bites and licks at the bite of the adult flea, swallowing the flea, the tapeworm eggs are released from the digested flea's body.

Tapeworms get their moniker by looking like a measuring tape, segment after segment seeming to calibrate contamination. They can reach eight inches in length but they grow in segments —- dropping off the last segment to be flushed from the bowel. These sections remain mobile and are often seen wiggling about the anus. The dog or cat may scoot its behind along the floor to rub at the irritating parasite pieces. Although tapeworms do not usually cause serious illness, it is gruesome enough to think of their presence. Eliminating them and fleas makes a lot of sense.

How? Just hold your nose...

It is imperative that you hold your nose and come to grips with the task. Follow the dog to the yard and the cat to the litter box and squidgy some b.m. into the plastic container. Your pet will reward you with a much healthier bowel and body condition.

Phase one of a pet's life can be well protected by initial vaccination and worm control.

This phase embodies the 'baby' weeks. That's right, weeks, not months or years. A human baby is an infant until it reaches two or three years of age. A puppy or kitten is no longer a baby after the tenth week. It has become a child. These first few days then, give only a brief period in which some important health controls can be implemented. One of them is the worming process. Check out the appendices for details as to specific times and treatments necessary for the dog or cat you have under your care.

If your pet happens to be a horse it is just as imperative to rid them of their wormy passengers. A fecal sample is not hard to find in a horse stable. Just make sure you know which pile came from which horse.....

10:00 AM ...Discuss Breeding with Mrs. Traney

...Trip's scandal

We've realized for a long time that Trip is popular with clientele. He has a drawl and a demeanor that, along with that dark curly lock that drops down his forehead, give him a charismatic aura. At least that's how the female staff and clients see him. I tell him to brush his hair!

Nicole Traney is a recent youthful and comely widow. Her youth and comeliness touches on about forty plus years and a good deal of make-up. Her figure draws first glances. Fronted by a robust bust and followed by a wriggling rear she causes neck injuries in both directions as she walks in Heron Point. A rather large estate was left for this aggrieved dowager. It happened that she lost her mate and her dog in the same car accident two years ago. We tried to save the poodle — at least Dr. Tipper did — as he was on call that fateful night.

But the damage was simply too severe to pull the dog through. Nicole was as heart-stricken about the dog as she was her husband. To supplant lonely days and nights she finally invested in a new male companion — the canine variety. On Dr. Tripper's advice, she purchased a Blonde Retriever puppy as a Christmas gift to her-self.

Now, Nicole had become eternally grateful to Trip for his heroic attempts. So she named her new dog, 'Trip'.

Trip, the dog, today, was now six untrained months of age: a Golden Labrador with power and youth at his beck and call, utterly unmanageable. Mrs. Traney had to chase him down the street as soon as they got out of the car in the clinic parking lot. Her short skirt gave the local chiropractor significant revenue on that brief dash.

Trip, the dog, once inside the waiting room boomeranged from cat to dog to cat huddled at their owners' feet. Wendy Flitz's Persian cat Pershing jumped three feet high, all four feet at once when the black and gold nose and muzzle bounded onto Wendy's lap. Cats and dogs scattered at random until we were able to herd the pup and the skirt into the first examination room.

Mrs. Traney, obviously, asked to see Dr. Tripper. After all, the dog was named in his honor. Clients and patients settled down, eyes glancing at one another as their heads shook from side to side in disapproval of the pup's behavior. Staff and clients looked at one another with silent statements of impropriety, until even more lucid scandal emanated from the other side of the exam room door.

"Trip, get off of me!...Ohhhh, Trip you devil!....Trip stop that!"

Now, no one in the waiting room knew that this new puppy was named after the good doctor. Most everyone knew that Dr. Tripper was happily married. Jeannie Tripper was much appreciated in the town for her community work and interest in the Heron Point Literary Group. To hear the widow Traney scream such scandalous verbiage induced shocked looks from one person to the other, and many glances to the ceiling with each cry from beyond the door...

"Trip, stop licking me!...Trip get your nose out from under my skirt!...WILL YOU STOP THAT!"...

The appointment continued with intermittent shrieks audible to the entire clinic until finally Nicole, Trip and Trip came out the door. Trip, the dog, bolted out, rosy tongue drooped to its knees and dripping in drool from the excitement. Nicole's arm suddenly wrenched her forward as the leash tethered to the dog's neck yanked her into the waiting room — almost onto John Doyle's lap.

Trip, the vet, locks adhered to forehead dampened with sweat and wrinkled with frustration, gave the chart to Leslie.

"Thank you sooo much Doctor," oozed Nicole Traney as she struggled with Dr. Tripper's instructions and the straining leash. "I guess it just wouldn't be wise for me to breed..." The eyes of every person seated in the waiting room bulged in shock, staring straight ahead unable to look at one another. Mrs. Traney continued,"I just thought that he was such a beautiful dog and I wanted him to father a litter before I got him fixed." Then again as one, the heads in the waiting room bent in relief as Mrs. Traney pulled at the leash and said, "TRIP! SIT DOWN NOW!"

Trip, the dog, sat down. Eyes gaped again in sudden revelation that a dog finally minded his master, albeit one who had led them down a perilous path of scandalous thought.

Trip, the dog...

Everything in their power to please you.

$Let's\ talk$...Nothing could illustrate better the need for immediate training of puppies and kittens. Yes, cats can be trained as well. With their indifferent and diminished attention span it takes a lot more patience.

> Cats, unlike dogs, are more civilized, so they need not be trained beyond house training and the imparting of key words and attitudes so that you can let them know when you are angry for their indiscretions.

Dogs though, will be an embarrassment if not schooled in life's lessons from the outset. Although attention span is short they will do everything in their power to please you. Use this eagerness as the opportunity to learn. Puppy training begins with their first step into their own puddle. When they look down at the dampened paw and sniff the urine, let them know that the deposit on the floor is not appreciated. It needn't be extremely harsh. Puppies are ultra sensitive and you could generate an anal retentive canine if you overdo it.

11:18 AM... Mrs. Wendy Flitz, vaccinate two cats

"I've got a great memory, it's just short!"

As I get older, I realize that some of my brain cells have taken permanent vacation. Remembering takes a lot longer than it used to. Sometimes, I have to review the entire day's events before I can recall why I had previously and purposely come into a room. But Wendy Flitz is the epitome of forgetfulness. A saccharine personality, she pours redolent devotion onto her Persian cat 'Pershing' and her Calico Cat 'Calicat'. A stout woman in her mid-forties and with short dark hair and ebony skin she rushes through life like a tornado, twirling aimlessly from one incident to the other.

In addition to her cats, she has two children in elementary school. Her husband is a salesman who is on the road most of the week so she rushes around town in her '79 Volvo station wagon as chauffeur or ambulance, depending on the event or crisis at hand. Time management is not her forte. She is invariably late for appointments, almost 20 minutes behind today. And there's an adventure with her automobile with every visit.

The Flitz cats first autoventure...

Today she has brought Pershing and Calicat for their annual vaccinations. This being mid-winter, she did remember to bring an electrical cord to plug her block heater into our outdoor socket (her wagon doesn't start all that well, so she takes every precaution to keep the engine alive). However, she forgot where she put the block heater cord. Instead, she found a seventy-five-foot outdoor extension.

I hadn't arrived at the clinic yet thanks to the Biddle lecture series, so Samantha looked after the cats. Mrs. Flitz loses herself in conversation especially with her new-found kindred spirit, Dr. Skeen. Sam's husband too, was always busy with the farm. So, in addition to the work at the clinic, Sam had to look after their 'kids', the two Yorkshire Terriers and their pups, and the household chores. Wendy and Sam compared notes throughout the examination and vaccination of the cats.

As Mrs. Flitz went to the counter to pay the bill she continued the discussion. "Oh, I know," she said. "If it's not one thing it's another. Today I had to rush the kids to school, stock up on a few groceries, clean the house and bring these babies in for their needles. I hadn't counted on this late snowfall. Not only was I late in getting out of the house I had to shovel the driveway! Now I have to pick up some things at the hardware store before going back to the school before twelve. You see, I forgot to make the kids their lunch, and now I have to run it over to them as soon as I'm done here. Some days I feel like I'm playing Beat the Clock!"

"Well, you've got this chore done," said Samantha. "These guys are good for a year now, so that's out of the way."

Mrs. Flitz gave Dr. Skeen a weak, grateful but unconvinced smirk as she carried two struggling cats to her car. They were just as eager to get out of the clinic as are most animals, who don't enjoy being prodded and pricked by the strangers in this building.

In her battle to get Pershing and Calicat safely into the car, Wendy was so pre-occupied in accomplishing the task, that she forgot to unplug the cord to the block heater. Glancing at her watch, she muttered aloud, "Oh my heavens, look at the time". Gunning the engine, the car went into reverse and roared back out onto the highway. Samantha and Leslie heard the extension cord 'pop' out of the socket and ran out to see a seventy five foot serpentine cable bouncing behind the vehicle. Pershing and Calicat watched through the rear window as the cord twisted and bounced, clearly wishing they could swat at this playful string that mommy brought. A portent of many more Mrs. Flitz's 'autoventures'.

2:15 PM... Mrs. Redding, recheck growth

A reprieve for Boz

"Hello Mrs. Redding, how's Boz Budgie today?" I said. It was my turn to take the afternoon appointments. Dr. Tripper had opted for country calls while Dr. Skeen cleaned the drainage tube from Gumper Walton's abscess. She also wanted to give Rambo Burtle special attention as he recovered from his surgery.

"Hello, Doctor Runcibal," said Mrs. Redding. "Well, he appears to be healthy but

I wanted to see what you thought about this lump again. It seems to me that it's getting bigger. And I was wondering whether or not it could be removed."

I reached down to pick him up so that I could get a good look at the growth. Boz grabbed my finger with his beak and crunched. "Wow!" I said with a wince and a tear. "I can tell you for sure, that he still has his strength."

"Oh now Boz, you little rascal, don't you hurt the good Doctor," admonished Mrs. Redding with a wagging finger. Boz's head went back and forth with each wag, my finger still firmly in his grip. I bit my tongue with each rotation. Finally, he realized that I wasn't going to let him go, nor was I hurting him, and he released. I put Boz back into his box.

"Yes, you're right, Mrs. Redding," I said shaking and rubbing my digit. "The lump is a bit bigger than the last time you were here. It's not growing rapidly but it's definitely larger."

I looked at the box for a moment or two before speaking. "I have to be honest with you, Mrs. Redding. At some point that lump should be removed. But we don't operate on that many birds to make us experts in avian surgery. I could refer you to the College or to another specialist in the city who looks after birds and exotic animals. I'm reluctant myself to operate. I'm especially concerned because of Boz's age. The surgery doesn't bother me as much as the anesthetic."

"I understand Doctor. I'm prepared for the worse. I would hate to lose this little rascal, he's such a companion for me on long lonely days. But heck, if I lose him I can always get another bird. And I don't really want to bother seeing a specialist about this."

"Look," I proposed. "As long as he's eating and singing let's leave the tumor alone.

As soon as it starts to bother him we'll try to remove it. Okay?"

"That's fine Doctor." Mrs. Redding and Boz left with a reprieve from the surgery that we all dreaded.

2:45 PM... Julie Baldwin's cat and litter check-up

A queen protects her own.

We cherish the times that a new litter of puppies or kittens are brought into the hospital. Everyone pitches in when we deliver a litter either by instruments or Cesarean. At first our spouses and some of the staff found it 'icky' to be rubbing the gelatinous cream off the bodies and faces of the newborn — even more difficult to press a mouth over the face of a puppy or kitten to blow life into a weakened, limp and fading body.

But a kennel or box full of writhing mewling puppies or kittens is a wonder and a joy. Particularly so, if you've had a part in the survival of all concerned. Julie Baldwin and Maxine had reason to be grateful to the staff of the Ark and Bark. Six weeks ago Maxine was in dire straits. Weakened by hours of pressing on a breech birth she had been rushed to the clinic at three in the morning. Julie didn't realize the birthing was taking place that night until she was awakened by howls reminiscent of 'The Exorcist'. She found Maxine, her orange tabby, screeching painfully in the far corner of the kitchen pantry.

Dr. Skeen was on call and since this would be her first Cesarean, Mary and I, even Leslie, had come into the clinic to help out. There were tense moments since Maxine had weakened dangerously. The breech kitten could not be revived and four others were delivered barely alive. Our team passed the mouse-sized bodies from womb to towel to be rubbed vigorously and dried. Each took turn blowing life into the squeaking faces.

Today was the first we'd seen the litter since that early morning surgery three fortnights ago. Samantha was understandably keen to admire her very first Cesarean delivery. Mrs. Baldwin brought the basket of mewing critters to the counter. "Look at these kittens, aren't they adorable?" Leslie, Sam and I butted heads as we peered into the nest of mother and kittens. Samantha reached into the cradle to pick up an orange tabby clone of Max...

Maxine was not the most pleasant personality prior to the litter. She had no choice

Cats in a box...

six weeks ago but to let us sedate and operate. Today she would have no part in human intervention — for her or her brood. As soon as Sam put her hand into the basket to pick up one of the kittens Maxine snapped furiously. The quarters were so close that the bite was huge and tight. Sam instinctively pulled her arm back. Unfortunately there was a cat attached to the end of it!

Samantha stood fixed in shock. She held her hand in the air. Maxine had her jaws clamped onto the flesh of her hand below her baby finger. You could hear the feline's canine fangs scrape together inside the muscle. Maxine hung straight down from her grasp of the hand in front of everyone sitting in the waiting room, blood dripping slowly onto the floor below. Joyce Walsh swooned and fell back into her chair, Allanis Scriven uttered a subdued gasp, her hands grasping her cheeks.

Dr. Skeen was in shock (thankfully this prevented undue pain). The cat was determined to remain with its vice-grip hold of the hand. I tried in vain to force the jaws apart. Clearly the only way to remove the cat was to sedate or anesthetize. I sat Sam down on a stool beside the surgery table. We had to keep Maxine suspended in the air because as soon as she was able to get a foothold on the table she wrenched her head from side to side to further punish this person she had attacked.

A tourniquet, alcohol and raised vein allowed me to slowly inject a fast-acting barbiturate into the cat's blood. Maxine began to go limp although her mouth remained firmly clamped on Sam's hand. Sam lowered the slumbering feline onto the table as Julie Baldwin and Leslie eased her arm and the cat to a comfortable position. I was then able to wrench the jaws apart.

The unorthodox procedure completed, Samantha, Leslie, Julie and I ... fainted.

Caution: New litter!

Let's talk...Queens and bitches protect their young. Some dogs and cats have dispositions that make them less than 'best friends'.

> When a dog or cat has a litter they can become overly protective no matter what their temperament.

Children and adults must realize the hormones and motherly instincts rushing through these animals pre and post partum make them dangerous and unpredictable. For the most part, they will maintain the same mood whether pregnant, nursing or childless. It is prudent to be cautious around a new litter nonetheless.

6:50 PM ...puppy hit by a train

Bounce limps into my life

Bounce was a happy-go-lucky Old English Sheepdog that lived his name. I first met him when Al Latimer, the manager of the feedlot west of town brought him to me to be put to sleep. A puppy that was only four months old he had already been dealt a severe blow to his young life.

"I found him crying beside his mother," said Al with a shaking voice. "He and Sherpa were hit by a train." He explained with some difficulty. "You know that the feedlot is close by the tracks. Well, he and his mother must have been crossing the track to come up to the house just when the 5:20 was going by. He was the only pup left as we'd found homes for the rest of the litter. This pup was like her shadow as soon as his last sister had left."

"What about Sherpa?" I asked, knowing already from Al's tearful expression what the answer would be.

"She was killed instantly...I couldn't believe...it was just terrible..."

I knew how attached Al was to Sherpa, the pup's mother. I had made several calls to the farm over the years and the two were inseparable. Wherever you saw Al, you saw Sherpa, either sitting in the truck beside him, walking through the fields to check the cattle or following the plow, back and forth, all the day long as Al tilled the soil.

The pup lay limp on the cold steel of the exam room table. His eyes showed fear and despair yet he seemed to look up at me with affection despite his pain. Sherpa was a pure-bred Sheepdog. Clearly this pup's father was otherwise. The puppy's fur was longer, curlier, but black-and-tan like a German Shepherd. But his short Sheepdog-like ears flopped to each side of his head. Dark brown eyes searched past the curly locks that feathered his face looking for relief and explanation.

There appeared to be a fractured humerus, the main bone of the front leg. The pup licked my face as I leaned down to check it's gums for any sign of internal bleeding. "It looks as though it's just a fracture, and I can fix that," I said stroking the injured orphan.

"No dog can ever replace Sherpa," said Al wistfully. "And this litter is not pure-bred like her. I don't get paid enough to cover surgery for a mongrel pup." Al was obviously suffering from all kinds of emotions and this poor pup was a victim of a time of great loss. I didn't like the thoughts of having to put this cute little creature to sleep.

"I'll tell you what," I offered. "This guy looks to me to be too good an animal to put away, so I'll fix him free of charge. If you decide you don't want to keep him, then I'll give him a home." Al looked up with a smile of relief. I knew he didn't want to lose this pup too, but he had too much loss crowding him right now.

Grief is a complex set of emotions related to the separation of a loved one. Sherpa was Al Latimer's loss. I didn't want two negatives to come out of one. I would rather see at least some benefits sooner — and I would see more later.

Six weeks later Al brought the pup in to remove the pin that I had used to stabilize

Bounce, sitting...

the fracture. Although well cared for, the puppy didn't get the attention it demanded since it brought too many memories of Sherpa. I seemed to be the one the pup responded to best as it was full of excitement every time I dropped by to treat one of their cows. In June I was called out to the farm to check a sick cow. It was a joy to see this little pup come bounding up to see me as I got out of my truck.

"We've decided to call him 'Bounce' ," said Al as he came out from the barn to greet me. "I've never seen such a happy dog in my life. It's as though he knows he was given a reprieve and he's overjoyed at the prospects each day brings. He doesn't walk or run from place to place — he bounces!"

Al was right. Bounce bounced. He bounced down the lane every time I went out to the beef-lot on a call. I maintained secretly that it was me he was delighted to see every time I went there. He bounced along the laneway as I drove out, as though he was saying 'come back again'. I looked forward to every call to this beef herd just because I was going to see a dog that was so happy with life. My reward, I was to learn later, would not just be the satisfaction of preserving a deserving creature. This dog would be evidence enough that love can be a four-legged word....

Size dictates their lifespan...

Let's talk...I watched this dog bounce through a couple of life phases before the next step in our relationship. As you can see from the daybook the variety of cases we see on any given day reflect the many stages that animals go through in their lives. It also includes the accidents that befall even beasts. Is disease an accident as well? Or can we prevent so many of the conditions that diminish quality of life? Certainly we can minimize problems.

Dog and cat breeds have come to us from around the world and generations of breeders who were genetic manipulators before the term was invented. Furred friends were bred to suit particular needs. The Chinese created ragmop lapdogs to add to the aesthetics of their palatial surroundings, the French and English created hunting dogs, some as terriers to mole out creatures from the ground, others as deer hounds to outrun the quarry.

> As a consequence we have dogs in all shapes and sizes. And their size more than anything dictates their life span.

Toy dogs (Chihuahuas, Yorkshire Terriers etc.) may have a higher rate of metabolism, higher heart rate and so burn out their bodies sooner. Giant breed dogs (Great Danes, Newfoundlands) have a slower system but seem to run down just as quickly as the tiny breeds, perhaps because there is so much extra work for them to do just to keep the motor running. Since dogs especially, come in so many shapes and sizes, there are distinct differences in their stamina and longevity. Small dogs (Bassets, Poodles etc.), other than the diminutive toy breeds, seem to live longer than tiny and giant breeds. Medium-sized dogs (Setters like Ruby, Labs like Smokey) live as long or longer than small dogs.

And breed determines behavior and disorders...

> Every breed of dog or cat comes with it's own set of inherited traits, behaviors, diseases or disorders.

Mongrel dogs and mixed-breed cats have been procreated more by chance than design. Even though there may be an element of 'survival of the fittest' in impure hybrids, one may still find genetic disorders. Your veterinarian and specific pet breeder can advise on the suitability of a breed of cat or dog to your personality, home amenities and lifestyle. Don't rule out a mutt or barn cat though. They can love just as much as the pedigreed.

As a result of the compressed and differing rates of metabolism, puppies and kittens require significantly specialized nourishment during their formative weeks. If they've been lucky enough to nurse from a healthy bitch or queen, they are at least starting off the first few weeks correctly. Many dog and cat mothers however are improperly nourished, often parasitized, to be unable to provide quantity and quality of suckled milk. One can see by the hair coat of mother and babies as to the general state of health of the brood. If the skin is dry, coat dull, listless and scaly, perhaps both mother and children need treatment and prescription diets.

Regardless of the suckling diet, puppies and kittens, once weaned from the mother, have material nutrient requirements. . For this little ball of fur has already doubled or tripled in size by the time it left mom. It will repeat the feat during the baby phase of its life.

> At the very least they must be fed a name brand puppy or kitten food. Ideally, your veterinarian should be consulted to help you choose a diet specially formulated for the rapid growth these creatures will endure.

There's a difference between a dog and a cat

Dogs and cats are as different an animal as can be imagined. They live parallel roles as pets not as beasts. Dogs are thought to be carnivores. They actually are omnivores. Ever wonder why dogs eat grass? Cats are obligate carnivores. In other words, they rely on meat by necessity. As a result they have have a higher protein requirement than the dog.

> Do not feed cats dog food, nor dogs cat food.

This can lead to dangerous deficiencies, even death. Dog diets are deficient in the amino acid, taurine for example. This compound is an essential amino acid to the cat, without it the cat will perish.

Because dogs and cats compress several human years into a few weeks or months and because there are so many different breeds of dogs and cats, nutrition has become one of the most important areas for continuing education for the practicing veterinarian. Neither your family doctor nor your veterinarian was likely given an adequate education in foods and feeding. Even worse, research daily turns current wisdom into proven fallacies.

Some pet owners turn to holistic approaches. While the premise for a whole-body preventive attitude is laudable, we still don't have all of the answers to be able to make herbal and nutrient supplements the requisite health style.

There are valid arguments for many of the holistic supplements. Research, still needed to prove or disprove many such theories, will help separate the fiber from the fat. I propose a healthy combination of traditional medicine and nutrition with a modicum of research-proven holism.

The science of nutrition is going the way of pharmaceuticals and it has been suggested by some that we are entering an era of 'nutriceutics'. The more we learn about the chemistry of the body, the differences between man and animal, the differences within species, breed to breed, the closer we will come to prescribing a computerized, balanced natural sustenance.

Your veterinarian remains the primary source for medical and nutritional advice. Some lean towards holistic approaches while others remain traditional.

CHAPTER THREE

Ark and Bark

Animal Clinic

CHAPTER THREE

Ark & Bark Animal Clinic
Tuesday May 22, 1989

Morning Emergencies:
Mrs. Patrick - dog seizures
Tony Vicusso - calving

Morning Farm Calls:
Beth Rocklin - x-ray lame horse
Glen Kemp - geld horse

Morning Surgeries:
Dockerty - Cocker Spaniel to demat
Jock Campbell - St. Bernard to spay
Mrs. Redding - budgie: remove growth

Morning Appointments:
10:00 Jean Harcourt - dog's hair keeps coming out
10:15 Billie Smith - cat sneezing
10:30 Mrs. Switzer - St. Bernard's eyes sore
10:45 Mrs. Johnson - euthanize poodle
11:00 Winters - cat has diarrhea and vomiting
11:15 Cathy Barlow - first shots for puppy
11:30 *Constable Holtby - Spook to vaccinate*
11:45 Bud Wright - Cocker's ear
12:00 Russell Smoke - dog wheezing

Afternoon Farm Calls:
Henry de Vost - LDA
Riley Sitter - RP

Afternoon Appointments:
2:00 *Mrs. Dinty - mynah bird won't stop talking*
2:15 Julie Hubner - vaccinate Kinter
2:30 Mrs. Jordan - cat straining to urinate
2:45 Mrs. Kasper - annual vaccination
3:00 Keith Baler - dog has worms
3:15 Mrs. Alice Frank - cat with fur ball problem
3:30
3:45 John Archer - first puppy shots
4:00 Karen Marsh - anal glands

Evening Emergencies:
Ruby Beasley - porcupine quills

Tighter Titer...

Tuesday May 22, 1989 8:00 a.m.

Boz Redding - remove tumor

...'Ether' this or that.

"Leslie, would you come into the surgery to give me a hand with Mrs. Redding's bird?" Finally, today we had to operate. Mrs. Redding came in Monday in considerable distress. The lingering lump had grown to about the size of the end of my thumb. Boz was now leaning to the left. He was even falling off the perch!

Mrs. Redding felt though, that, "If Ronald Reagan could undergo surgery to remove a polyp when he was 73, her old bird could do the same."

"Just hold him under the light, so I can best see the tumor." I instructed Leslie as I passed the nervous bird into her hands.

"Y'know," I thought, "Let's use ether to put him down for the surgery. It's got to be the safest...really the only anesthetic that might be safe and quick for a bird. He'll come around quickly, if he survives the surgery."

Leslie prepared the instruments. She was ready to prep the area with soap, alcohol and antiseptic. I took a wad of cotton from the jar and poured ether into the pad. Then lowered the vapor-fuming pad to the bird's beak. Boz, after a minor struggle, started to drift off.

Leslie and I started to drift off.

Leslie was leaning on one side of the surgery table, elbows on the surface to support her hands that came together to hold the bird in a nest of cloth and vapors. Her face was immersed into the harsh fumes. She looked up at me with a smirk, each eyeball headed in opposite directions, then her head dropped back into the bed of vapor. To me, she looked perfectly normal, for by this time I too was bending down into Boz's berth of cotton and gas to examine the growth. By the time I looked up at Leslie my lower lip drooped uncontrollably. Either I was swaying gently from side to side or the table suddenly had grown wheels.

I finally realized that I was going to be asleep soon. I shook my head and walked back and forth to get my senses. "We're gonna have to get this done as soon as possible or we'll be on the floor.....Y'know," I thought out loud. "I've got that new electrocautery unit. It will nip that little growth off in seconds." I leaned over to peek into Leslie's hands to examine the surgical site, taking a deep breath of the soporific fumes ".....And there will be no blood...... Then it will take just a few more sheconds to put a shtitch or two....."

I staggered over to the cautery machine, turned it on. I stood in a trance with a face contorted and numb. I stared as the electro-scalpel became red hot looking more like the clinic jester than the hospital surgeon. I beamed with satisfaction that I had hit on such a great technique. Then I stomped flat-footed to the table. I lowered the hot iron into the fumes surrounding the sleeping bird.

Abruptly, a great white flame erupted in our faces.

POOFFF!!!

In that instant the ether, and Boz, exploded.

A fine white mist wafted over us as particles of black soot and feathers filled the air.

"Phffft, phfff." Suddenly startled to wakefullness, Leslie and I wheezed and coughed as each of us blew feathers out of our mouths and noses. We looked at each other, our faces blackened, as white and blue feathers wafted gently and profusely around us.

Immediately staring into each other's blackened faces our thoughts simultaneously whirled to the real victim of the detonation.

We looked anxiously and fearfully down into Leslie's cupped hands at a blackened Boz'. Staring wide-eyed and surprised more than us glared a charcoaled feathered, significantly denuded, formerly beautiful budgie. Mostly naked from the head to its breast, covered only with a handful of singed feathers the bird gave a barely audible coughing 'peep' as if to say, "What the hell happened?"

"Oh my god!" We sang in unison. I felt asinine and angry as I realized what did happen. How could I have not remembered that ether is highly flammable. Obviously, the ether had numbed us as well as Boz.

After a few minutes outdoors to get some air and composure, I realized that I had

Boz was here...

an even greater problem. I had to tell Mrs. Redding. I grudgingly shuffled into my office and dialed her number.

"Hello?"

"Hello,.....Mrs. Redding?"

"Yes, Doctor Runcibal?"

"Yes...Mrs. Redding...you know that I told you of my biggest fear in doing the surgery on Boz ?"

"Yes, I know... he didn't make it did he?"

"Nnno...He's still alive, but he had a bad reaction... from the anesthetic."

"Oh dear, you must be just heartbroken Doctor."

"You can't imagine," I agreed. "I just wanted you to know that we would take care of little Boz.....for a while." There was no way I wanted her to see the state that this cooked bird was in. I waited with baited breath praying that Mrs. Redding did not want to take her charred bird home.

"That would be kind of you, Doctor." She finally said. "I'll come by this afternoon to settle up the bill."

"Oh no," I said, "that won't be necessary, I certainly can't charge for this. I'm going to remove the tumor this afternoon after I get some advice from an expert on birds. When Boz is ready to go home I'll call you."

Boz Budgie became a clinic guest for several weeks before he looked half-way presentable and I was willing to let Mrs. Redding see what I had done to her precious little bird.

I did call Mrs. Redding a few days later. My conscience wouldn't stop making me feel guilty. Interestingly, Mrs. Redding was more comforting to me than angry. She clearly felt my regrets and appreciated my personal admonishment. Hereafter, I would admit at the outset, any deficiencies I may suffer and refer to an expert whenever indicated.

There is nothing wrong with anyone saying, "I don't know." If you find a veterinarian willing to admit this, you have a keeper.

Preventive care equals longer life

Fundamental to avoiding disease is the life-time vaccination program.

$Let's$ $talk$...Keeping a pet around longer demands strict attention to preventive care. We recall the tears and fears of inoculations at the hands of the public health nurse in the school gymnasium. Pets and veterinarians alike have experienced syringe scares...

12:00 noon - Officer Holtby, Vaccinate Spook...

Behind closed doors, there waits a demon.

Trip continues to have disaster visit on a regular basis. He seems to come within a hair's width from demise on his recurrent adventures. "Ah'm wondrin", he said earlier today. "Whether I was a cat in a previous life. A cat who died before it's nine lives were wasted. And Ah'm wondrin' just how many lives that cat had in reserve cause ah'm runnin' through several of em".

Trip's sixth or so, remaining cat's life expired when the twelve o'clock appointment came. Constable Darren Holtby, of the local constabulary, brought his German Shepherd 'Spook' to the clinic for vaccination. Darren has trained this furry partner for drug busts and airport duty in the city. Spook would only respond to Officer Holtby. And he was trained to attack.

Spook was a dark and moody black and tan Shepherd. If it were late at night you would likely not see him lurking in the shadows. If ever you were unfortunate enough to be contemplating crime and you met Spook in a dark alley, restitution and prayer would immediately be on your lips. If Spook were to stand on his hind legs resting his front paws on the shoulders of a six- foot man, his massive head and teeth would be looking down at the felon-turned-casualty.

Spook would not let Trip get close to him. He growled menacingly with every movement. No, it was more than a growl. The walls of the clinic shook. It was an eruption, a warning that if you so much as blink, you can say good-bye to your forearm.

After several half-hearted attempts to edge near enough to Spook to be able to break into that space, Trip finally said. "I'm simply not going to be able to give Spook an examination. The only way I could, is to give you some tranquilizers for his food...."

"That won't work," interrupted Officer Holtby. "Spook's trained to turn down any food that's adulterated. Isn't there some way that you can just give him his needles? I can tell you that he's healthy, if that makes you feel better. Hell, he's stronger than anyone on the force."

Not exactly what Trip wanted to hear, especially the latter part, as he had only one method of inoculation that might work. "I've been able to vaccinate guard dogs before by having the owner stand on the other side of a closed door while holding the chain and collar tight against the closed crack in the door. That allows me to get behind the dog to give the needles."

"Sounds like a plan," agreed Officer Holtby. "let's do it!". Trip could feel his skin tingle as the method of his next feline death was arbitrated. The officer walked out of the room holding a leash that seemed to Trip to be such a fine thread to hold so huge a dog, at a time when heavy gauge chain was needed. Holtby closed the door behind him and Spook looked at Trip as if to say, "I know what you're up to. Start praying pal!"

Trip got his inoculations ready to inject the two needles rapidly. Then Officer Holtby pulled the door and the chain taut. Once again, Trip remained trapped in this small room. This time, with an enormous canine. His only escape was being held shut by an equally muscular officer.

Spook grumbled menacingly. The windows rattled. Then Trip said nervously. "Now hang on to the door and the leash as tight as you can." With the words, 'stronger than anyone on the force' still resonating in his ears, Trip knelt down behind Spook to pray, meow, and vaccinate.

Spook pulled at the door and the leash. You could hear Holtby's face smash into the door. But he didn't let go. The leash held. The door warped. And Trip lost another life.

Because of the intensity of the sounds that Spook made, the two appointments sitting in the waiting room abruptly left in terror.

But Spook was vaccinated. Officer Holtby, disheveled, but looking much better than Trip, was about to put Spook into the cruiser when he called back, "We'll see you next year". Those words still possess Trip, who has now asked for the entire month of May 1990 for vacation time.

Sent down to the mynahs...

2:00 Mrs. Dintey has a Mynah Bird that won't stop talking...

...sent down to the Mynahs.

Animals imprint. If they are raised by humans they will follow and mimic their parental substitutes. Birds are intimately affected, particularly if they are raised from nestlings. Such a feature of animal behavior befell Mrs. Bernice Dintey.

Bernice was a spinster octogenarian. She had lived alone for most of her adult years. She did have a brother who lived in Saskatoon. It was his passing that led her to our clinic door.

"Doctor Runcibal, I really don't know what I'm going to do," said an exasperated Mrs. Dintey. With spectacles that hadn't been renewed for decades leaning on the edge of her diminutive nose, she peered over the rim to look at me with considerable desperation. "You see I lost my brother Bertram in his ninety first year, just last December. He really

didn't have a lot of belongings but the one treasure that he valued most was this foolish bird!"

Inside a cage the size of the Sky Dome sat a colossal black Mynah Bird with ebony dark feathers and a yellow beak. He looked curiously at his new surroundings and said, what at this point, was unintelligible... "Eessoosseessoorrrsss".

Mrs. Dintey dropped a sigh of distress at this and continued. "That's just what he does. Constantly. I can't get a moment's peace. My brother asked in his will for me to take care of this creature. It was his dying wish, but I swear, this bird will be the death of me. I thought birds just sat there. I never expected that they would never shut up!"

"Yaaaahhhhhh..." said the bird.

I thought for quite some time before speaking. I have had plenty of people ask why their bird wouldn't sing or talk. "The only thing I can suggest Mrs. Dintey, Is that we keep the bird here for a few days. Let's see if the change in venue makes a difference. I also want to keep an eye on its demeanor to see if it is extraordinarily nervous for example. There must be some reason for such churlishness."

"You can keep it for a week, a month if you like," agreed Mrs. Dintey, relieved to be rid of this babbler for at least some breathing space. "I hope you can find something that can help."

I took the Mynah back to the treatment room. "Hi there bird. Want a cracker?" I said in a lame attempt to get it to talk.

"Arrriigghht....Arrriigghhht," Said the Mynah.

By the next day we were ready to ring the bird's neck. Our hearts went out to this hapless lady saddled with a motor-mouth mynah. It wasn't until the end of the day that it became clear what the problem was. The dark-feathered loud speaker finally became less of an enigma when he said, "T'ose Russians oughta go home!"

Then everything he said and how it was said became crystal clear.

"He shoots, he scooorres!.....Arright now listen up youse guys....Yaaahhhhh (crowd noise)....T'ose ref's t'ose ref's, they gotta get in tha gammme..."

Mrs. Dintey had inherited a Mynah bird that had likely spent the majority of its life sitting in an old man's parlor beside the television set. The most dramatic constant in it's life has been Hockey Night in Canada! And its most emphatic imprint has been on Don Cherry!

I phoned Mrs. Dintey to give her the news. "I'm afraid there isn't much we can do about it. The bird has a fixation on Don Cherry. I would recommend that you consider finding a home for it where it will be well cared for and by people who watch hockey on TV, unless of course you do."

"Oh I don't watch hockey Doctor Runcibal. I just think that Donald Cherry is so annoying. And hockey is so violent! Oh, I couldn't keep a bird that reminded me of those two things all the day long." said Mrs. Dintey.

So we found a hockey haven for the Mynah, a minor hockey coach with three kids in love with the sport. They called the bird Molson. He immediately fell into the family fun of watching the Calgary Flames win the Stanley Cup by beating the venerated Montreal Canadians two days later. Molson learned to mimic Don's plaudits 'Laaanny MacDonald...that's a hockey player boy!' I'm sure Molson is still calling play-by-play...

The appointment book today had several new patients. Billie Smith brought two kittens in for vaccination. Unfortunately, one was sneezing so we had to treat it for a possible upper respiratory infection before going ahead with either inoculations. She found them abandoned on the side of the road. John Archer has a poodle-cross female that had an unwanted litter. He's had their tails docked so that they resemble as close as possible the type of dog he hopes they become. I expect he'll get

Mandy spayed soon after the pups are gone. Cathy Barlow brought a lively puppy in for it's first needles.

Why vaccinations?

Let's talk...Each person asked differing questions along the same theme: what are these vaccinations all about? John was frightened that he might have to get the first needles for six puppies in order to entice people to give them a home. That expense alone justifies the spay.

In the first phase of life a puppy or kitten go through their baby years in just eight short weeks. A newborn child cannot walk or talk till it is 18 to 24 months of age. New-born pups and kittens can be weaned after six to eight weeks.

> The mother's milk and placental residuals have been protecting the litter from infectious diseases. That umbrella slowly unfolds as each day goes by until finally there is very little protection remaining.
> The first vaccination is essential.

At eight weeks of age the first 'distemper', 'cold and flu' combination must be administered. Just as newborn children must embark on their scheduled boosters for diphtheria, hepatitis, whooping cough, polio, and tetanus —- human afflictions now prevented with effective vaccines —- puppies and kittens need their vaccinations.

Vaccinations/Preventive Prescriptions for Dogs:

Recent veterinary graduates rarely see a case of Canine Distemper. When I began practice it was a common condition. Young dogs would be brought into the clinic with pus encrusting their nostrils and eyes, footpads hard and callused, and painful coughs. Eventually the dog would develop nervous symptoms and begin twitching uncontrollably. Euthanasia was inevitable. Now canine distemper as a disease is under relatively good control. It is still a worldwide prevalent problem, from unvaccinated stray dogs on the streets of North and South America, to the pet dogs in Africa. The disease is even prevalent in wild dog breeds such as hyenas and jackals.

Canine Hepatitis is caused by a virus that is usually contracted by way of mouth. It's target is the liver. This Hepatitis cannot be transmitted to humans, though it can be as deadly to the dog. Sudden vomiting, painful abdomen, spiking fever, make the dog acutely and severely depressed.

Not a virus, but a bacteria called Leptospira can penetrate the skin after exposure to discharges of the organism from the mouth, nose or urine of an infected animal, often other dogs or rats. The resulting disease, Leptospirosis thrusts the animal into a high fever, vomiting, reluctance to move and abdominal pain.

What could be called a 'canine flu' but more often referred to as 'Kennel Cough' is generally caused by a trio of organisms: Adenovirus Type 2, Bordatella and Parainfluenza. The dog joins us in our miserable symptoms of cold and flu season with a cough and runny nose. The viruses are commonly transmitted in boarding kennels if there are unvaccinated dogs allowed. And the barking greetings dogs make to one another results in an exacerbated 'kennel' cough, much like the barking laryngitis humans get when they talk too much despite having a sore throat.

Parvovirus is the most recent scourge of dogdom. This bug first appeared in the late seventies. Our clinics became converted war hospital scenes with dogs lining the hallways on stretchers or on the floor with intravenous units snaking down to their veins. Had it not been for relatively rapid production of an effective vaccine we would have lost a lot more dogs than we did. The virus still rears its ugly head from time to time. Some breeds (Rottweillers, Dobermans, Labradors, German Shepherds, Springer Spaniels, American Pit Bull Terriers and Yorkshire Terriers) seem to have a difficult time developing immunity. So some veterinarians feel compelled to give boosters to these dogs more often —- although others express concern about vaccinating too frequently since this may be producing immune-mediated problems.

Some vaccines, if not most today, include Coronavirus. This is an intestinal attacker that also causes diarrhea and vomiting. Although less severe than Parvovirus it is considered to be the second leading cause of viral diarrhea in dogs.

We are probably just at the beginning of identification of viral and bacterial organisms that can cause disease, some of which we can prevent with effective vaccines. Annual check-ups and determination of which viruses, bacteria, parasites are in your area of the country are the least you should do.

For example, you may also wish to discuss the prevalence of Lyme Disease and Heartworm Disease in your dog's environment.

Lyme Disease, primarily a danger to humans, is known as Borreliosis thanks to the organism Borrelia burgdorferi. The bug is carried by deer ticks. (Not the usual brown dog tick often seen sticking it's vicious head into a dog's skin). When the deer tick bites your dog or you, that.bug mentioned above that's hard to pronounce, gets into the bloodstream. Fever, arthritis (with a painful lameness) and lethargy follow.

This is also one of the reasons I stress grooming. Finding any tick demands immediate and careful removal (ideally with tweezers or a gloved hand after dousing the mouth parts imbedded in the skin with rubbing alcohol). Pull gently, firmly up and away from the skin avoiding squeezing the body of the tick or you'll inject the stomach contents into the blood of the dog. Take the tick to the veterinarian for identification —- or take the dog to the clinic to have them removed of you feel unsure of your ability to take them out yourself.

Heartworms are carried by mosquitoes. This parasite is prevalent in the warmer climes although gradually spreading across Canada, at least in the southern parts. Microscopic larval worms (called microfilaria) injected into the dogs blood by the mosquito, gradually end up in the heart where they grow in numbers and size. The inside of the heart and major vessels can become packed with scores of 12 inch white wriggling worms. The unfortunate affected dog becomes sluggish with all these worms diminishing its circulation. The dog starts to cough   The heart enlarges. Without treatment the dog can die, or suffer miserably.

Your veterinarian can test for heartworm presence in your dog's blood. A small sample would reveal the microscopic microfilaria. If present ,the worms can be killed with medication. If not present, they can be prevented from proliferating from the outset of the bite from the mosquito by giving a daily or monthly pill. This is essential for dogs that live in a heartworm endemic (prevalent) area.

Vaccination for Lyme Disease and medication to kill Heartworm microfilaria are now available and imperative if these parasites are endemic.

Feline heartworm

Cats can get infested with Heartworm as well. Recently, a test has been developed that allows the veterinarian to see whether the parasite has been injected into the cat by the mosquito (mosquito's carrying the

Your puppy needs needles...

organism don't just bite dogs, they bite anything with blood). It is recommended having cats tested for heartworms in an endemic area for the disease.

Vaccinations for Cats

What we used to call feline distemper, is now known to be caused by a number of viruses each with deadly consequences. They may even be more difficult microbeasts to defeat than those of dogs, but vaccines are becoming increasingly more effective against most of them. Cats can be totally and immediately debilitated by the bugs. It is most discouraging to have a cat so afflicted, in lateral recumbency, with no evident will to live. They are so devastated that it becomes impossible to raise a vein in order to give life-saving intravenous fluids. We resort to subcutaneous, oral or intra-abdominal administration, but often to no avail.

Cat viruses are disparate, dangerous and deadly. A vaccine incorporates diminished strengths of viruses, often killed viruses, that, once injected into the body stimulate the immune system to make antibodies against each disease. We vaccinate cats for a host of Upper Respiratory Viruses (the feline cold and flu bugs); Feline Leukemia Virus (until newly refined vaccines, this was the leading cause of death in cats); and Feline Infectious Peritonitis (A Coronavirus that causes a chronic wasting state leading inevitably to death).

Feline Leukemia Virus causes a cancerous lymphosarcoma. The virus can be detected with a test but there are caveats. There can be positive results to the test that are actually negative. On the other hand a cat might have the virus but the test could show negative. And a negative test means that no virus is detectable at the time the test is taken. It does not mean that the cat has immunity to the disease. Further, a cat that tests positive is not necessarily going to come down with cancer. It simply means that at some time the animal had been exposed to the disease. If this cat is otherwise healthy it is wise to test for the virus regularly and watch for signs of illness.

There are two cat diseases that as yet, have no effective vaccine - but certainly need them:

Feline Infectious Anemia (caused by a bug called Hemobartonella felis that attaches and destroys the cat's red blood cells; and Feline Immunodeficiency Virus. This one is referred to as Feline AIDS, but a completely cat-specific virus that destroys the immune system as does it's counterpart in humans.

However, neither can affect the other's host. Like AIDS though, this Retrovirus suppresses the body's ability to resist infection resulting in a number of secondary problems and eventual death.

Indoor Cats

Indoor cats that are not vaccinated run a great risk. They would have little or no immunity against these deadly diseases. A chance encounter with a roaming cat in the neighborhood —- through the screen door for example or an accidental escape from the house —- can bring the viruses to your cat's doorstep. Indoor cats should receive routine vaccinations.

The Case for Rabies

Acute Encephalomyelitis is known the world over as Rabies. The causative virus can attack any mammal. It can penetrate the body if exposed to the blood or saliva from an infected animal. The virus travels up a nerve to the spinal cord to begin destruction of nervous tissue and the result can either be paralysis or frenzy. An affected wild animal can change personality from feral-and-fearful of humans, to pet-like. The danger of petting a fox that seems to be as friendly as a puppy is enormous. The virus is present in the saliva drooling from the mouth. All it takes is a quick snap, breaking the skin, and the viruses rush into the new human host. The diseased animal can also act phobic, afraid of anything and everything, roaming aimlessly, biting at animate and inanimate objects in its path.

Why give a series of vaccines? Won't one 'shot' do? Here's why:

> The maternal antibodies, (protection from the mother's milk
> and placental blood) do not suddenly stop protecting.
> The protection gradually subsides.

If and when vaccination is given in the presence of these antibodies, the effectiveness of the vaccine is diminished and the higher the level of mothers' protection, the lower the 'take' of the artificially injected level. A series of injections stimulates an increasingly simulated response of protective antigens that eventually take over the mothers protective essence. The first injection becomes the sensitizing dose, priming the immune system, allowing the second and third shots to produce greater and greater protection.

Frequency of vaccination after the initial puppy and kitten inoculations may see some debate over the next few years. Most veterinarians believe that annual boosters give the best protection while others express concern that such repetitive vaccines may contribute to immune-mediated disorders.

Ongoing research on these viruses and on the immune system are going to provide the answers. Companies making the vaccines are developing even more effective versions of their products. A three-year Rabies vaccine is available, although annual vaccination in endemic areas is still advised. Ideally, we may some day be able to replace some of the vaccinations with blood tests that will tell us the 'titer' or level of antibodies in the body that are available to fight the disease in question. A high titer means no booster is needed. If low, the animal needs the vaccine. Tighter monitoring of titer could be the guide to individual vaccination programs.

If there is one critical procedure that is needed to launch a pet from its first phase of life successfully, it is that first vaccination. Subsequent regular boosters are the insurance policies that you pay to keep the demons from the door...

7:10 p.m. - Mrs. Beasley has Quills

....There are dumb dogs and smart dogs.

Every creature on earth has its own level of intelligence. Sometimes I've shaken my head over some people I've met, wondering how anyone could have been so short-rationed on brainpower, but from time to time Trip reminds me about my exploding budgie escapade. I've met some animals that could equal or better, such brainless antics.

The prizewinner was Ruby the Irish Setter.

Ruby was a portrait-perfect Setter, with a glossy russet coat, long feathered ears,

Ruby wears a bald porcupine's quills...

tail and legs. She had a regal look as she pointed her head in the air at the slightest sound. But, as with some monarchies, there must have been significant inbreeding to have produced Ruby.

The call came at about 7:00 p.m. just as Mary and I were about to sit down for an extraordinarily early dinner. "Dr. Runcibal, please come to the clinic as soon as possible, Ruby has tangled with a porcupine!" came the distraught call to action from her owner, Mrs. Beasley.

"Are you at the clinic already?" I asked, as was the inference in her call. This happens a lot. Pet owners get so excited about the incident, that they rush off to the veterinary hospital without thinking that they should have called first.

"Yes, can you come soon?" she said. I'll be right there. Is Ruby in much discomfort?" I asked as Mary handed me my coat. My wife and I have become resigned to the fact that the descriptor of veterinary life is existence-interruptus.

"No, she's just sitting as though nothing were the matter." She said with incomprehension. "But she must be in such terrible pain as her face is just full of quills."

That was my first clue as to the mental capacity of Ruby the Red Setter.

When I got to the office, Mrs. Beasley was waiting at the front door with Ruby sitting on the steps, her rear end on the landing and her front feet on the step below. A light dusting of snow was falling. Mrs. Beasley had a haggard, worried look on her face but Ruby was flitting her head at every snowflake that wafted past her nose, ignoring the mass of quills in her face. I admitted Ruby and sent Mrs. Beasley home, with assurances that the dog would be fine after I took out all of the quills. Since it would require an anesthetic to safely and painlessly tug each quill, one at a time, from her muzzle, tongue, face and cheeks, Ruby would be spending the night sleeping at the clinic.

Wandering somewhere that night, was a very bald porcupine. Ruby didn't just get the routine mouthful of porcupine quills. Her face and head were made into a porcupine clone. Most dogs learn the hard way by cautiously sniffing or snapping at an irate porcupine. The normally complacent beast doesn't 'throw' its quills as legend says, but it does release them into the mouth of any unfortunate dog, fox, or wolf, dumb enough, or hungry enough, to try to attack it. Ruby must have thought this porcupine was a fuzzy toy, just come its way to play. The only way that quills could have gotten so embedded into skin and mouth, even far down her throat, was for her to have had an intimate and continuous relation-

ship with that porcupine. It took 3 hours and several small incisions to ensure
that every quill was accounted for.

My dinner that night was cold but ravenously devoured. Little did I know, that
this was not the end of my encounters with Ruby...

They can learn...

Let's talk...In my view the evidence is clear, personality is heritable. Ruby personifies many of the Red Setters I have met, though perhaps
not as flighty. Setters make great companions but deserve attention to
their inbred need to hunt. Lap dogs love sitting in laps, hunting dogs must
have freedom to roam.

Each breed of dog and cat has an inherent personality.
Choose your pet carefully or you'll find your environment
at odds with the dog's personality.

Cats on the other hand have two possible dispositions. They either adapt
a dog-like mentality or a laissez-faire attitude. As a simulated-dog they
will allow you to pet them, follow you around and seem to act as obedi-
ently as a dog. Don't be fooled. When they have had enough of your
caressing as they drape their limp body across your lap they will shock
you out of reverie with a snarl and a nip. They will rush off victoriously,
happy to see your stunned face saying, "What did I do?"

The laissez-faire, disinterested cat will reluctantly be petted. You can
never own this cat. They own you and everything in your house. Their
attitude is, "You may stay if you wish, but don't bother me." Worship this
cat and you may be allowed to grovel and serve.

From birth, no matter how traumatic, animals have an emotional imprint on
our lives. Yet they are animals. We are supposed to be the superior beings
(cats' attitudes notwithstanding). How do we establish the proper pecking
order: Me Tarzan, you just a pet! The solution is in the training.

As pets grow into the second phase of their life they are old enough to
go to school. In human equivalents they are children who can certainly
start to learn. The debate will go on forever as to whether animals can

think and reason. I believe that they can, to some degree, but we will need to communicate with them not at them in order to resolve this puzzle. But they can learn.

First training focuses on minimizing house-soiling, asking to go outside for dogs and hitting the inside of the litter box for cats. They can be taught. Some cats can even be trained to use the toilet. But after childhood potty training, come the lessons in life. Some lessons are more difficult than others. A dog has a hard time understanding why master gets so angry at him when he cools off in the flower garden. "What's the big deal? This sand is soothing and cooling." Being partly color blind, there is no appreciation for the strange grasses (flowers) now trampled in an otherwise comfortable sand bed.

But training can and should be done as early as possible. Ideally from six months of age on. An obedience school is helpful because of the knowledgeable approach to training, persistence and most importantly, social acclimatization with other dogs and people.

Cats will have very little to do with training. And the more you try, and seem to succeed, the sooner you will realize that they have effectively trained you!

Training demands a tough-love approach. Consistency of verbal commands for the same desired effect is essential. Dogs have a short attention span so regular short training sessions are often the only way to get the message through. I have no idea how long a cat's attention span is. They can stare at a mouse hole for hours but turn away from any attempt to get their attention by you within seconds. If you mess with them too much you're dead meat.

Old wives must never have had an old dog because you can teach them new tricks. It may take longer because you are dealing with other habits that get in the way. Your friends will appreciate your efforts of training a well-disciplined pet. Especially when they who don't get knocked over when they come to visit. Pets enjoy pleasing their owners. Remember however, you are the servant to the cat, you are the servant to the cat...

CHAPTER FOUR

Ark and Bark

Animal Clinic

CHAPTER FOUR

Ark & Bark Animal Clinic
Monday June 5, 1989

Morning Emergencies:
Mr. Brice - injured Canada goose found on the road
Take clinic truck in for service, check the brakes

Morning Farm Calls:
Jocko Sweener - cow calved 3 days ago, remove afterbirth
Kasper Button - pig ruptured
Boyce Harrel - check horse in field (Monday Morning Disease?)

Morning Surgeries:
Iris Raitt - castrate Tippy and flush ears
Mrs. Waldie - spay Puddles, dental - prophy and extraction

Morning Appointments:
10:00 *Major & Mrs. McQuig - Chiwawa has a sore leg*
10:15 Reg Kettle - 2 cats, 2 dogs - shots
10:30 Mrs. Marscott - cat going bald
10:45
11:00 John Doyle - Sparky won't eat
11:15 Koos Popalicious - Doberman with a thorn in its paw
11:30 Mrs. J. Furrow - Coco - scooting on hind end (worms?)
11:45 Rose Walton - vaccinate new kitten
12:00 Caroline Rose - cat has swallowed needle and thread

Afternoon Farm Calls:
Stokely Harper - cow with plugged teat
Jeremy Dickson - herd health call
Parker Barrow - pony foundered

Afternoon Appointments:
2:00 Jane Jones - Gretchen - spaniel can't sleep
2:15 Ms. Winters - cat with ear mites
2:30
2:45 *Wendy Flitz - Calicat vomiting fur balls*
3:00 Cathy Barlow - Willy (pup not feeling well)
3:15 Billie Smith - 3 cats coughing up worms
3:30 Mrs. Lockern - Twinkle - lumps in abdomen
3:45
4:00 Gloria Logel - chinchilla not eating, smells badly

Evening Emergencies:
P J Palfrey - board Wolf - cross for a few days
Heron Point Kennel Club - Dr. Runcibal's talk on hip dysplasia

Monday June 5, 1989

Tempest in a Teacup

The day opens with news of the Tiananmen Square Massacre still echoing in our minds. Petty problems are set aside as visions of tanks and flames and bodies of young idealists take precedent. We can do nothing but watch and listen. We are left to cope with issues in our own world somewhat diminished by man's inhumanity to man.

Animal Lovers don't discriminate in their veneration. The pet dog sleeping on the porch at home, the cat on the window sill, both benefit from pats, coos and meals. Feral beasts profit from sympathy at the least, activism at the most. An animist would swerve to miss a frog hopping across the road rather than create road-kill. A dead raccoon on the side of the road immediately conjures the whereabouts of a nest of baby raccoons somewhere nearby. Anyone would cringe to think of those poor creatures starving to death.

This affection for wildlife encompasses birds of the air, and is especially enforced when the aviator cannot fly...

7:15 AM... the early bird emergency...

...a Canada goose walking north

Early June the Cumbersome foothills north of Heron Point, reverberate with new-born bristling leaves flapping happily in the warm gusts of spring. Only Mother Earth as Gaia could write a score of music that builds and subsides with the wind, trees, birds and frogs. Lost in early-morning reverie as this rustic symphony builds, I sat on the front porch sipping the final draughts of coffee listening to the orchestra of nature surrounding me. From the orchard whistles the single and double note phrasing of the Northern Oriole, followed by a loud and clear, 'Wheet wheet wheet..wheet-cheer wheet-cheer wheet-cheer' of the crested male Cardinal. Then, as though it had always been there, a faint chorus echoes from the distance in the south. The choir sounds a repetitive phrase in unison and at random at the same time. The burly voices sing a continuous low phrase immediately followed by a louder version.

Suddenly the chorus is overhead as a wavering wedge of Canada geese adds their rustle of feathers to this spine-tingling aria. Such a serene moment should never have to end.

On Highway 21 the fluff of enormous wings and indignant honks, by the victim and passers-by, shattered any serenity there and eventually at my porch chair. My sunrise coffee klatch was interrupted by the distressed call from Knowlton Brice. Answering service suggested that I rush to the clinic immediately. The background commotion on the call sounded like World War Three had broken out. As I drove into the clinic lot, I could see a man in the front seat of a new-model Chevy surrounded by flying feathers.

Knowlton Brice, a gentleman of 52, was the local jeweler. Always meticulous, with a slim build on a five-foot-eight frame, he was always the picture of composure. Knowlton would come to the clinic regularly with his cat Sapphire. His speech was erudite like the diamonds he gleaned day to day. At first I didn't recognize that this flailing mass of arms, wings and legs was the one and the same Mr. Brice. I rushed to the front door as the confabulation fought its way into the clinic.

"I just couldn't believe what I was seeing, Doctor," gasped Knowlton, as he struggled with the squirming goose wrapped in a London Fog topcoat. "This bird was walking north. The poor thing must have a broken wing or something because it can't seem to fly."

"But that wasn't going to stop him from following the flocks," he continued. "I was driving to my store, south on Highway 21, at approximately three point five miles from the town line, when I saw this goose waddling the opposite direction at the side of the road. I just had to stop after I had passed it, because it wasn't trying to fly but was looking up in the sky and making an awful racket."

Knowlton recovered his breath as the goose finally submitted to its captors. "I turned around and drove about 100 yards ahead of him. I got out of the car and kneeled down directly in his path as he walked towards me. He was honking a blue streak and not paying any attention to me, looking into the northward sky. You could hear what it was that had him so upset."

"Sure enough," he continued, " There was a flock of Canada Geese above us, heading north. And this goose, even though he couldn't fly, had all the intentions of at least walking to the northern nests. I could see that there was definitely something wrong with him as he came closer. See here, his left wing is distorted and twisted behind his back.."

I confirmed Knowlton's observation as the goose gave a squawk of pain wher. manipulated the wing to determine the extent of the damage.

"He was so engrossed in the activity in the sky that he walked right into my arms. It surprised both of us. I never knew what hit me because as soon as he bumped into me I realized I had a tiger by the tail."

" I guess now you know why some country folk use geese as watch dogs," I said as I gently wrapped my arms around the disconsolate goose. The regal eyes glowered menacingly at Knowlton and then at me. The long neck swayed for a moment then the beak savagely hammered at my arm. Injured wing or not, the goose was determined that these strange beasts would not keep him from his mission in life.

"That's for sure," he confirmed. " But I knew that if I let him go I would never catch him again, so I held on for dear life while he pecked at me and wriggled to get loose." By the look of the cuts and scratches on this man's face and the disheveled suit of clothes there was clearly evidence of a terrific struggle. "And I really wanted to get him in to you because I was afraid he would either be hit by a car or attacked by a dog."

"That's likely what would have happened," I agreed.

"Once I got him into the car with my coat snuggled around him he seemed to settle down, though he nattered at me all the way to the clinic. You should have seen the looks I got as I drove down '21' with this goose in the passenger seat!"

I can picture it, but can't imagine what people would be thinking when they saw this car speeding down the road with a passenger with a long neck and narrow face wearing a top-coat. The number of double takes must have set a record.

"Unfortunately my wife is not going to be too happy when I get the car home," he groaned. "I have a white and streaming donation on my front seat."

"I'm afraid you've also got some of it on your pants," I said, reluctantly nodding at a white streak down his trousers. "Has a sharp, acid smell, doesn't it?" I added.

"Well I guess that's the price I've paid for stopping him on his mission," Knowlton conceded as he winced and wiped at the stain with a damp cloth I had handed him. Now, Knowlton Brice was known to be particular about dress and demeanor. To refuse to begrudge such a smudge was the sign of a true animal lover. "Can you fix him Doctor?" he asked. "I would be willing to pay you if it weren't too much."

"Don't worry about that," I assured him. "Our policy on wild animals is that we all have a responsibility to care for them. I can't promise anything because it's not the same as treating a domestic animal. They can die from just being handled, or they can starve themselves to death out of spite for being taken out of their element. Let's see what we need to do first. If he had enough gumption to walk north surely he's got the stamina necessary to survive this injury." Knowlton left content that his part in the saga was over.

Percy, the persistent goose.

"What should we call you?" I mused, as this determined goose looked anxiously at me and its strange surroundings. "How about Percy, the persistent goose!"

"Come along Percy," I whispered gently to the goose as I carried him back to the treatment room. After taking a radiograph of the injured wing we were unanimous in our disappointment. Percy would never fly again. He had a fractured humerus although thankfully it was not shattered. A truck or car may have struck him as he and his mates took off from a pond at the side of the road. Since there were no other injuries, the wing must have been hit by a single strong blow. There are no tall buildings in this area so he couldn't have bumped into a man-made structure as happens to so many birds today.

Thanks to Boz Budgie, I had attended a course last month on anesthetics for birds. I also maintained a set of pins small enough for fractures in puppies, kittens or pocket pets. So Percy went under the knife. An hour and a half later I was wrapping his wings to his body. The bandage would prevent Percy from moving the injured wing. If he were to try to fly it could put undue stress on the surgical correction. If we could keep this bird from moving the wing for at least five weeks perhaps this fracture would heal.

What Percy needed now was a good home where he could recuperate. And I knew just who might be interested. Knowlton Brice had a few acres about a mile from Clear Lake. His heroic efforts to save the goose in the first place justified more than a progress report.

"Mr. Brice, I thought I'd better bring you up to date on the Canada goose you brought in today," I began. "We've named him Percy for his gritty perseverance to walk north."

"Most appropriate," he agreed. "How is he, Doctor?"

Determined to walk north...

"Well, he sustained a fracture of the humerus in his left wing. I've repaired this by putting a metal pin inside the hollow of the fractured bone, which allowed us to keep the strength of the bone as well as oppose the two broken ends to one another. We've wrapped his wings close to his body so that he doesn't separate the fractured sections. If we can keep him confined for at least a month we should be able to see the wing mend. It's possible though, that he'll never fly again."

"I was afraid of that," he said.

"What we need now is somewhere to put the goose rather than in a cage in the clinic," I continued. "I'm afraid he would just pine away in a kennel." I waited anxiously for a response.

"Well," Knowlton mused. "I've got a little shed that I used to use for chickens. Why don't I keep him here?"

"That would be perfect," I agreed. "Let's do that."

Percy stayed with Mr. Brice for five weeks. But just when it came time to check the bandages, Percy decided that his destiny could be interrupted no longer. Knowlton had allowed the goose to waddle outside the shed from time to time but only when he and his wife were working in the yard. Percy must have been plotting his escape for some time as he seemed to pick his moment well. While Percy and Knowlton were pecking away at the garden with beak and hoe, the phone rang. By the time Knowlton came back outside Percy was gone.

Apparently, Percy maintained his sense of direction. Later he was seen by Knowlton's neighbor to the north, at the Siffton farm. Glenn Siffton was ploughing a field when he saw what looked like a Canada goose in a white tuxedo following behind in the freshly turned furrow.

Percy waddled a mile to the lake and then must have swam two more miles north as he had been spotted by people in Mildale. At that point he met up with 20 or so other Canada Geese that had stopped for the shelter and minnows of a creek that emptied into the lake. The local cottagers tried to catch him because they had read about Percy in the local paper and the bandages were starting to unravel. Knowlton found out that his goose was up the creek at Mildale so he rushed to intercept him.

Knowlton was delighted to find the goose still at the stream. Percy seemed to recognize his Samaritan. The gander honked a salutary greeting towards Knowlton then turned to give a plaintive wail as his companions began to ruffle their healthy pinions and take to the air. The bandage had completely unraveled by now, giving

Percy the freedom, at least, to take flight if he could.

Percy tried. His left wing was straight and firm. But it was weakened enough to make it impossible to fly more than a few feet. Percy splashed and circled in frustration with melancholy cries. As the last glimpse of his feathered family receded in sight and sound in the distance, Percy gave a final solitary moan.

Knowlton walked slowly to the edge of the creek with a handful of grain. He spoke softly and called for Percy as he always did when he carried feed to him in the pen. With a blaring 'Honk' of recollection, Percy swam over to the edge, trundling right into Knowlton's arms, this time not by accident. Somehow, Percy knew that Knowlton's care was now his revised destiny. There was no struggle and the honks were low hums of conversation that Knowlton crooned back with reassurances, "Don't worry Percy, we'll look after you, that's all right my friend...."

Percy was never able to fly more than 100 yards. But he's content now with his own kind at the town's conservation area where a group of Canada geese live year-round. Knowlton Brice is a regular visitor.

Morning Surgery: Spay and Dentistry for Puddles Waldie

Puddles Waldie is a slightly overweight female Beagle. Unfortunately for her, Bernice Waldie has been killing her with kindness. Not only has Bernice been feeding mostly table scraps, but Puddles has succeeded in training Bernice to give her candies and cookies. A simple whimper and stare at the fridge or cupboard brings Bernice running. Two cookies to a dog that should only weigh in at 25 pounds is like a human eating the whole box!

I was finally able to convince Bernice to spay Puddles and at the same time do something about the teeth. It was the bad breath that finally forced Bernice to take action. "I can't stand to have her lick my face anymore, Dr. Runcibal. Her breath just about knocks me over!"

I agreed. It made me open the window for air when I had to stick my face and hands into Puddles' mouth to examine the teeth and gums.

"Whew," I said. "I can see why. There are serious problems in here. See, the teeth are caked thick with tartar...notice at the gum line of several teeth, here..." I continued tracing my finger along the diseases gum line to show Mrs. Waldie the infected state of affairs. "You can see how the gum has receded from the tooth. The gingiva or gum should have been continuous along the base of the teeth about here." I paused to allow her to see the red swollen tissue. "But the infection and tartar has caused it to fall away, exposing the roots...see here on this molar...and even worse the gum in extremely inflamed and swollen on the other side." Mrs. Waldie winced and choked on the odor as I showed the severity of the dental disease.

"You can just imagine how painful this must be for Puddles." I said. "You know, we've ignored the need for dental hygiene for our pets while adding to the problem with the treats we've been giving them. We now advise clients to brush their dog's teeth."

"Brush a dog's teeth? You must be joking!" Bernice admonished skeptically.

"Yes, yes," I returned. "You see the results of not brushing...and smell them, here in Puddles's mouth."

"But dog's have never had to have their teeth brushed before. Is someone going to run through the woods now chasing after wolves with a toothbrush?" Bernice questioned, obviously not convinced of the concept. "I have enough trouble getting the kids to brush more than once a day! Heck, I'm so busy that I don't brush as often or as long as the dentist tells me that I'm supposed to. And you want me to brush my dog's teeth?"

"I know, I know," I returned somewhat apologetically. "I grant you that this idea is a tough one to get a grip on, but it is a fact of modern pet ownership. Dog species like the fox and wolf in the wild, eat raw meat and chew on bones to help clear the mouth of plaque and tartar. But I would still venture to say that they have their share of dental disease nonetheless. Our pet dogs and cats have been eating canned foods and table scraps that have not been as efficient at fending off the tartar and plaque build-up. As a result their oral hygiene has become more human. Just think of what your mouth would be like if you didn't brush your teeth for a year, eating what you like to eat."

Bernice grimaced as she whirled her tongue slowly under her lips at the thought, trying to wipe phantom scum from her teeth raised by the disgusting vision I had created.

"The first culprit is plaque, really a coating of the bacteria that normally inhabit the mouth. These germs cover the teeth and when they mix with food and saliva they harden into tartar. These layers of tartar keep building up until the gums become infected and inflamed. Pockets of infection, gingivitis around one or several of the teeth as we have in Puddles' case, eventually destroy the bone and ligament that secure the tooth in place. The only recourse is removal of the tooth."

"I will save as many of the teeth as I can but Puddles is in a lot of pain," I continued. "'See, some of the areas around the gum line are bleeding. No wonder Puddles has been picky lately."

It was the woeful brown-eyed stare that Puddles gave to Bernice more than my explanation, that convinced Bernice to go ahead with the dentistry. She had only wanted to have the dog spayed. She was getting tired of trying to find homes for 'Heinz 57' beagles, even more upset at chasing all the neighborhood males away from the doorstep every six months.

Yes. Dentistry for cats and dogs

Leт's тalk... Many continuing education conferences today provide our profession with courses, even hands-on sessions, in veterinary dentistry. There are even those practitioners who have completed Board Certification to become Veterinary Dentists. As we head into the millennium we are beginning to win the battle against periodontal disease. At this point in time, over 80% of dogs and cats over four years of age have it.

Every dog and cat should undergo a complete dental exam
from the age of six months and
at least annually after that.

The pet owner can minimize the problem with daily brushing. Not all dogs and few cats will tolerate this. Certainly not every pet owner will tolerate it. But plaque, the layer of bacteria, should be removed daily. The pet owner needs a special toothbrush, but more importantly, a toothpaste made for dogs and cats. Human toothpaste can cause stomach upsets.

To acclimatize the pet to the procedure, first spend some time rubbing the teeth with a finger, getting the dog or cat used to something foreign against its teeth. After a day or so of this, put some of the animal toothpaste onto the finger to get the pet used to the taste and texture on the teeth. After a few more days introduce the brush against the teeth without the toothpaste, then add some toothpaste. It may take a week or so to get your pet used to the procedure.

If the teeth are already caked with tartar, perhaps not as bad as Puddles, we can do a scaling to clean the teeth so that follow-up brushing by the owner can maintain the cleanliness of the mouth. In Puddles' case Dr. Skeen-Wilson is performing a scaling, root planing (scraping inside the gum along the tooth surface), and subgingival curettage (scraping gingiva surrounding the teeth), followed by polishing.

Fortunately we will not have to do any root canal work as the teeth are not worn down as yet in Puddles' case. But we will have to extract at least two of her teeth. Their ligaments have been so damaged and the gums receded so far away, exposing the roots, that there is no alternative. We also have to dispense antibiotics to make certain that the bacterial infection in the mouth is controlled. If bacteria from an infected mouth were to enter the blood stream we could be faced with subsequent infections in the other parts of the body. These could include meningitis (inflammation and/or infection of the 'meninges' or tissue surrounding the brain), to endocarditis (inflammation and/or infection of the endocardium or tissue surrounding the heart).

You have to catch me first...

Bernice was still skeptical when she came to pick up Puddles. I was explaining what she could/should do, now that the teeth were clean. It was a joy to see Puddles greet Bernice with licks to the face, even more gratifying to see how Bernice could endure what was impossible to endure before. "I've never seen Puddles' teeth look so white. And her breath is great! Even sweet. But you're still not going to get me to brush her teeth. Uh uh, no way!"

I explained the alternatives, feed dry food in addition to canned, any foods that make the dog chew more to wash away the plaque build up; chew toys and oral hygiene products.

But Bernice was disinterested for the moment, greeting a refreshed Puddles. It was the buzzing of the printer and the tear of the invoice that convinced her. After the shock of reading a bill for $465.50, Bernice asked meekly. "Got any of that toothpaste, doctor?"

10:00 AM... Major and Mrs. McQuig...

Be brave, soldier.

Major McQuig (retired) is a veteran of the Canadian United Nations Forces that served in the heady days of Cyprus. A native to the area, Major and Mrs. McQuig returned to Heron Point to enjoy retreat from military life. The Major's physical demeanor certainly suited the title. At least six feet in height at full attention, broad square shoulders and a brush cut to his grayed and thinning auburn head, it was indisputable that one paid attention when the Major spoke. Surprisingly, the commander's dog was the antithesis of what you would expect from a burly militarist. The Major's poise whenever he visited the clinic with his dog somehow demoted him to less than a military authority.

"This is Sergeant Lopez, Dr. Runcibal," said a trembling Major. Mrs. McQuig, following matronly behind the Major, kindly smiling as she clutched her purse, seemed more concerned about her husband than the teacup-sized dog balanced but shaking in his quivering hands. She extended an arm alongside his, set her handbag onto the table in order to nestle both of her hands under his to help support and steady the Major's grip. As the Major slumped, Mrs. McQuig took charge. Clearly she was the matriarch, the true commander in this family and her husband at least second in command. She may have looked like everyone's Auntie Bee, but she knew when to take charge.

Staring wide-eyed and anxious from the Major's wide palms and shivering uncontrollably while being jostled by four pairs of hands, all the while trying desperately to maintain equilibrium, sat a two-pound adult Chihuahua.

Sergeant Lopez was one of the smallest Chihuahuas I've seen. He could easily fit into a teacup with two or three tea bags besides. Off-white on his chest with light tan short fur on the rest of his body he looked as though he would freeze to death with the slightest cool breeze. Perhaps it was his persistent shivering that gave the impression of frigidness despite this warm June day.

"And what seems to be the problem with our tough Sergeant?" I asked as Sergeant Lopez swayed back and forth in his perch. The dog's ears rotated like antennas to whomever was speaking, as though trying to pick up enemy signals with auricles as large as satellite dishes almost the size of the animal himself.

"I think his leg is broken," blurted the Major. Although only an inch or two taller than I, his frame had far more muscle and power than mine. His presence imposed inert power yet somehow there was an edge that was missing. Instead of broad erect and stiff shoulders he hunched submissively over the diminutive treasure in his grasp.

"Now Herbert, don't go jumping to conclusions," interrupted Mrs. McQuig. "I'm sure it isn't that bad."

The major's slumping body trembled fitfully, giving Sergeant Lopez a ride that must have resembled a ship adrift off Cape Horn. Two wild eyes bobbed and weaved in disbelief as the miniature Mexican searched the horizon for a safer shore. "I'm so sorry, I'm so sorry," cried the Major, with an infantry of tears rolling down his cheeks. "You see Doctor, I...I..."

"Oh Herbert!" sighed the Major's wife, somewhat in sympathy but with enough impatience to demonstrate who commanded the McQuig battalion. "You see Doctor," she continued for the Major, "Herb thinks that he stepped on Sergeant's paw. I didn't see it happen but I certainly heard it."

"Ohhh," winced the Major at the recollection of the Spaniard's howl. Sergeant Lopez swung his head to gaze intently into the Major's face. He whimpered his reassurance but the Major took the sound to be moans of pain and went further into self-blame and pity.

"Herbert!" commanded Mrs. Major. "Set that dog down right this instant and go out

Tempest in a teacup...

and wait in the car. You're of no use to us in that state. Now go!"

I gently relieved the Major of his weapon as Sergeant Lopez snapped at my fingers trying to wrap around his Lilliputian body. I placed a rubber mat on the examination table so as to put the dog down to test his ability to place his feet. The major skulked away dejectedly but somewhat eased to have been dismissed from duty.

"I'm sorry Doctor," whispered Mrs. McQuig after she waited to hear the screen door of the clinic close. "Herbert just loves this dog but he just can't stand to see the little thing hurt. He may have commanded men through tough times during his stint in the army but he's a push-over when it comes to this dog."

"It's easy to get that way," I explained with reassurance. "Pets, especially tiny ones like Sergeant Lopez here, can appear to be utterly dependent on us. One might think that bones that are pencil thin like a Chihuahuas could be easily fractured. And in truth, they can more readily sustain injury. But provided their nutrition is sound, the strength of their bones relative to their body size is quite stable. At any rate, I don't think the Major should worry. As you can see the Sergeant is standing comfortably on all fours."

Sergeant Lopez looked up at us rotating his head with an inquisitive expression as if to say, "what is their problem?" I palpated each appendage carefully to determine whether there was any evidence of pain or distortion. I then held Sergeant Lopez in my hands and made him place each of his feet on the mat to see whether there was any need to radiograph, based on tentative placement of one of the paws. Sergeant Lopez pushed each foot confidently onto the table and looked up at me bewildered at this strange test. "He's fine." I said finally.

"I'll get Herbert," said a mollified Mrs. McQuig as she rushed out of the examination room and front door. Sergeant Lopez's ears seemed to become miniature satellite dishes as they turned towards the doors intent for the return of his masters. He whimpered quietly, his eyes widening and searching in tandem with his waiting ears. He sank down as though to leap for joy when he finally heard the major and his wife return.

"You must think I'm nothing but a coward Doctor Runcibal," sulked an embarrassed Herbert McQuig as he re-entered the waiting room dejectedly.

"Not at all," I said with certainty. "I think that I would have felt just as bad if I thought that I inadvertently hurt a tiny friend like this." The Major grew in stature to meet me eye to eye, pet lover to pet lover. "In fact, you did the right thing by bringing Sergeant Lopez in for attention. You see, if there was an injury, it would need attention as quickly as possible. These animals may have relatively strong bones but they do require special care if they ever do have problems." The Major Beamed with satisfaction as Sergeant Lopez jumped eagerly into his arms.

"Thank you Doctor!" said a now proud commander.

Mrs. McQuig held me aside and murmured into my ear with a glint in her eyes. "You did a great job treating both patients, thank you..."

Farm call to Parker Barrow's...

...The pony who thought he was a dog.

Parker Barrow and his wife Ina, were a retired couple who moved away from the city after years of busy executive roles. Parker had worked for IBM and Ina for the Board of Education. Even in country clothes they looked like executives. Outward appearances may have remained but inner solitude emerged and grew with each year in the country. They had spent all their working lives in a metropolis. Moving to their 25 acre spread with its utter lack of urgent lifestyle, completely changed their lives. They became executives of their country retreat, with serenity rather than stress.

What it didn't change was their regard for animals. I made routine calls to the farm to treat Pokey the pony and their Cairn Terrier 'Tartan' and two cats, 'Laura' and 'Heathcliff'. I was summoned to the 'farm' to vaccinate and de-worm 'Pokey' once a year. Pokey was as much a member of the family as their grown children, the dog and cats. Parker and Tartan would lie down under a tree, Parker to read a book on a warm summer's day, the Terrier to slumber close to his master. Pokey would lie down beside them. He would compete with the dog for attention by forcing his head onto Parker's lap so that the master would rub his ears in addition to, or instead of, Tartan's.

Pokey was a mixture of genes from a small horse and a large pony so that he was slightly taller than the typical Shetland pony. His shoulder reached a height of almost five feet. Although a drab mottled gray coat that was peppered with sprays of white on his forehead and lower legs, it was his long flowing mane and tail that caught your attention. Then you would become captivated by the knowing, pet-like look in his eyes and the twists of his ears to your every word that made one wonder if this beast truly understood the human language.

Pokey would follow Parker and Ina on their walks, without a lead, and when they reached a crossroad he would look both ways with them. If the other horses in the barnyard were to break down the fence to escape into the neighbors more verdant pasture, Pokey wouldn't go over with them. He would run up to the house and squeal, not whinny, at the window as much as to say, "Hey, the horses have gotten out again!"

A bonus for them on their property, was a mature but productive apple orchard. A bonus for me whenever I visited them was a slice of warm apple pie. But this bounty was to turn out to be a detriment to Pokey.

Today Ina had called to see if I could come out to see Pokey. She was quite concerned as he seemed to be in a great deal of pain. Normally, he would follow her all around the barnyard. Today he would not leave the barn. He was standing stiff and sore, with his head down and his neck tense.

When I arrived Ina met me anxiously in the drive and walked me over to Pokey. He was standing in the middle of the barn walkway, pain evidenced by his arched back and stiffened shivering muscles. "Has he gotten into anything?" I asked.

"No nothing," she said trying to search for some explanation for the cause of Pokey's distress.

I looked around for evidence. A hamper of last years apples was upset in the corner with half eaten as well as whole apples strewn across the floor. "Could Pokey have eaten these apples?"

"Yes, but we give him apples all the time," she said.

"It could very well be that he's overindulged on apples," I suggested as I passed my hands over the horse, especially feeling the feet. "His hooves are swollen and warm and he's in extreme pain. I'm afraid he has foundered."

"What's that?" Ina asked, unaware of the problems of overeating in horses. Parker walked up to us, wrinkled worried brows indicating his concern, just as I was explaining.

"Medically speaking, it's a condition called laminitis, where the laminae or layers of tissue making up the hoof become inflamed. The cause is often something like getting into fresh grain or hay — or too many apples." I drew a little diagram in the dirt by Pokey's feet to show how the inflammation was making it painful for Pokey to stand. "Horses essentially walk on one digit and the nail of that toe normally give the firmness necessary for standing and walking. Pokey's 'nails' are completely

Pokey, the pony... or puppy?

inflamed." I hesitated to go further but I had to. "I'm afraid this can be far too painful if it persists, to warrant treatment." Ina gasped at my next words. "It's possible we might have to put him down."

I've had clients doubt my words before, but Ina won the prize for hurling wrath upon the messenger. "Put him down!" she screamed. "Put him down! We'll do no such thing! We'll have someone else treat him if you don't think you can! How dare you speak of putting him down." Tears were streaming from her eyes as Parker tried to calm her.

I tried to explain further. "I certainly hope that this can be avoided but I've seen cases like this where the horse was in constant pain. I know how much Pokey means to you and it's his welfare that I'm thinking about."

"Well, we are not going to put him down and that's that!" Ina said indignantly.

"What I would suggest for now, is to call Jake Willows. He can make some comfortable shoes for him. I can give him painkillers and anti-inflammatories. What he needs from you right now is nursing." Jake was the local farrier, the modern-day blacksmith.

"We'll do whatever is necessary." Ina scowled caustically.

Later that day Jake the farrier (a modern-day blacksmith) came over to the Barrows. He had seen as many or more of these cases than I have and I'm certain Ina double-checked my diagnosis and treatment with Jake.

He placed soft pads on the base of each hoof then, with what would seem like a glue gun, injected a silicone-like gum between the pad and the frog — the frog being the center portion of the bottom of the hoof. The pad would keep Pokey from walking directly on the laminae that were inflamed and painful. But Jake didn't want Pokey to be walking or even standing for a while, at least until the silicone hardened.

Ina took this as literal. She managed to move Pokey from the open sun where he was standing to the shade of the maple tree on the lawn. Both Jake and I had told them that warm salt baths could help soothe the inflammation. So Ina brought a bucket of Epsom salt, and gently forced Pokey to lie down on his side. Then dissolving some of the salts in some warm water in heavy plastic bags, she immersed his hooves and tied the warm bags with twine above each hoof.

She faithfully changed these water bags at least three times a day for several weeks. Pokey remained a contented patient under the maple for the duration, pleased for relief of the pain. But after the first 10 days it is was clear that he was liking the attention a little too much. Ina, and sometimes Parker, would sit beside him to rub his ears for hours. Ina would cover Pokey with a horse blanket on chilly evenings. And on my urgings they would roll him from one side to the other to keep him from getting cramped leg muscles.

Soon Pokey became famous in the neighborhood. The kids in the area would come to see him, sit on him, pat him and give him treats. Pokey was getting so much attention that I'm sure he laid out there far longer than necessary. He milked that attention for every drop.

It was several weeks later when one of the Parker's horses had torn its right shoulder breaking down the fence again that had me out to the farm. The laceration needed urgent attention so Ina, Parker and I were concentrating at the problem at hand at the front of the stable door. Their big Hunter, Brutus was tethered to each side of the open stable so that his cut was best visible in the sunlight. Parker had a firm hand on the nose twitch to take Brutus' mind off of the stitching. The procedure took quite some time because Brutus had gotten the underlying muscles torn as well. None of us had yet looked over at Pokey although we discussed his progress.

On the final few stitches as Ina, Parker and I had our heads down in close inspection of the repaired wound, a fourth head nuzzled in to block out the sun completely. We all looked to the side to see Pokey as intent on the process as each of us.

He curled his lips in a meek smile as much as to say, "So this is why you've been ignoring me! By the way, where's my treat for today?" He had gotten up on his own and hobbled over to the stable to get the attention if it wasn't coming to him.

To this day Pokey is getting along very well. He can be seen on a warm fall day going for walks with Ina and Parker following faithfully behind like a dog without a leash — the pony that thought he was a dog.

2:30 PM - Wendy Flitz and Calicat's fur ball...

Did anyone get the license number of what hit me ?

 This morning little Willie Flitz, was stung by a bee, and little Wanda sprained her leg. Pershing slept through the panic that ensued, but Calicat had to be involved. So this little red and black striped cat decided that today she would discard the fur she had been accumulating in her stomach. She would also advise her harried owner that she did not enjoy the affliction of a lump in the gut. So just as Mrs. Flitz was about to rush her two wounded children to the emergency clinic, 'Cali' went to the litter box and let out a painful howl.

Wendy grabbed the cat, threw it into the back seat of the car with the mewling off-spring and sped out of the driveway. She rushed first to the medical center to get attention for Willie and Wanda. Her priorities had to be established — unfortunately for Cali who continued to howl and wretch in the back seat with the kids. Willie and Wanda cried from their own pains but cringed to their respective windows not knowing what to expect from this feline's devilish moans sitting between them.

Dr. Hillin treated Willie, while Wanda was checked by Dr. Stryll. Wendy had an understanding wherever she showed up with her panics, that one simply attended to the crises as swiftly as possible, because Mrs. Flitz was usually in a hurry to rush off to the next disaster. Cali's wails from the parking lot were testament to today's list of predicaments. Patients and doctors peered from the clinic windows to no avail as Cali could not be seen in the back seat of the Volvo.

With Willie towed by mother's hand, Wanda hopped hurriedly to keep up with mom and brother. The eight-year old daughter tried to place the new crutch Dr. Stryll gave her under her arm to help keep her sprained ankle from touching the ground.

Wendy hurried the kids into the car, Cali still retching and ralphing. In her zeal to rush to the pet's medical center she had stood the crutch between the tailgate and the bumper and quickly forgot that it was there. She roared away from the medical center down the road for five miles and into the veterinary clinic lot with a crutch wedged between her car's back bumper.

People she had passed in March as she sped down the road with a 75 foot electrical cord may have smiled and nodded that, "Yes, that can happen." But she drew many more stares and concerns by people who wondered if this lady had backed over some poor cripple who was now lying helpless without crutches, somewhere on the road.

Wendy carried Calicat into the clinic as Trip came out to greet her. Wanda and Willie were left sitting in the back seat swatting at each other with sibling zeal and squeals. A convoy of vehicles drove slowly past the clinic, drivers staring with concern for evidence of blood or appendages on the wheels or bumper. Trip waved at some of the people he recognized then wandered out to look at the back of the wagon to see what had caught their attention. A recognition of a 'Flitzism' immediately affirmed the purpose of the concern as he saw the splintered crutch wedged between the bumper and the wagon.

Wendy was waiting impatiently in the examining room as Trip sauntered in with a smirk on his face. On cue, Calicat retched a massive fur ball onto the examination table. After discussing the history and giving Cali a complete physical, Trip assured Wendy of the cat's good general health. "Just a fur ball upsetting the tummy," Trip said smiling at the frazzled Wendy Flitz. "Better get home for a soothing cup of tea. It looks as though you could use a quiet break."

"Yea right!" admonished Wendy. "As though I can ever get a tea break!" Trip dispensed a tube of lubricant to help Cali with her fur balls and watched with shaking head as Wendy drove off with the crutch still wedged into the bumper. He felt it would be better that she found out about it when she arrived home. She was in no mood to be told now. Besides, it would draw more attention as she passed people on the way home, crutch scraping pavement all the way...

7:00 PM Fox Palfrey - boards his 'dog'

The case of the smiling dog.

One dog smiled at me every time it came to the clinic. If you didn't know him, you thought you were a 'goner'. He would curl his face in a snarl, show his teeth — then wag his tail. It was the tail that gave it away. His owner was Fox Palfrey, an Ojibway who had worked in the mines in Northern Ontario. Fox was now a consultant who traveled the world advising on drilling equipment for mining. He maintained his heritage through a ponytail of dark hair, one string of beads tight to the neck and a leather jacket. The rest of his attire and deportment was strictly business.

Nueejewaagun was his dog (phonetically accurate rather than spelled). "That's 'my friend or partner' in Ojibway." Fox advised me. Clearly Nueejewaagun was this man's best friend. The huge hulk panting with the heat walked brazenly at the side of his master — no, in this case the man did not seem in any way to be master. It really seemed as though two partners were walking together, proud of each other's company.

I was at first frightened when the wolfish head looked up at me, wrinkling it's upper lips and folds of skin and baring his teeth. I backed towards the wall instinctively. "Oh don't worry." Fox said quickly to interrupt my recoil. "He always smiles like that when he greets people. He probably thinks you might join his pack if you like him."

Nueejewaagun was part wolf — more wolf than dog. I had worked on wolves before, and they have much larger teeth, paws and head than even their cousins like the German Shepherd or the Husky. I'm sure Nueejewaagun's smile was a carry-over from his wolfen genes. If he were approaching you in the woods with lips curled up and great white teeth exposed, you would be reciting every prayer you've ever known and relieving yourself uncontrollably.

But if you looked at Nueejewaagun's dark eyes, you would see that they were squinting slightly with a sparkle of friendship. And as soon as you spoke to him, the feathered tail confirmed the good intentions of his greeting.

Yet it was Nueejewaagun that I have to thank for protecting our clinic. He was brought in to be boarded because Mr. Palfrey had to go back north to visit family.

"He has never been in a cage before, Doc," explained Mr. Palfrey. with great concern. "I can't take him with me, and I don't have anyone who could look after him while I'm gone. Is there any way that you can keep him here, but not put him in a kennel? He's my best friend and I couldn't stand the thought of being so far away with him caged up. It just wouldn't be natural for him."

This was a difficult request. Most dogs and cats are quite content to be in a kennel. They seem to assume it's their own little house and settle down very nicely. But I could understand what he was saying. I knew that I couldn't, in good conscience, confine Nueejewaagun to a cage. So I agreed to simply let him have the free run of the clinic. If I had done that with some dogs, the next day I would find torn clinic towels, chewed table legs, and emptied and scattered garbage cans. Somehow I trusted Nueejewaagun to be content. So that evening we left the smiling beast to roam the confines of the clinic hoping we were right and wouldn't find the woodwork chewed to pieces.

What I did find the next day was most unexpected.

At first there was a whimpering, sobbing coming from the front desk. Following the sounds, Trip and I, who had arrived at the hospital at the same time, immediately realized what had happened in the night when we saw a ruffled sniveling wanna-be thief cowering under the waiting room counter.

Nueejewaagun was lying on his stomach facing this frightened and regretful intruder. Sometime during the night, this man had obviously intended to break in and

An Ojibway's friend... and ours.

steal some drugs and the cash box — not knowing that we deposit all cash each evening, and that the controlled drugs are locked away.

Not knowing either, that he picked the wrong night for his escapade. "Please don't let this wolf kill me, please don't let him kill me!" he pleaded. He cringed in the corner where Nueejewaagun had crowded him. Every time he moved Nueejewaagun would smile. But to this burglar — and I'm sure it was even worse in the darkness of night— that was no smile. That was the threat of death. This hapless felon was never happier to see Darren Holtby come to take him away. That evening Nueejewaagun was treated to a big juicy steak!

How to teach an old dog new tricks.

Let's talk...Sergeant Lopez, despite diminutive stature, was an authority in the McQuig household. Nueejewaagun probably learned to 'smile' in response to a reinforced gesture signifying that his grin appeased his owner, his friend. Eventually the smile became routine.

> Dogs learn primarily by conditioned responses. If they are given positive or negative reinforcement for almost any action they will repeat it. Positive actions are repeated usually because they see pleasure in their owner. Negative actions are repeated usually in self-defense.

Do dogs think? Do animals have enough brainpower to reason, to understand?

Many pet owners believe the affirmative. Dogs' innate abilities and quickness to pick up inbred tendencies and learned behavior make it difficult to decide whether they have learned simply by reflex. Watch Border Collies shepherd a group of sheep towards an enclosure in the middle of the field. Shepherds usually work with one or more collies who respond to their calls or distinct whistles. To the onlooker, it seems it seems as though the dogs are thinking carefully, "If that big ewe steps out of pace with the others as she appears to be ready to do, I will move to her left and intercept."

Others will say that dogs, or any other animals cannot reason. They will insist that animals can only respond to situations based on instinctive and reflex-learned reactions. Only the human animal can think and rationalize because of the larger brain and opposed thumb. We have evolved far beyond the lowly animal world.

What is the truth?

Are we too arrogant for our own good and someday the apes will take over to make pets and research animals out of us? Humbug! Stuff of fiction and movies! Is the brain of that dog sleeping at the doorstep simply a programmed tape of commands and lessons to be played for our pleasure?

We may never know.

And in the end, I don't really care. I would rather believe that my dog understands at least some of the lessons that I have taught, and those that life has provided. I would like to believe that my dog dreams from memories of good times we've had together. Even during those seemingly nightmarish reveries, I would like to think he's chasing the bully dog off our property to protect his own lair.

Research into the neurons of the animal world is difficult to assess since we have no means of communication. We may never be certain whether the beast is thinking thoughts or has an empty vessel. We must accept though, that the dog does and can learn, conditioned reflex or not. By understanding this, we can train the pet dog to be a more behaved and contented companion. Some dog trainers use treats as the 'conditioner.' Others use language. Either will work.

> The key points in training your dog to do anything are patience, persistence and opportunism. But there are other tips to keep in mind.

Short, repetitive lessons:

A dog has a very short attention span. It can last for a few seconds to a few minutes. Spending an hour or more at a training session is likely a waste of forty five or more minutes. Spending ten minutes once or twice a day and your dog will learn the required trick or task within just a few days.

Consistent commands:

Persistence also demands consistency. Teaching your dog to 'sit down' and 'lay down' as commands may confuse him particularly if you emphasize 'down' with both commands. 'Sit' and 'Lay Down' as consistent commands for the desired purpose, will help the dog to discern the correct response for the command given.

Emphasis:

Individual words can be learned provided that you stress the key words. Eventually you will be able to speak to the dog in a normal tone of voice, in sentences, and the pet will respond positively. For example, my dog knows that when I say 'Back Door'. He may be standing at the front door wanting to get into the house with muddy feet, but he knows that if he runs around to the back door of the house I will let him into the mudroom where he can dry his feet on the rug. (Sure, he doesn't know all about muddy feet and drying them, but he knows he's got to get to the back door!) And now, when I speak to him in a normal tone of voice at the front door saying, 'I'd like you to go to the back door please.' He bounds around the house to the back door!

Training a dog begins with Housebreaking. It should never end. Your dog will always want to please by learning what human words are supposed to elicit in response.

Get the point?

Cats on the other hand, require far more patience persistence and discretion. Training for them begins at the outset. They must learn the word "No!" but they require a much less aggressive approach. A gentle rap on the bum and a firm loud and meaningful "No!" at every indiscretion will give you at least a little bit of power over them (or so you'll think).

Cats may not develop the vocabulary that dogs seem to be capable of. (But doesn't it just seem though, that the cat on the window sill is thinking human thoughts?) Here are just a few of the words a dog can learn:

Vocabulary for a Dog:

Dogs have a reasonable capacity for a repertoire of tricks and good manners. I would recommend most of the following:

Good Dog

Bad!

Sit

Stay

Come

Lay Down

Shake a paw

Roll Over

Heel

Stop

Speak

Sit Up

Jump

Go get your dish

Would you like a cookie?

Please go to the back door

Lay on your back so I can clean your feet

Would you open the fridge please?

Please bring me a beer

Old Dogs, New Tricks:

Dogs learn faster when young. As they age there are other lessons they've learned in life and a confusing array of human language that makes further lessons more difficult. But they can learn new activities at almost age. It just takes a little more time, patience and persistence

For Cats Only...

How to train a human.

Cali Gimps was only trying to give Wendy and her family a little gift. Ideally she would have wanted to deposit the treasure onto the living room carpet. The bile stain is somewhat difficult to remove from polyester. And she would revel in the remarks as the family crowded around the deposit with distorted disgust on their faces: "It looks like...it looks like..y'know, it's round and formed like a piece of..." "No, no, no Willie it's just a dead mouse. Cali' ate it whole and it would dissolve.." "Oh Walter, it can't be a mouse, we don't have mice in our home...do we?...' 'eeuuwww..gross!"

Fur balls are a relatively normal phenomenon of the cat's digestive process. They spend hours every day grooming themselves. The barbed tongue pulls dead loose hairs from the coat to keep it clean. Unfortunately, the only place for the fur to go is down to the stomach. Most of the time the fur passes through the gut and ends up in the stool. But hair cannot be digested by the acids and enzymes of the bowel so there are times when the cat can get constipated ——- or worse, when the lump of fur can cause a blockage. Chronic vomiting, lethargy, straining, loss of appetite can signal a fur ball problem. The fortunate cat can simply retch the clump to the ground, as did Calicat.

I can see Cali sitting contentedly around the corner in the hallway listening to the family diatribe over her screams and vomits, licking her paw. She would stop to listen tentatively if the conversation faltered only to resume licking (and laughing under her purrs?) when the next 'yucky' comment ensued. "I got them again," she would mew.

It will be of no use for the reader to continue for the next few paragraphs.

What is to follow is better left for the feline family member to read. Oh I know, you might think that they cannot interpret the written word. Yet cats around the world must have read the same manual on "How to manage and maintain superiority in the household".

Their expertise is universal and consistent. You may read this section to your cat if you wish, but I would suggest that he or she will only show indifference —- stopping to snicker and then saunter out of the room just as Cali did. If they could jolt back a fisted paw with a resounding "Yessss!" they'd do it. If you are totally submissive to your pet cat simply leave this page open for him or her, or them, to read at their leisure.

Did I say 'pet cat'? Sorry. I don't usually like to use oxymorons. In reality we people are 'pet humans' tolerated by the imperious feline. I realize that those cats out there that are now having their owner.. attendant, read this to them —- or those that are disinterestedly perusing these words, may have no great need to reiterate instructions on the manipulation of the Homo sapiens (sorry cats, another oxymoron?). But it may help your servants to understand that they must simply submit to your will. There is no way out!

Cat Lesson One: Preparing a Meal

In order to ensure that your human servant is properly qualified and trained to meet your every whim, it is critically important to follow some basic rules of feline petiquette.

First, be inconsistent. When your human coo's and purr's to you indicating that they have bought you a new brand of cat food show profound excitement. Raise your head to them glancing patiently into their eyes and then eagerly to the can they are nervously opening. Circle their feet all the while that they are trying to shuffle between the cupboard to the bowl. You get extra points if you manage to trip them. Before they are able to get the bowl to the floor dive headfirst into the gruel with a passion. Make growling purrs as though you've just taken down a prize gazelle in a successful hunt.

You now have them snared for the next step.

Your servant will now be so overjoyed at having found the 'right' food that they will rush out immediately to buy a truckload of the stock. They will tell none of their neighbors as they will want to hoard the treasured find for you and you alone. On the second feeding however, give them the whammy. Let them coo and purr. Circle their feet with zeal and make your mews reach the ceiling to show your keen anticipation for the pending feast. Rub the ankles harder than before (they really like that!) and they will likely be drooling and shaking more nervously than the meal before. Stand on your hind legs as they bend over with the dish of succulent food pawing anxiously towards the bowl.

Now, kick them in the toe. As soon as the dish gets to floor level put your head back in surprise and shock. Be sure to sniff at the food with head raised and neck arched back. Raise your tail perpendicular to your head for a symmetrically appalled effect. Flick the tip of the tail vigorously as you trundle away as if to say, "Hmmphh!" No need to look back. The servant will slowly fall backwards onto the kitchen chair, mouth open, lower jaw particularly low, can opener drooping perilously from a weakened grip as juice from the can drips on their shoes. Eyes will then gaze with abject bewilderment to the counter where two cases of the food now sit, waiting for indefinite storage.

Cat Lesson Two: Now for the double whammy.

Show enough interest in the multiple purchases of both canned and dry foods that the servant purchases over the next few weeks. Draw it out as long as you can, ideally until cat food has replaced most of the human cereals, dry and canned goods in the cupboards. Now you are ready for the peaks of resistance!

Your servant will now be so intent on pleasing you with a diet that you like that they will purchase seven bowls. At the apologetic meal they will dish out four types of canned food and three types of dry. This is their ultimate taste test. You must show moderate interest in their nervous banter. Let them tremble a little more than usual by giving just a few interested purrs and mews. Rub their legs ever so slightly so as to send a quiver of unfulfilled excitement up their spine. Wait until all seven bowls are placed onto the floor. Look up as if to say, "Is that all?" By this time they will be on their knees looking furtively at you, then to dish number one, dish number two, to you, dish number four....

Go to any of the bowls that pleases you, sniff tentatively, take a bite and chew a morsel, just enough to give the servant the sense that victory is at hand. Then quickly raise your head to peruse the field of battle, wander amongst the bowls of booty, tail raised but eyes firmly fixed on the horizon. Then walk away and out of the kitchen to leave your victim in tears and despair. Now you have them firmly in your grasp. They will feed you anything you want, anytime you want it!

Cat Lesson Three: How to Litter Train a Human

The principles for effectively frustrating the human servant remain the same when it comes to establishing toilet needs. Be inconsistent.

Serve me . . .

Your servant will purchase a ton of kitty litter over the years, one small bag at a time. As with their zeal to find the food that pleases you, they show the same enthusiasm to determine what litter 'works' best. You will find shredded paper, sawdust, clumping granules, non-clumping granules, scented and unscented kitty litter. They will also purchase open plastic trays and hide them in closets or under stairways, and closed and covered boxes for privacy in an open room (or double privacy in a closet.)

There are two basic maneuvers to make your servant subservient. One relates to odor, the other to placement, not mutually exclusive.

From time to time you want the entire house to smell like a litter box. It is gratifying to see visitors who enter the home for the first time be taken aback immediately by the sharp, acrid and penetrating smell of cat feces. The house owner will have become acclimatized to the odor, particularly if you gradually leave more and more of the deposits uncovered over the span of a few days.

It will only be when a precocious child visitor blurts out, "Whoa it sure stinks in here!" that the servant will notice the stench, and embarrassed, rush off to clean and disinfect the entire house. You will subsequently be blessed with scented litter for the next few weeks and the litter will be cleaned daily for a month.

Placement will really get them. Despite the cleanest, freshest litter box and litter you can always ensure that the servant will religiously maintain your throne if you occasionally leave an especially pungent and runny mess just beside the box. A well formed deposit can be placed several inches away.

Do this especially when they have neglected to clean the litter regularly. You might really befuddle them by placing it under their bed! If you feel a more fluid movement coming, it's best effect can be had by draping it from the litter box, across the floor and down the hall. Be careful how often you do this however, as the paranoid servant will have you to the dreaded vet in no time.

Cat Lesson Four: Training for Petting —- and Setting the Trap

Once again, surprise is the goal. We felines enjoy being petted. Humans are known to have their blood pressure decreased from patting and caressing a dog or cat. Think about that. You have a human settled in a couch, stroking your fur in a state of bliss, their heart rate and blood flow being subdued by this gentle, restful activity. You can put them even further under your control by closing your eyes and setting your purring motor to full volume. As their speech begins to slur and their eyes glaze over, unsuspecting, eject your claws from their retracted state and dig them into a leg. Scream a sharp cry to make them think this outburst was their fault, and snap at their stroking fingers, just enough to leave a scratch and draw a hint of blood. Jump off the lap and run to hide leaving the astounded human sucking at the lacerated fingers while the mistress of the house is saying, "What on earth did you do to Kitty?" You get extra points if their blood pressure spurts back high enough to get them to keel over.

Use your tail as an early warning device. At least this will give the most intelligent of the human species a chance to move quickly enough to minimize the size of the scratches.

Standard tail maneuvers include:

1. The Flap: When you've had enough petting or you are really not ready to be held in the human's arms, flap the distal one third of your tail hard against their lap. Be totally inconsistent as to the number of times that you use 'the flap' before you bite or scratch. After all, there's no fun in giving them an easy early warning signal.

2. The Indignant Flag: Whenever you wish to ignore the human (this is especially effective when they have called for you to show you off to their friends), look at them as though you are ready to pet and coo, then turn

royally away from them, raise your tail straight up into the air perpendicular to your back and saunter away indignantly. A great frustrator is to hide under the couch with only the very tip of your tail showing. Stay there for the entire visit of the house guest. It's a delight to hear the owner say, "She really is a beautiful cat, please believe me."

Such techniques were surely instrumental in feline godly reverence during the time of the pharaohs. Petroglyphs in many cultures show servants catering to the cat set on a pedestal of royalty and deity. These very talents trained the ancient Egyptian. Some day soon, modern humankind will again be buying pedestals.

CHAPTER FIVE

Ark and Bark

Animal Clinic

CHAPTER FIVE

Ark & Bark Animal Clinic
Tuesday July 18, 1989

Morning Emergencies:
Cole Grafton - milk fever
Mrs. Beasley - Ruby is in a traffic accident

Morning Farm Calls:
Duke Stump - check mare - in foal?
Jarred Shjott - herd health and check lame cow

Morning Surgeries:
Mrs. Clarose - Jeepers - spay and remove dew claws
Mrs. G. Sempl - Igor - plate fractured leg

Morning Appointments:
10:00 *C. Fearm - Lucifer hasn't eaten for 6 months*
10:15
10:30
10:45
11:00 T. Lloyd - cat vomiting yellow foam
11:15 *Lamont Wilker - poodle with a broken nail*
11:30 Mrs. Tuttle - Bonnie, cat frothing at the mouth
11:45 Peter Smith - collie can't stop panting
12:00 Mrs. Walker from the antique store - siamese is sneezing

Afternoon Farm Calls:
Mr. Biddle - check Winston - coughing

Afternoon Appointments:
2:00 Mrs. Strong - Mitzie has hiccups
2:15 Mr. & Mrs. Buchersal - annual needles for Casey
2:30 *Peter Archer - another frog*
2:45 V. Choo - Bruce Lee - remove bandages
3:00 Mrs. Gadd - Burt, 6 year old dog very sick
3:15 Agnes Huskins - canary attacked by her cat
3:30 Jacob Jurdin - sick dog and shots?
3:45 *Edna & Barry Berry - Trinity is retching*
4:00 Ellis Milter - dog with a smashed paw

Evening Emergencies:
Jake Burtle - Rambo terribly swollen

Tuesday July 18, 1989
- Lucifer Clears House...

Ruby, Tuesday

...Who can hang a chain on you?

As the sun peeked over the hills to kiss the dawn, Trip and I were bleary-eyed but intent on getting some practice business done before the crises of the day switched the emphasis from office matters to medical urgencies.

Just as we were adding up yesterday's invoices to see whether we could pay some bills, Wendy Beasley burst through the clinic doors, screaming, "Ruby's been hit! Ruby's been hit!" We rushed outside to where Ruby was lying in the back of the station wagon. She had certainly been hit by something. There were obvious fractures as a front and hind limb both lay at right angles. Scrapes and cuts oozed fresh blood and were embedded with stone and gravel.

"How did it happen?" I asked as I began to check her gums to see if there was any internal bleeding. There was evidently no sign of shock as Ruby, with consummate indifference, perused the setting unconcerned, as if she was saying, "What's all the fuss? I'd like to go back home to play."

"I just can't seem to keep her tied up and out of trouble," said a frustrated Mrs. Beasley. Tied to Ruby's dog collar was a frayed six foot length of rope that at one time had kept her, for a moment anyway, tethered in the yard. "One minute she was chasing back and forth at the squirrels in the tree — I'm certain that they were taunting her — and the next moment she was bounding away with the rope dragging behind her. She quickly forgot about the squirrels and started running blindly away, flitting after anything that happened to cross her path. I ran after her and called and called, but she just ignored me. Then when she got to the main intersection, she just ran out into the traffic. She put two cars into the ditch before a motorcycle hit her."

"Well, don't worry for now," I said as I had completed my preliminary exam. "It appears as though her injuries are fixable. I'll know better when I've checked her inside and get some x-rays. I can feel some broken bones but there doesn't seem to be any internal damage. We need to make sure that things like a ruptured bladder or diaphragm haven't happened though." Leslie had brought out the animal

Ruby, the dangerous offender...

stretcher so that we could carefully carry her inside.

While I'm certain the bodywork for those cars was more costly than the bodywork I performed on Ruby, the repair bill for the dog was bad enough. Veterinarians are very sensitive to the cost of their services and often don't charge what the work is truly worth. Just as I hadn't charged Mrs. Beasley for all of my time the night that I spent removing quills, I couldn't bring myself to charge for all of the time we spent fixing all of Ruby's injuries. In a way I would be repaid many times over because these incidents would be regular occurrences. Ruby was to become one of my most steady patrons. During his investigation into the traffic accident and discussing Ruby's many scrapes with disaster, Constable Holtby decided to declare Ruby a dangerous offender.

10:00 AM Mr C. Fearm...

...Lucifer clears the building

After the commotion from Ruby's calamity subsided, it was time to discharge the morning appointments. From the outset there seemed to be whispers of concern and quandary. Janice Patril had just come in for her 10:15 AM appointment, carrying Gordon, her orange and cream domestic long haired cat. I had asked previously whether 'Gordon' was a name common to the family only to be shown the obvious. The cat had one paw that was pure white, thus deserving the moniker of Janice's favorite singer, Gordon Lightfoot.

Clients often come in early for appointments. Today, the waiting room was crowded with people and pets, casually chatting to one another about their reasons for being here. Barbara Minners greeted Francis Best as Minny Minners and Gordon sniffed the air in each others' direction. Soon there began an undercurrent of distress and distrust. Sitting at one end of the room was a disheveled young man. Long, dark and greasy hair fell haphazardly onto his shoulders. A few days of stubble gave him a menacing appearance. His eyes were somewhat glazed as he sat staring into space unaware of the fleeting and sidelong glances aimed in his direction.

The concerns were induced by a distinct characteristic of his dress, rather than purely his unkempt nature. It was a blistering, humid July day, with a temperature of at least 80 degrees Fahrenheit. Yet this young man had a cumbersome overcoat draped over his shoulders and dragging to the floor, a garment that must have come from the back rack of the Sally Ann.

Trip, Sam and I were brought curiously to the front counter to join Leslie when we heard the patter and natter of squeals, nervous coughs and exclamations. Janice and Barb Minners had left their seats on either side of the young gentleman in the heavy overcoat. Shouts of , "Oh!" and "Ooooh!" and "Oh my!" ensued.

The coat was moving!

The man sat perfectly still while undulations wavered along his shoulders and chest. Suddenly the explanation for the bulging, mobile garment peaked its head from under the lapel. The room exploded with frenzy!

Mrs. Patril screamed, Gordon echoed in harmony. Barb Minners grabbed her Yorkshire in dreadful fear that Minny was about to be eaten alive. Francis Best who had just sat down to await her 10:30 AM appointment, after socializing with Janice, nearly fainted with fear.

Staring out at them from his secure nest inside the vest was Lucifer, a ten foot Boa!

Lucifer waved his jagged tongue at the unsettled audience who were now standing in a clump for protection, all clasping pets close to their chest and face. Suddenly,

Lucifer in his Summer coat...

Lucifer's tail fell from the left coat-sleeve confirming that this demon was big enough to devour each one of their charges.

Three people and three pets found that they could not fit through one doorway at the same time. Decorum and courtesy fell by the wayside as each grappled with the other to be the first through the door and outside to safety. Trip, Sam and I watched helplessly as they ultimately warped the screen door to fit themselves through, en masse and en route.

Our sidelong glances at one another, not wishing to look the other in the face betrayed a collective question as to who was going to look after this appointment. Sam quickly rushed back to surgery muttering, "Well, I'd better finish cleaning Ruby's wounds!" Trip patted me on the back with a smirk saying shamelessly, "I'm on my way to Duke Stumps to preg' check his mare. Guess you're the lucky one!"

Leslie, who had slid her chair away from the counter handed me the chart. "Okay," I said reluctantly. "Mr...er, ah yes, Fearm...would you bring Lucifer into the examination room please?"

"Now what seems to be the trouble today?" I asked ensconced on the opposite side of the table while Chuck Fearm removed the topcoat to reveal his serpentine scarf.

"Lucifer hasn't eaten for about six months," he said with obvious concern.

"Six months?" my voice squeaked. I pressed my back to the sink and counter as far away from the table and patient as I could.

"Yea, and I've been buying mice like it was goin' outta style," he added, though I could never fathom it stylish to be brokering in mice.

"Well," I conceded, " Let's have a look at him." Although certainly not an expert in snakes and amphibians, there are enough creatures brought to the clinic to realize that the fundamentals of medicine apply to any creature. This one looked healthy. His eyes were bright, his skin was firm and his demeanor was bright. He looked hungry! "Would you excuse me for a moment?" I asked.

After the experience with Boz Redding, I had learned that it was better to check with the experts whenever I was out of my league. I called Dr Jacob Treat at the Exotic Pet Referral Clinic only to find that Boas can go for several weeks or months between meals.

"There could be an underlying infection," he told me. "But if you feel the snake shows no sign of disease, he could just be due to eat. Give him an injection of Tylocine if you feel antibiotics are indicated. Have him brought over to me if he isn't eating within the next few days. I'll run some blood tests, perhaps take a radiograph in case there is an obstruction or foreign body."

I went back to Mr. Fearm and Lucifer to reiterate the expert's instructions. I decided to give the injection, perhaps to feel that I may be doing some good and for the experience of giving a needle to a snake. "Now make sure you call if Lucifer is not eating by next Tuesday. You needn't bring him here again," I added, to ensure that we didn't have another hospital clearing. "We'll give you the directions to the Exotic Species Clinic in the City. Let me know either way."

Mr Fearm called on Friday. "Lucifer just ate a big live rat!" exclaimed an elated pet owner. "You can see it's bulge sittin' halfway down it's gut!"

"How wonderful for Lucifer," I said with little conviction. How terminal for the rat.

11:15 AM.... Lamont Wilker - Poodle with a broken nail...

talking to no one.

"Dr Runcibal, Nathan Biddle is on the phone. He says he has one quick question..." Leslie raised her eyebrow and crimped her cheek in disbelief as she handed the receiver to me. I held my hand over the mouthpiece as I asked Samantha to cover the rest of the appointments knowing that I could be on the line till well past noon.

"Hallo, Mr Biddle..." I greeted as I settled into a comfortable chair for the duration, while Dr. Skeen carried on.

"Hi, Mr Wilker? I guess you're next," Samantha extended her head past the exam room door to glance at Lamont Wilker and Precious, his toy and very pink poodle.

"Hello Doctor!" Lamont returned as he hurriedly carried his miniature pedigree to the table. Mr. Wilker suffered from a lisp but somehow it never detracted from his otherwise perfect diction. Precious was recently trimmed and dyed pink by the Cuddle-and-Cut Pet Groomers. A bouffant headpiece and bouffant piece at the tail framed her shaved torso. Two purple ribbons adorned each ear, tied to a braid in the middle of a fuzzed flap.

"I'm just tho glad that you are able to thee Prethious today. I have been very worried ever thince I thaw her limping this morning," began a concerned and anxious Lamont. "Thee, look at her paw. There, right there on the middle digit. Her poor little nail ith broken right off!"

"Ah yea..." mused Samantha as she looked at the nail dangling from a paw held up for observation by the precious poodle. Sam spent little time on ceremony and simply grabbed the nail with thumb and forefinger, snapped it away from the paw in one stroke. Precious yipped slightly and Lamont leaned against the wall as if relieved that the painful nail was now removed.

"That does it," Sam continued confidently. "I'll just put some antiseptic on the nail now, to make sure it doesn't get infected. This may sting a bit Precious but it must be done..." Sam busied herself between the shivering poodle on the table and the alcohol jar, cotton swaps and antiseptic spray. She explained the procedure to Lamont, and respectively to Precious, who seemed reluctantly willing to endure the procedure.

"The entire nail was sticking out wasn't it? That made it easy to be able to rip it away from the toe, though. Just a bit raw now where the nail was supposed to cover the tissue. I think I'd better put a little bandage on the paw." Lamont, leaning against the wall held his head down, as though unwilling or unable to watch what seemed like a painful procedure.

Dr. Skeen continued to discuss the condition of the paw, engrossed in her work and apparently not realizing what had just happened to Lamont. "The bandage will make sure that Precious doesn't bump the exposed tissue against anything that could make it bleed again. See, there's a bit of bleeding from tearing the nail off." Lamont began to slide down along the wall, seemingly to respond to her request to look at the blood — although slowly sliding further than necessary...

"I would also like to give her a shot of penicillin. That way we'll be certain that there will be no infection. We've exposed the blood vessels under the nail enough to warrant some antibiotics." Finally, Sam stopped to scrutinize Lamont's reaction to her ministrations. He was sliding, back to the wall, knees supporting his frame, further and further down, inch by inch. His chin rested on his chest. It looked as though he was staring at something on the floor, and was going down to examine it further.

Sam looked at the floor at Lamont's feet. "Did you lose something?" she asked, searching the expanse of the floor around the table legs. "Do you wear contacts?" She persisted trying to help him look for whatever it seemed he was probing for. Samantha kneeled down head to head with Lamont staring at the same spot on the floor. Precious looked down at them out over the edge of the table wondering why she'd been neglected.

"I don't see anyth...oh my!" Dr. Skeen, knee to knee with Mr Wilker raised her head to seek enlightenment when it hit her. Lamont had fainted! The wall had supported his slow descent to the floor. "Leslie! Jonathon! Give me a hand!" she shouted.

We carried Lamont out to the front steps of the clinic for fresh air after waving smelling salts under his nostrils. All three of us hovered over Mr. Wilker concerned for his recovery. His first words brought us back to duty, "Prethiouth?"

"Oh My goodness!" Sam said as each of us instinctively bolted inside, Lamont almost falling over again from the sudden lapse of supporting hands. We had visions of a toy poodle splat on the floor with more than a broken nail. Anxious and nervous in the middle of the table sat a dejected pink poodle with purple ribbons, one paw held slightly elevated, waiting for the remainder of the treatment. She cocked her head to one side as we gave a very deep collective sigh.

Samantha drove Lamont home while I finished bandaging a precious pet. He would pick her up this evening after he had recuperated from his ordeal.

What's going on down there?

Dr. Skeen-Wilson was only able to work the morning appointments today as she and husband Jim were vaccinating their swineherd in the afternoon. She planned to return towards the end of the day however, to check on Igor Sempl the shorthaired Weimaraner that underwent orthopedic surgery in the morning. This sleek gray-coated, aristocrat of a dog, had been struck down by a three-wheeling drunkard as Mr. Sempl and son were hunting grouse north of town. A fractured femur demanded a metal plate to join the severed ends together. A plate to the side of the head might be appropriate for the drunk.

Trip was content to take the afternoon appointments and let me spend mid-day, and then some, at Nathan Biddles. He and I conferred over sandwiches at lunchtime. Lucifer and the multitude of exotic and fad pets were the inevitable topics.

"Ah can tell you that Jeannie would never let me keep a snake, she's scared to death of 'em," Trip said. "There's precious few exotic animals that she would grant a home for."

"Yet some people, like Mr. Fearm, seem to get quite attached to the 'unusual' pets," I observed, thinking of my fearful reaction to Lucifer. "Ferrets, pot-bellied pigs, pocket pets like hamsters and white mice are all fair game for pet ownership."

"Yea, but we've also seen a lot of problems as a result of people not realizing what they've gotten themselves into," Trip said, almost reading my mind. "It would make me feel better if anyone who was thinkin' of buyin an unusual pet, would study the needs of the animal first, even call us or other experts or owners for advice. Ah hate having to euthanize a little creature whose only problem was an owner ignorant of the care necessary to keep them healthy. Why there's as much to caring for an exotic pet as there is for a dog or cat!"

"You're absolutely right!" I agreed, getting up from my chair. "But right now I've got to head out to Nathan's for a lecture and a laceration."

2:30 PM ...Peter Archer...

Pocketful of Pets.

Trip was gratified to see Mitzie Strong today. Mitzie is a Jack Russell Terrier that suffered from bladder stones, at least a month ago now. Trip diagnosed the problem and in his usual southern drawl, broke the news to Mrs. Strong. "Ah'm wondrin," Trip had said, "Just what you've been feedin' this little terrier, Ma'am. Why she's got so many stones rattlin' round in her bladder that she's just a walkin' gravel truck!'

Today Mitzie was fine,except for hiccups. She recovered from the surgical removal of the stones, now sitting as a trophy on the Strong mantelpiece. No further recurrence of the problem was evident. Except for the hiccups. Mrs. Strong delights in telling us how very smart Mitzie is. "She knows everything. She brings her ball whenever she wants to play. If we try to get her to play ball and she doesn't want to, she grabs the ball and hides it behind the couch. She can tell our footsteps from a stranger's footsteps at the front door. She rushes to greet Dick when he comes home from the plant, but she'll bark like the dickens if a salesman knocks on the door. And when Josh, our son, drives his car into the driveway she rushes from window to window just as excited as can be. Why, dear me! Her hiccups have stopped!"

Mrs. Strong bustled out of the examination room in a bit of a huff, Mitzie securely tucked under her arm. Trip scratched his chin, trying to figure out why she was so haughty, unaware that he was hiccuping. His diaphragmatic spasms stopped when he looked across the waiting room to see who might be next.

Sitting patiently beside Mr. Buchersal was little Peter Archer. He looked up at Trip with a smile that tried desperately to join his ears. Suddenly a frightened look swept away the grin. He thrust his hand into his left pocket then slumped assured that whatever seemed to be missing was still there.

Peter was a regular visitor to The Ark and Bark. About once every three or four weeks Leslie would see nothing but a baseball cap bobbing up and down on the other side of the counter. It was Peter bringing another find to the clinic. "I'm gonna be a vet when I grow up!" Peter would say assuredly to whomever would listen. He's advised Leslie, Trip and me as well as any client who's been sitting beside him during any of his many visits.

Under his cap a head of rusty brown curly hair seemed to be trying to force the hat off his head. Red dots of freckles testified to his youth but belied his apparent wisdom. He would pour over books from the library and any that we could lend to him so that he could learn everything possible about the animal world that so fascinated him.

Peter would salvage a squirrel that had been hit by a car, a young robin that had fallen from its nest, a bunny whose nest has been exposed from raking leaves along the edge of the brush. His left pocket carried the victim of the day. In his right pocket were the coins he would use to pay us for our medical care.

"You're next Peter," Trip said. "And what have you got for us today?"

A small hand fished around the left pocket while his tongue swayed from side to side onto his lower lip. Finally he grasped the patient. "I found this here frog, Doctor Tripper... He was crawling on the side of the road over on Cedar Street. See, he's got a crushed back leg...car must've run over it."

"Yes, Ah see," Trip said to the hat that was all he could see at the edge of the table. "Ah think we can help 'im. It wasn't so much crushed as bumped, fortunately for the frog. "Ah'll put some antibiotic salve onto the sore digits. Ah'm thinkin' that if you can keep him in one of your aquaria for a day or so, he'll recover and you could soon let him go — maybe into the creek over by Cedar. In the meantime, make sure you trap some flies for him."

"Yup. I already got some," said the hat. Trip leaned over to hand the frog to the vet-erinarian-to-be. Peter slipped the frog into his pocket. "Thanks Doctor." he said, as he turned to go he faltered and looked back at Trip. "I'm gonna be a vet someday!"

"Yes, Ah think you are, Peter. You've already got a forest-full of patients that appre-ciate your help."

Peter beamed happily as he limped, straight-legged, to the counter, taking care not

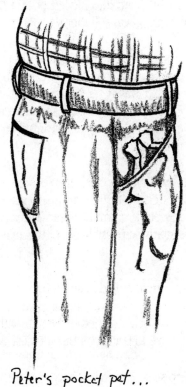

Peter's pocket pet...

to press his left leg hard to the ground for fear of crushing the frog-in-the-pocket. A shiny nickel slid from the edge of the counter towards Leslie. "Thank you Peter," she said, "Here's your receipt."

The young man with a destiny walked proudly out the door, with an early start on what was certain to be an enjoyable career...

Let's talk...Peter and Trip have had many talks about the pros and cons of picking up injured animals along the road. Right from the very first frightful event presented by the budding animal doctor. Several months ago, actually just a year ago now, Peter flashed his proud smile below Leslie's counter. Cupped in his hands was a black and white scent gland —— a skunk!

Peter found this baby skunk after its mother had been struck and killed by a car. Since he lives just a block away and had become familiar with our hospital after a classroom tour, it seemed to him the natural place to bring us a baby animal in need of attention.

The skunk's front teeth were cracked and shattered. Trip had a lot of fun practicing new skills in dentistry he had learned at a short course . This case brought those new talents to bear, along with a few innovations.

Trip later made a point to sit down with Peter on the front step, especially after the first assertion of, "I'm gonna be a vet when I grow up!" Trip thanked the boy for bringing the baby skunk to the clinic but told him that if he really liked animals he had to understand the ground rules: "Never pick up a mammal that is injured. Frightened wild animals, especially if they are hurt, can bite. Their bites can carry disease —- such as rabies —- and these diseases can make him very sick."

> Never pick up a mammal that is injured. Frightened wild animals, especially if they are hurt, can bite. Their bites can carry disease and make humans very ill.

From then on, Peter would bring us 'safe' road-kill survivors like snakes and frogs, turtles and birds. His parents brought in injured squirrels, rabbits or skunks. Peter became the custodian of the untamed wounded of Alder Street.

Trinity, Trinity, Trinity . . .

3:45PM ... Edna and Barry Berry

Trinity is retching... retching, retching

Nathan's lecture today was cut short by his wife's insistence on a trip to the city so I was able to cover the final appointments for the day. Trip and Sam were now checking Igor. Precious Wilker rested comfortably sporting a bandaged paw decorated by another purple ribbon. Appointments for the remainder of the day progressed uneventfully until I met Barry Berry and his wife Edna. I realized very soon how Trinity had been named. She was a six month old English Bulldog. Though still a pup, she looked menacingly at us with her broad shoulders and splayed stance.

Let's talk...The Bulldog, originally bred for bull-baiting has become a gentle and faithful companion for families, especially gentle with children. Don't let the massive head, muscular body and stentorian snortles fool you. These dogs are excellent pets.

There are times when a client's assistance in describing symptoms is most helpful, especially when clients try to mimic the sounds they hear at home. Repetition of coughs, yelps, wheezes and whistles all register a particular disorder. Then there are people who have the nervous habit of repeating everything two or three times. Put these together and you've got a bit more than desired...

"I see that you are concerned about Trinity's retching?" I questioned as I closed the door behind Mr. and Mrs. Berry. Barry Berry, in coveralls and suspenders, with a plaid hanky prying from his pants pocket, set Trinity on the table. Although not retching at the moment, I had heard Trinity's attempts at throat clearing in the waiting room as I was completing my previous appointments. Her wheezing gags were voluminous and protracted, intermittent and repetitive.

"Yes, yes, yes!" said Mr. Berry, emphasizing the concern with inflections on each affirmation. Edna, shorter, stouter and sporting a straw field hat, nodded three times.

Trinity plopped her hindquarters onto the exam table, rolling a few folds of girth onto her haunches. I stooped down to smile into her winsome face and she snorted and sneezed her affection and her saliva, back into mine. Wiping the mucous from my face I took my stethoscope that had been draped over my neck, to begin auscultation. "Has she been eating well?" I asked.

"Very good, very good, very good," Said Edna.

"We feed her puppy food, feed her puppy food, feed her puppy food," added Barry.

Trinity and I cocked our heads to the side, Trinity in wonderment of the pieces of tubing coming out of my ears and myself wondering where the echo was coming from.

"She keeps going Chhhgghhhgghhh, Chhhgghhgghhh, Chhhgghhgghhh. All the time, all the time, all the time," continued Barry Berry.

And Phhhsshhhgghghh, phhhsshhhgghghh, phhhsshhhgghghh," chimed Edna.

"Shhnarff, shnarff, shnarff," added Trinity.

"Is she going to be all right, all right, all right?" asked Barry mimicked by Edna's lips moving on each all right, all right.

"Her chest is clear, her throat is normal, and she appears to be healthy," I answered. "These sounds that she makes are relatively common for a Bulldog. It's not only their face that scrunches up to give them such a charming appearance. Their vocal cords, larynx and uvula at the back of their throat are equally squashed together. As a result, they tend to build up considerable fluid from time to time and have to clear their throat and/or sinuses. That's when you hear the snorting."

"So she's okay, okay, okay!" exclaimed a relieved Barry Berry.

"She's fine, fine...er, she's quite all right," I said. "But I do want you to bring her back if she ever goes off her food, seems to cough rather than snort, or seems to have inordinate amounts of sputum. Bulldogs, because of the variation in anatomy of their nasal sinuses and upper respiratory tract, can be predisposed to infections. I want to treat her early if she ever does have trouble."

"Don't worry doctor, don't worry doctor. We'll be back, be back, be back." Edna and Barry repeated every phrase till they left the clinic. Trinity tripled her snortles and sneezes. Here was a trio of individuals with a lifetime of echoes.

For some reason, although I had been feeling pangs of hunger before, I had lost my appetite and knew I would be picking at my dinner tonight. I seemed to have the urge to spit...

Rambo Burtle's Torsion....

Jake Burtle's inclination.

At about 6:PM Jake Burtle's truck jumped the curb and accelerated to the side door. Jake leaped from the cab to greet Samantha and Trip just as they were leaving. I had agreed to wait for Lamont Wilker who would be coming in later to pick up Precious.

"Doc Tripper, Doctor Skeen, please help. Something terrible is wrong with Rambo!" cried Jake. Rushing to the passenger door he flung it open almost to the point of tearing it off its hinges. He hefted a clearly distressed Boxer into his arms and waited expectantly for the two doctors to open the door of the hospital for him. "Where do you want him?" he demanded as he brushed by Trip and Sam almost knocking them over.

"Get him into the surgery, Jake," advised Trip, fairly certain what the problem was. Sam also noticed the distended abdomen that made it difficult for even muscular Jake Burtle to get his arms around. They both raced inside to prepare for immediate surgery if their first fears were correct.

"Did Rambo eat not too long ago?" asked Sam hurriedly as she held a stethoscope to his chest and abdomen.

"Yeah."

"Did he seem to eat rapidly?" hastened Trip, setting up an Intravenous drip.

"Yeah, he always eats fast...What's wrong?"

"It looks like a gastric torsion, Jake." said Sam hurrying to get a set of surgical drapes and gloves laid out on the counter. Jake stood helpless amidst the chaos as Rambo wavered on the surgery table, sometimes retching, sometimes moaning, abdomen seeming to blow up like a balloon.

"What's happening?" Jake pleaded. "Is he gonna die?"

Sam took Jake by the arm to lead him to the door of the surgery.

"It is relatively common for dogs with deep chests like Boxers, especially if they eat too rapidly, to eat too much at once and swallow excessive air in their ravenous attack at the food. This fills their stomach with air and acids that eventually forces the stomach bloat — then it can rotate within their abdomen. The deep chest allows for a lot of room for the stomach to twist. When each end of the stomach is cut off, more gas develops, but with nowhere to go. Rambo is bloating now to the point of shock. If we don't operate immediately he will likely die. You have no time for contemplating, I'm afraid Jake...but we still have a very good chance to save him..."

At this assertion, Jake too, was in a state of shock. Sam waited anxiously for Jake's permission to proceed. Trip had the intravenous needle in hand, already masked and gowned in anticipation.

Jake shook his head slightly to clear his mind to finally realize where he was and what has been asked of him. "Yeah, sure, cut 'im open, I don't wanna lose 'im." Sam was gowned and gloved, scalpel in hand before he had finished the sentence.

Walking back to the surgery with Precious under one arm, I placed a reassuring hand on Jake's shoulder. The speed at which Trip and Sam had established a diagnosis and instituted procedures for correction made me confident of the outcome. "Don't worry, Jake," I said. "Rambo's in good hands."

Jake looked over to thank me for the encouragement when he saw the pink shagginess under my other arm. "What the hell is that?" He asked, face distorted as though looking at an alien canine.

"Just a cute little poodle," I offered, snuggling the bright eyed pup to my nose.

"You call that a dog?" cried Jake incredulously. It looks like a...." Just then Sam had decided to puncture the stomach as the only apparent means to diminish the bloated gastric balloon. A small explosion erupted as a voluminous dispersion of pungent gases ensued immediately. Such fumes and smells can best be described as stifling and acrid. Heavy vapors filled the clinic and stomach contents oozed a bit from the puncture.

Jake, to whom acceptable odors were oils and vapors from engine fuels succumbed immediately. Precious and I managed to grasp his weaving body only to be able to settle him onto the floor while surgical necessities were completed.

Lamont Wilker who had entered from the front door just as Jake was repeating Lamont's earlier exhibition, looked concerned but actually seemed exonerated. I left Jake on the floor to deliver Precious to his arms. "Get out the thmelling thalts." He called back as he and Precious left the building.

Obesity and complications

Let's talk...Jake mentioned later that Rambo was just getting 'a little fat', but when he saw the distended abdomen he knew this wasn't the result of overeating. In fact, Rambo did have a bit too much fat deposit. But he wasn't as bad as many of the patients coming to The Ark and Bark.

Of the 16 dogs and cats we saw today, seven were seriously overweight. In many cases their obesity contributed to their problem. Igor Sempl had been stuck by a car yesterday and severely fractured his hind leg. Surgical correction with a plate across the fracture site should mend the break but Igor is at least 15 pounds beyond his optimum weight. A Weimaraner his age should weigh approximately 60 pounds, Igor was carrying seventy five. This represents 25 percent beyond healthy weight. That excess is going to give Igor some trouble in recovery from such a serious injury.

Mr and Mrs. Sempl wanted a breed from their native Germany but never provided Igor with the exercise that a hunter-retriever would need. They compounded that with providing too many table scraps of dumplings and cabbage rolls until Igor became as plump as both Joseph and Anna Sempl.

Did you call me fat?

Bonnie Tuttle, a nine-pound sealpoint Siamese kitten that should have weighed six, was frothing at the mouth because she had swallowed a sewing needle. Mrs. Tuttle had left her needlepoint to answer the phone and the playful kitten chased the threads across the couch. When Mrs. Tuttle returned Bonnie had eaten a needle, point-first. The telltale drooling and white thread hanging from the side of the mouth was the evidence that led us to radiograph immediately to see how far down the throat the needle had advanced. Trip is performing surgery to retrieve the dagger.

The surgery would have fewer risks if Bonnie was not overweight. Any surgery is complicated by obesity, from the mere fact that there is too much fat to cut through, to the real danger that breathing under anesthetic is compromised by internal and external body fat.

I've had to discuss the complications of obesity to each of these clients and five others today. Such discussions occur daily. We are killing our pets with kindness - and neglect. Kindness because pet owners are truly attempting to provide the best food possible. So palatability becomes a key goal in finding a diet that Igor likes. Neglect, by not giving adequate activity to burn the excess calories being fed.

Modern day attempts to simplify life may in fact be contributing to shorten the lives of our pets. We tend to be too 'busy'. So dry pet foods, unmeasured, and high-fat table scraps, provide quick and easy feedings for the dog or cat. Walks, runs and active pet lifestyles are only contingent to those who make the extra effort. Television has made most of modern society an armchair observer. As a result we eat too many calories, feed too many calories to our families —- including our pets, and are less physically active. If half of my patients are over-weight, very often, so too are their owners.

This makes weight reduction a somewhat ticklish subject to raise. But raise it we must.

If the Sempls are a bit embarrassed with the suggestion that Igor is a little overweight (putting it mildly), all the while Mr. Sempl's belt is lost beneath a significant fold in the belly, and Mrs. Sempl's lower arm waves it's significant mass with every gesture, so be it. My responsibility is towards Igor. I want this dog to live as long as his biological clock will allow. If I do not convince the Sempls to get him to reach his appropriate weight, I will be failing him and them. They will lose his companionship for the months or years that obesity will steal. If the Sempls gain some personal insight and benefit from my crusade for Igor's optimum health and reduce their own weight, even better.

It is really very simple. There are two essential rules that the Ark and Bark proposes for new puppies and kittens and to established clientele when it comes to healthy weight. First, prevent obesity for those animals that are not overweight. Second, achieve optimum weight for those animals that are obese.

Preventing Obesity:

Let's Talk...This involves training ourselves as well as our pets. We cannot leave it to the dog or cat to watch their weight. They eat what we put in front of them. The majority of any species must have discipline in the act of eating or feeding. Thus it is the discipline of the owner that dictates the success of the feeding regime for the pet. Here is a pet owners eleven-point blueprint for ideal feeding:

1. **As soon as you acquire a new pet, speak to your veterinarian about diet.** Start with your puppy or kitten. Veterinarians are becoming increasingly aware of the many dietary products on the market and their medical training incorporates enough nutritional science to make them credible advocates of the correct feeding regimes for pets. Take their advice as to the foods of choice, ideally a puppy and kitten food.

2. **Determine the weight and keep a regular log of weigh-ins.** This is particularly critical for large breed dogs, but essential for all puppies, kittens, dogs and cats. A ten percent surplus from normal weight for a dog or cat is dangerous, five percent can be unhealthy. Knowledge of what weight your pet should achieve at every stage in life is key to being able to maintain correct body condition and optimum health through nutrition.

3. **Feed according to the recommended guide** that should be provided on each bag or can of food. Based on the weight of your pet, feed the amount that is prescribed. For large breed puppies, and sedentary kittens, dogs or cats, feed at the lower level of the guide. In other words, if the guide suggests that a 40 pound St. Bernard puppy should get three to three and one half cups of food, give three cups. Puppies that grow faster than they should through over-feeding, especially in the giant breeds, can succumb to bone and muscular diseases such as hip dysplaysia and Osteochondritis Desiccans.

(Hip dysplasia is a degenerative disease of mid-sized to large dogs where the socket that accommodates the head of the femur or long bone of the leg, becomes shallow and widened —- thus no longer a ball and socket joint, but a ball in a joint with too much room. The result of the subsequent movement of the ball in the joint is painful arthritis; Osteochondritis Desiccans is a degenerative disease of the shoulder joint, also more often in larger dogs, with considerable pain and joint cartilage degeneration).

4. **Provide a mixed feeding program.** That is, give both canned and dry food. But determine first what the mixed amounts should be. Ideally, feed the same brand of food that is for the same purpose. In other words, give a same-brand puppy or kitten food that has both a dry and canned recipe and, I would hope, feeding guidelines for the combination. In this way, you can

determine how much of each to cut back on in order to provide both the same nutrients while achieving adequate levels of energy.

An all dry diet is not satisfactory, in my view, because canned food provides an additional source of dietary water. This is especially helpful for some cats that are minimal consumers of water or milk. Diminished body water turnover can lead to, and contribute to, numerous health problems. (Body water turnover is the balance of water consumed to water metabolized to water excreted.)

5. **Keep pet lean-and-median.** Develop an eye for assessing body conformation in dogs and cats. This requires palpation for pets that have long-hair coats. The pet that is at optimum health is lean, not thin; median, not fat. The best assessment is the ability to see and/or feel the ribs. This is not to say that the ribs should be sharply defined with depressions between. Quite the contrary, they should simply be visible and/or palpable. If they cannot be seen and can only be felt by compression of the rib cage there is too much adipose.

6. **Treats must be used strategically**. Two strategies are involved. First, small morsels may be used for training if you or your pet trainer agree with the use of rewards to establish compliance. Second, occasional treats for indulgences can help the bond you feel for your pet, but remember that too many of these will jeopardize health. In order to ensure that treats do not interfere with health, use them sparingly. And add more exercise to the days that they are used so as to burn off those calories.

7. **Minimize table scraps.** Notice that I do not say avoid, as many veterinarians do. If you are comfortable with a disciplined lifestyle that allows for a pet-food-only feeding for your pet, great! Many however, find it difficult to throw away table scraps and see the dog or cat as a logical disposal unit. If you must feed table scraps, plan the human menu so that there are fewer scraps to discard, rather than just assuming that Bouser will clean up after you. Make a pact with your pet that you will feed them 80 to 90 percent balanced pet food, with occasional treats from the human table. Reduce the amount of canned or dry food according to a guestimate of fats and foods sloshed off the plates into Bouser's dish.

8. **Maximize table scrap nutrition.** If you insist on scraping human foods into the doggy bowl, at least recycle wisely. Separate the fats, proteins, sugars, carbohydrates, and other nutrients according to a priority of benefit for Bouser. Throw out the skin of the chicken but scrape chicken meat into his dish. Throw out the pieces of cake but give him the fruit (if he'll eat it) and throw out the fatty sauces and gravy but give him the rice, potatoes and noodles. Throw out the vegetables he won't eat, but give him those he will. Establishing a nutritional menu for the humans in the family will better ensure

that the pet will be getting more nutritional scraps.

9. **Establish a human punishment plan.** For children and adults that feed the cat or dog unhealthy, indiscriminate morsels of food, that are also outside of the feeding guide for the family pet, administer swift and punitive justice. I recommend that whoever is caught in the act must take the pet for an active jog within ten minutes of the indiscretion. The duration of the jog must be commensurate with the size and fatty impact of the morsel. If junior is caught slipping his green beans under the table, this equates to a simple walk around the house since green beans are a healthy treat. But if hubby is detected with cookie in hand beneath the table while Bouser sloshes away at crumbs on the floor, they must both be banished for a one mile trundle.

10. **Weigh yourself.** An overweight master often sanctions the same habits that led to that state of obesity of the pet. Longer and healthier lives for human and pet can be attained first and foremost by treating the top of the feeding pyramid. Think about it.

11. **Enjoy an active life —— with your pet: Exercise burns off excess calories.** It also establishes some healthy triggers within the body. The heart must get it's share of exercise in order to keep muscle tone. The resulting circulation of blood and body fluids from exercise induced heartbeats, helps to fuel the multitude of body functions including the immune system and digestive system. Dogs and cats are able to lay around for most of the day. If they were in the wild, they would do the same. They must however, be stimulated for simulated hunts and games every single day. Chasing or being chased by your pet sets your cardiac muscle in motion as well. Can't hurt anyone.

There are over 50 million dogs and 50 million cats in the United States and Canada. There are over 30 million households that own at least one dog and almost 30 million that are tolerated by at least one cat. Yet I have driven roads through town, country and city at all hours of the day and night. Where are all these pets? If there are so many dogs, and they all require exercise, and their owners get home from work after 5:PM or 6:PM, why aren't the streets full of dogs in all shapes and sizes towing their owner from tree to tree?

I suspect, because I'm just as guilty, that the dog is plopped lazily at the hearth of the 90's video-flame —- television, as the male of the family hypnotically stares from flickering channel to flickering channel. Now we have the Internet drawing people away from exercise towards more and more obsession with the cathode ray tube.

For the sake of the dog, and to minimize the pregnant paunch growing over the human belt buckle, I suggest someone hide the remote, set the VCR onto 'record' and shove master and dog into the cold, leash in hand. Lock the door until there is proof that they've covered significant ground in at least an hour. Just think. House after house with a man and his dog standing on the porch, dumbfounded, separated from the precious tube god. They may just start to exercise in order to replay the VCR (as their reward).

CHAPTER SIX

Ark and Bark

Animal Clinic

CHAPTER SIX

Ark & Bark Animal Clinic
Thursday August 24, 1989

Morning Emergencies:
Mrs. Bossingen - Taffy HBC

Morning Farm Calls:
Harry Seeg - vaccinate horse (only one in the barn)
Norty Glip - soundness examination for quarterhorse
Joe Hooker - check steer that is walking in circles

Morning Surgeries:
Mrs. Philiper - Duke and Duchess - neuter and spay
Bob Balina - Rex, debride granuloma

Morning Appointments:
10:00 Mr. Harwoode - rope burn on dog's neck
10:15 T. Someson - iguana with a lump
10:30 *Mr. & Mrs. Pardan - cat acting funny*
10:45 David Hiden - annual shots for Willy
11:00 Mrs. Bier - budgie, feathers falling out and scratching
11:15 Kay Leftma - wire haired chasing it's tail
11:30 Mrs. Firtzz - Silly Cat - sores on backside
11:45 Mr. & Mrs. Taft - Taffy, eczema
12:00 *Mrs. MacDonnal - house call, several? cats sick*

Afternoon Farm Calls:
Hunter Brothers - losing too many baby pigs
Henry Spansall - remove stitches, check guinea hen that is egg bound
Steven Beech - herd health (pregnancies only)

Afternoon Appointments:
2:00 J. Doyle - Sparky's vaccinations
2:15 Mrs. Patril - recheck Tara
2:30 Buffy Knowles - yearly shots for 3 cats
2:45 Mrs. Boltran - cat Simba - broken leg?
3:00 T. B. Smith - Bruce Bulldog, itchy
3:15 Bob Cormace - Siamese is cross-eyed
3:30 Darren Soul - second shot for Cody
3:45 Mrs. Sepl - recheck Igor
4:00 *Wendy Flitz - Pershing is straining*

Evening Emergencies:
Mrs. Closter - heifer with calf bed out

The Rape of the Guinea Fowl

Thursday August 24, 1989 9: AM. Harry Seeg, Vaccinate horse, only one in the barn...

...just try to get to it!

Trip and I met for coffee with the appointment scheduler between us to divvy up the day's events. "Did you hear on the CBC this morning that George Adamson was killed by poachers in Kenya?" I asked. Adamson was the author of Born Free, an African game warden who, along with his wife, had an international impact on the awareness of conservation and care of animals in their habitat.

"Yeah," said Trip. "Sad, isn't it, that he should become victim of those he kept from destroying so many animal lives... Ah'm wondrin...if he's gonna lie down with the lions in peace. After 83 years he deserves to meet up with those friends he saved..."

"Ah'm more certain than ever that in my past life Ah was a cat!" Trip drawled and reaffirmed as he flipped the appointment scheduler to the day's date. He was on call last night and had been chased around Henry de Vost's barn by a cow with Nervous Acetonemia. "That cat that was to become me in this life, died for certain, a sudden death in my past life. Ah've inherited the eight lives he would've had if he'd've lived. Least, Ah hope he had eight lives left! Why, for sure, one of those lives passed outta me last night or Ah'd've never been able to jump that nine foot wall to get away from the mouth of that cow...she was bent for hell with me in the lead!"

Trip's finger stopped on the morning's country calls. "Now here's a few calls Ah can do that won't do me bad," he said as his left cheek puffed and a breath of relief passed from the side of his mouth. "If ya don't mind, Ah'll just take the easy road t'day see'n as how last night and early this mornin' Ah was goin' t'beat the band."

"Not a problem, Dave," I countered, glancing through my bifocals to see that he did indeed have a prolonged evening last night and a very early call this morning to tend to Taffy Bossingen. I had just checked her vital signs earlier and she was stable thanks to Trip's comprehensive critical care. "You've talked to Mary Bossingen?"

"Yea, Taffy's gonna be okay, but Ah'd like you to watch her for the rest of the day. The only detectable problem was shock and a ruptured bladder. Likely got hit by the car before she was able to relieve herself. Ah went in to repair the tear and flush the abdomen. She's on fluids and antibiotics. May be a good idea to check her for signs of a diaphragmatic hernia a little later." Trip rambled as he laid out his unconscious judgments before me so that I would pick up on his train of clinical thought.

"I agree," I said. "Remember that it's just you and me this morning. Leslie has had to take her Mother to the retirement home this morning. Samantha isn't coming in at all this week. So as soon as you get those 'easy' calls done, come in to give me a hand."

"Righty!" Trip shouted as he bounded for the door content that, for the morning at least, life would be kind and gentle. A quick vaccination and a routine soundness exam would be a snap. Joe Hooker's cow should be seen as soon as possible though, since that steer may be a case of Listeriosis. Joe's place was just past Seeg's so he could vaccinate the horse quickly, then drop in to treat the steer.

What should have taken no more than two hours for those three calls squandered an entire morning. One of Trip's remaining feline incarnates was about to meet death-by-dog.

An oft neglected skill in reading the appointment scheduler is the paying attention to detail. A notation beside the Seeg call says 'only horse in the barn'. Now that likely means that there will be no one home to hold the horse. Sure, it's certain that Harry would put the horse into the stall, and under normal circumstances one could simply walk up to the side of the horse, grab the halter and vaccinate into the shoulder muscle.

But Harry isn't home. He has a full time job driving truck for Anderson's haulage. Mrs. Seeg works at the Donut Shop. Harry guards his property with dogs...Dobermann dogs.

I was fully aware of the notation in the day book. I was also cognizant of the Dobermans. I had met them last month when I called in to sew up a lacerated shoulder on one of their mares. I was well introduced to Satan and Frank (short for Frankenstein).

Satan and Frank are both 80 pounds of bold, fearless terror. This breed was originally bred from German mastiff stock to protect their master from muggers. Their creator was a tax collector. Obviously, he needed the most fearless and aggressive protectors he could produce. Mr. Doberman must have been one of the most successful tax collectors in history.

Trip sailed into the Seeg barnyard, spraying stones from the wheels of the four-by-four truck against the shed. Whistling blissfully and lost in thoughts of a warm summer morning and the leisurely schedule, Trip stepped from the truck to walk to the

Trip is held by twin evils...

tailgate. His back was towards the barn as he placed his hand on the latch to open the back of the cap to retrieve his medical case. His hand stopped mid-air. Hair bristled on the back of his neck. Something, an omen, a feeling, a sense of danger seemed to tap him on the shoulder.

He hadn't heard a sound. There was no breeze. It must have been nothing.

His hand lowered towards the latch once more. Suddenly he felt compelled to stop and freeze once more. What was so manifest behind him that exuded evil with such a sense of disquieted danger? Then he heard a short sharp snarl. His body tensed as he stared into a void suddenly realizing his dilemma. Harry Seeg must have had a guard dog and it had snuck up behind him.

Trip turned with the slowest of slow motion, centimeter by centimeter, to confront the sentinel. Sweat beaded on his forehead then each set of drops joined into streams when his eyes confronted twin evils. His back, not fully rotated to the front, squeezed against the rear of the truck, hands flat against the gate, chin deep into his chest. Staring up with curled lips and exposed teeth, no less than four feet from his knees, were Frank and Satan.

The Dobermans had eight paws planted in launch formation. Any slight move would fire them like rockets at the intruder.

A simple glance towards the left side of the truck, as Trip pondered the distance to travel and the speed at which he could leap if he were to make a break for it, elicited a lunge by each hound. They moved forward no more than half an inch, but their deep ribs, square body and long neck, seemed to advance by several feet.

Trip was trapped in that uncomfortable position for over an hour. If Harry had not forgotten his lunch it could have lasted the day. Worse, if Trip had attempted escape he may have spent a week or two in the hospital. At least Trip had sense enough to remain stationary.

Satan and Frank held their ground even as Harry drove his dump truck up to the house. Harry squinted towards the barn as he tried to discern what Trip was doing. Was he talking to his dogs? Was he trying to climb onto the roof of his truck, back first? Harry walked over towards the clinic vehicle. As he reached his dogs he realized the plight of the frightened veterinarian.

"Frank! Satan! Sit!" screamed Harry. Frank and Satan sat.

Trip slumped, half sitting, half leaning onto the bumper. When Trip had commanded them to sit they simply lunged forward, inch by inch. By the time Harry arrived he could feel their hot breath singeing his legs. Harry realized that Trip's perspiration-soaked shirt was not merely the result of humid weather.

"I'm awfully sorry about this Doctor Tripper," he apologized. "But I'm so proud of these fellows." Harry's attention abruptly turned to the attending guardians. Trip's jaw dropped as he saw the modicum of regret for his personal welfare transform into a heaping of praise onto his oppressors.

Harry dropped to his knees to nuzzle his face between the twin sentinels who now transformed into wriggling, gentle playmates, ignoring their captive completely. "Good boys, good boys, yes my Dobie's are such good boys!" Harry repeated with baby gibberishes as Frank and Satan bounced merrily around their kneeling praising master.

Trip started to move dejectedly towards the front of the truck then instinctively stopped dead in anticipation of an attack. No more. The demon dogs were frolicking with each other and Harry, content that their duty as watchdogs was secure. Trip shook his head and wiped the travail from his face and neck with his handkerchief. He climbed wearily into the cab and drove away leaving the horse to be vaccinated another time. Harry raced the dogs to the house to give them a special treat for their exemplary responsibility as guard dogs.

"Ah'll get over to Joe Hooker's before Ah go home to change," thought Trip as he drove away. His sense of duty was as strong as the Dobermans' given the stress he had just endured. He still had to tend to a sick cow whose intended treatment was unexpectedly delayed. At least he had a good idea what he would be treating. This steer would give him no trouble, a simple intravenous would start the course of therapy.

Little did he know, but would soon find out, that Joe Hooker's steer did not suffer from Listeriosis, but from furious Rabies. Dr. Dave Tripper was about to be chased once again by a mad and villainous bovine, it's brain destroyed by the Rabies virus, but with enough intent left to attack any moving object — and Trip, despite being worn to his limits over the past twenty four hours — would move remarkably quickly. Four more feline lives to go?...

11:20 AM Mr. and Mrs. Pardan...

...Who's on first?

Unaware of the reason for Trip's delay but intensely annoyed at the consequence, I muttered angrily under the pressure of the workload. "He knew Leslie was away...Why, I even told him!...Where are those files?....Where's my stethoscope?..."

I fumbled through the first appointments becoming further and further behind as the morning drew on. It was always patently clear how valuable Leslie was to the clinic, especially when she was away. This morning was no exception. I nodded to the next couple, new clients that I had never met before, that I was finally ready for their 10:30 appointment. Given that their files were not on the computer or hard copy, it was my duty to start a record on them and their pet. I peered at them and the necessary papers in my hands as they got up from their chairs. I gathered that the lady was hard of hearing as the gentleman bent over to her ear to shout, "Time for us now Mabel!"

Mabel was in her early sixties, stout though not grossly overweight. She seemed oblivious to the surroundings as she focused intently on the bundle in her arms. A grey ball of fluff wrapped in a beach towel peeked from the enclosure, uncertain as to why it's head was bobbing through this unfamiliar environment. The man was late-sixtyish, bespectacled, somewhat beyond his age in attitude as he shuffled his feet and doted after his companions. He held his arm hesitatingly behind Mabel to ensure that she rose from the chair safely. His baggy slacks and drooping cardigan seemed to place him and his charges into another era.

The mood at the moment, was as serene as the music that was playing in the background. Soothing patients and clients in the front room as they waited was Pachelbel's most famous composition. Mabel looked up at her husband as they walked by me towards the examination room. "I know that tune!" she blurted. "That's the Taco Bell Cannon!"

"Just place your cat on the table," I said as I lay my papers on one end of the examination counter.

"Ehy?" said Mabel, looking up at the gentleman, I assumed was her husband.

"Put Puddy Tat on the table!" shouted the gentlemen directly into his wife's ear.

"Oh..." she verified understanding by placing an equally disquieted cat onto the table. Puddy opened her mouth almost involuntarily to elicit a subtle cry of pain. I was drawn immediately to the cry, ignoring the paper work for the moment. After assuring that the cat was going to survive the interrogatory session I resumed the data entry.

"Name?" I asked routinely, pen poised to fill in the blank spaces on the data sheet.

"Pardan," was all the gentleman said.

I looked up from my page in a double take. I thought it was Mabel who was hard of hearing. "Name?" I said again, volume up a notch.

"Pardan," he said again, equal volume.

"Ehy?" asked Mabel, looking from my face to her husband's. He simply waved her inquisition off with his hand.

"What's your name?" I asked again, trying not to sound as irritated as I was becoming and probably louder than I needed to be.

"Pardan!" he said again, clearly irritated with my tone and inflections.

"What!" I said incredulously. Surely he understood by now!

"Pardan!" he shouted.

"Pardon?" I asked, pen and paper drooping from my hands in exasperation.

"Yes!" he shouted.

"Yes?" I asked.

"What's goin' on?" questioned Mabel. He gave her a double-handed wave-off this time.

"My name is Elwood Pardan!" he bellowed as though I was hard of hearing.

"I know that!" cried Mabel, shaking her head in disgust at Elwood. Then she looked towards me. "Why aren't you lookin' to Puddy Tat?" She demanded with an angry raspy voice, evidently concerned that Elwood and I were lost in glares at one another — mine an embarrassed realization of the meaning of the preceding dialogue, and his an angry challenge to continue the tirade.

I shook myself out of this agitated state to return to duty. There was now enough data, difficult as it was to retrieve, to start the entry. I quickly wrote the client and patient names onto the chart. "I'll get the rest of the information later," I thought to myself. This client is not going to have a very good impression of me or my facilities if I don't take a look at their charge immediately.

"What seems to be the problem?" I asked as I bent down to pat and palpate Puddy Tat.

"Ehy?" screamed Mabel, concernedly, as she tilted her head to see what I was up to.

"He says, what's wrong with the cat!" shouted Elwood into her ear.

"How're we s'possed t'know! He's the Vet!" she retorted indignantly, referring to me in third party but directing the reply specifically at me. This was going to be a long day.

"I mean, what are the symptoms that you're concerned with?" I returned in explanation, though becoming as agitated with Elwood and Mabel as they were with me.

"Ehy?" said Mabel crouching into my face that was now trying to hide from the discussion by engrossing myself into an examination of Puddy.

"He wants to know why we brought her here!" hollered Elwood, leaning to reach her ear leaving all three of us crouched towards the cat.

Mabel roared directly at me this time. "She ain't eatin'! Why'd you think?" Then she slipped a side-long glance at Elwood. "You sure this guy knows what he's doin'? Don't seem to know much!"

I resolved now to find out what Puddy's problem was without their help. Checking the tender abdomen, palpating the entire body, determining the pulse, respiration, heart rate, rhythm and temperature, I was confident that the cat was not in any danger. The firm, dry impediment to my thermometer however, gave the definitive diagnosis. I rose from the research triumphant. "Puddy Tat appears to simply be constipated," I asserted. "I think we can relieve her with a mild laxative provided there are no obstacles such as bits of bone that might have caused this. We can keep her here to give a mild enema, although I might rather perform an x-ray first."

"What's he sayin'?" asked Mabel, standing aback with her mouth slightly open as if questioning the validity of what she didn't even hear.

"He say's she's constipated!" barked Elwood, this time as an aside rather than into her auricle.

"Ehy?" Mabel said her hand cupped to her ear.

"She's constipated!" Elwood barked.

"Constiwhat?" Mabel retorted.

"She's bunged up!" Elwood yelled.

"Bunged up? Hell I coulda told ya that! Why she ain't shit fer five days! Why'd ya think we brung her here in the first place?" The initial declaration was directed to Elwood, the final question directed with Mabel's nose to my nose.

"Come on Elwood, we're goin' home. I'm given Puddy that concoction I intended givin'. These new fangled vetinaries don't seem to know a thing." Elwood and Mabel gathered up their uncomfortable companion, somewhat more vigorously than when they entered. I followed with laxative and record in hand stumbling over words that might mollify the situation and get them to reconsider my prescription. To no avail, Mr. and Mrs. Pardan and Puddy charged out of the hospital indignant and still constipated.

An anxious Dave Hiden saw me come to the examination room door to ask. "Are you ready to see Willy now Dr. Runcibal?" I turned, dejected and confused and could only say...

"Pardon?"

12: noon: Mrs. MacDonnal...

...The Cat Lady

There are instances of affection-cum-affliction where love of animals has gone too far. My nostrils still twinge when I think of the call to Mrs. MacDonnal's trailer. She was an elderly lady, who although no more than 65 years old, looked to be 80 with her grey unkempt hair and tattered clothes. She said on the phone that she had 'several' cats that were ill and since she had no car she couldn't bring them in to the clinic. Would I please come out to see them.

The home was an abandoned trailer on a secluded lot on a side street of town. I knocked on the door thinking I may have gotten the address wrong. But the distinctive smells that wafted out the open door to greet me along with Mrs. MacDonnal told me that this was not only the right place, but that I was about to meet another 'cat lady.' Inside the trailer were more than 'several' cats.

There were cats everywhere! A big long-haired male swatted at my head from his perch on the top of the cupboard as I entered the domestic cattery. Six or seven kittens ran across the floor chasing one another through my feet. The couch and chairs were draped with a dozen or more felines of every description. Cats were sitting in the cupboards and lying in pots and pans on the stove.

The senses were overwhelmed with the smell of contributions to the multitude of litter boxes, and the chorus of sneezes echoed from every direction.

"Here is my Molly, Dr. Runcibal," said the kindly Mrs. MacDonnal, apparently oblivious to the chaos around her. She walked me over to an orange tabby lying in a cardboard box breathing heavily and lying in discomfort on her side. "She seems to be bothered the most. Now where did Fester go, I wanted you to check him too, and Tinker is a little under the weather but I can't seem to...oh there you are, come right down from there." She went on and on trying to sort out who needed attention and who didn't. The one who needed the most care in this bedlam was Mrs. MacDonnal.

"Ma'am, do you have any idea how many cats you have here?" I asked.

"Oh dear. Er, yes I think there may be about 100. No Sally had a litter last night so there are 109," she answered though still trying to remember whether there were new additions from her walks along the side streets.

Cat ladies seem to become obsessed with the comfort and caring of stray cats. Like Mrs. MacDonnal, they will go to any lengths to accommodate them, even to selling their house and moving to a dilapidated trailer home to afford the food and litter. The result is the most unhealthy environment for both cats and lady.

The multitude of cats, usually unvaccinated and never dewormed, carry internal and external parasites as well as a host of viral diseases that they spread to one another — and some to their benefactor. The enclosed quarters allows the infections to afflict virtually every animal. And the home is so unhygienic for the caregiver that her food and air can only be contaminated with dangerous organisms, Toxoplasmosis (an organism picked up by cats but transferable to humans) being only one of them.

Sadly, it was in Mrs. MacDonnal's best interest that I had to call the Health Department as well as the Humane Society to handle this case, knowing full well that many of these cats would have to be put down and that the breakup of Mrs. MacDonnal's 'home' would devastate her. And there is a good chance that this addiction would not go away, so that Mrs. MacDonnal could once again be surrounded by more than a 100 felines.

A houseful of cats...

Fortunately for Mrs. MacDonnal, Jeannie Tripper and Mary Runcibal are cat lovers, and both active volunteers at the Senior Citizen Home. They were able to place one third of the healthy cats (for whom they shamed treatment and vaccination out of Trip and me) into homes throughout the community. Molly, as well as more than 40 others had to be euthanized as they were simply too ill, parasitized or malnourished to be salvaged. Tinker and Fester, Mrs. MacDonnal's favorites, were adopted as clinic cats that would become regular visitors to the nursing home.

Late Afternoon, Lady in Distress...

...The Worried Guinea

In addition to the Muscovy duck, another common feathered friend of the farm is the guinea fowl. I've had many older farmers tell me that, "If you wanted to be safe in the country, get a pair of guineas!" This was advice given to us when my wife and I moved to the country. "At night time it's a lot darker out there than in the city where the street lights give that warm sense of security."

Guinea fowl will sit in the trees right by the house and if an intruder comes near they let out a staccato, "Yak yak yak yak yak yak yak yak yak," to alarm both the intruder and the household.

Henry Spansall bought a pair of guinea birds for just that purpose. Henry was the Heron Point Treasurer who moved north of town with his family about a year ago. I visited their place fairly regularly as they had a clumsy horse they had bought for their daughter who seemed to get lacerated by anything sharper than a bread knife.

Whenever I would call, the birds would be roosted in the pine tree beside the house. As it got closer to winter Henry taught them to go into the barn for warmth and grain, fearing that they would freeze to death sitting in that pine tree.

Then one morning in late August, Henry went to the barn to do the chores before heading into town. There on the floor of the barn was a guinea hen lying on its back, feet straight up as though stiff and paralyzed. With no farm background he could only run to call for someone who could help.

First he checked the animal husbandry books but there was nothing on the guinea hen. So he called the clinic for advice. "Dr Runcibal, "he began, "I've got a guinea hen here that is stiff and seems to be quite sore. I found her on the ground completely unable to walk. Now I looked up in the books I've got here and under 'chickens', the symptoms seem to suggest that she's suffering from being either 'crop-bound' or egg-bound'.

I know the animal husbandry books are the bible of the hobby farmer so I suggested that either of those conditions could be the problem, though it was impossible for me to know without seeing the hen. "It just happens," I said, "That your name is in our book today to come out to remove Blackie's stitches. I'll have a look at the hen when I get there."

When I arrived on the farm and had taken out the sutures from Blackie's shoulder, telling her to stay away from wire fences, I went to the house where Mrs. Spansall had taken the hen. I noticed that the male guinea seemed considerably agitated as he followed me to the house, and even more indignant when I closed the kitchen door in his face.

Mrs. Spansall had the hen in a wide low tub on the table, obviously the bath she had used for her daughter when she was a baby. The hen was on its side now but legs stiffly pressed out as though it had just returned from a taxidermist. Veterinarians are trained to treat birds but we tend to see far fewer birds than we see other species so this was probably as much a mystery to me as it was the Spansalls. I was able to narrow the diagnosis to 'egg-bound' by palpating a hard oval lump in the genital area.

All the while that we were examining the hen we could hear the male guinea calling out for his mate, wondering what fate was befalling her inside the kitchen.

"YaYayayayayayayayaya," he screamed. The hen tried to answer back. Each cry from her made the male all the more animated and loud. He was at the back door screaming "Yiayiayia yiayiayiayia." He was frantic. As I continued to manipulate the hen's orifice to try to deliver the egg she screamed as though she was being murdered. The male started running around the house.

Now guinea fowl look funny enough when they run. They look something like an ostrich where their head, neck and body remain steady while their legs pace recklessly. A guinea bird looks like a short, fat version of this. When you add a look of panic, the bird becomes a demented road-runner cartoon, racing around the house, legs paddling, body still, at break-neck speed around each corner, yapping steadily.

Every time he reached the kitchen window his head and neck would pop up to steal a look inside. His eyes bulged out and they seemed to scream, "What are they doing to her?"

In order to help this hen to un-bound and pass the egg, I had to lubricate her. As

A distraught guinea bird at the window...

soon as I began the process she let out the most indignant screech I've ever heard. The more I massaged the more she screamed.

And the poor worried guinea cock outside was driven to a frenzy. He ran around the house in one direction. Then he turned 180 degrees to make it back the other way in record time, all the while crying, "Dahtdahtdahtdahtdahtdahtdahtdahtdahtdahtdaht!!!" Mrs. Spansall was totally distracted and she ran from room to room shouting, "He's at the dining room window!" Then, "He's at the living room window." Here was this weird guinea head and neck popping up at every window all around the house screaming at us at the top of his lungs, as his mate screamed at me to stop, and at him to save her.

I finally felt comfortable that the hen was lubricated enough to stop and I asked Mrs. Spansall for a hot water bottle. Carrying the exhausted hen outside we found a little indentation out in the yard where I placed the hen on the warm water bottle. We put leaves and debris around her to make a little nest.

The male was looking anxiously over my shoulder, constantly muttering. He came over to sit down beside her as soon as we backed away then privately nattered at her as though to ask what had happened. I'm sure he looked back at me, as though he was saying, "What kind of a barbarian are you? Doing that to my woman!"

They finally nested together, content. I decided there was little more that I could do so I resumed the rest of my calls. I was to learn later that they walked away that evening, leaving a large dark egg in the middle of the nest — that they would have nothing further to do with.

The Spansall birds were to produce a whole flock of guineas after that painful incident, without further incident.. But Henry found that he could never get a good night's sleep with a dozen hens cackling at the window every night. It seems that in a flock of 12, at least one bird is going to see something that disturbs it, at any given moment, during any given evening. And if one starts the alarm, the others join in until they almost shake the needles from the pine. So Henry sold the entire flock in favor of a German Shepherd.

4: PM Wendy Flitz - Pershing is blocked...

....Wendy blocks traffic

Leslie had returned from depositing her mother at the retirement home and seemed irritated to see the mess Trip and I had made of the clinic. Records were incomplete (especially the Pardan charts), pens were missing, day-book in the examination room where it was not supposed to be. Trip and I stopped apologizing, explaining, searching and Leslie stopped complaining when Wendy Flitz drove into the parking lot. We all scrutinized the bumpers and fenders of the vehicle through the venetian blind to see if there was evidence of bodies or bumps. This time all appeared orderly so we nonchalantly resumed assumed duties peering into charts, computer screens and pretend cuts on fingers as Wendy entered.

"Doctors, Leslie," cried an anxious Wendy Flitz. Pershing echoed her cries with a loud and painful, "Meeoowwww, meoowww." Ow! being the operative sensation.

"I'm so glad you're all here," Wendy continued, rushing Pershing without asking, directly into the examination room. "I had to hurry home to pick up some papers for Jason. He's in Calgary and I needed to fax some important information on a client he's meeting there. I must dash over to his office as soon as I can to get that off to him." Wendy began a prolonged explanation of this new dilemma as she gently placed a distended cat onto the table. "As soon as I came into the house to get the papers I heard this agonizing moan. At first I thought it was Cali but then I saw her resting comfortably on the windowsill. I followed the cries to the kitty litter and there was Pershi squatting and wailing. He's in terrible pain!"

Pershing's abdomen was painfully distended and taut. Ever so slight palpation increased the volume of his shrieks. His pupils were slightly dilated, pulse rapid and weak, hydration slightly diminished and he was becoming steadily weakened, evidenced by tremors of the head. His normally bright and smiling eyes were glazed and dry.

"It appears as though Pershing is blocked," I said as Trip rushed to the surgery to prepare for emergency procedures. "We have no time to lose, Wendy. I'll give you the situation in a nutshell." Wendy placed her hands on her lips and her alarmed eyes glassed over as she set herself for the diagnosis and apparent prognostic side bar to come. "Pershing has Feline Lower Urinary Tract Disorder," I continued. "Essentially, bladder and/or urethral stones. Being a male cat, there is either too many or too large a build up of these stones in his lower urinary tract so that he is unable to pass urine. The resulting back-up of urine is causing his bladder to distend. Now, he's essentially going into shock." Wendy slowly lowered herself into the examination room chair recognizing the seriousness of both voice and phrase.

"Is he going to die?" she asked hesitantly, her hands now clutching her scarf on her lap wringing as hard as she could for a negative answer.

"He could," I had to say. "But you've brought him in right away and he's still alert despite his pain and discomfort. We see too many cats with this problem but thankfully we are able to save most of them.   First, we must attempt to reduce the blockage in order to get the urine out. He will need fluids and perhaps surgery if we can't pass a catheter. We may even need to tap the abdomen to withdraw urine if catheterization fails." Trip had Pershing already prepared for the procedure as Wendy gave consent to go ahead. There was no question that Mrs. Flitz would place her trust in our intent to do the best.

I left Leslie and Trip to work on Pershing while I spoke reassuringly to Wendy. I was as anxious as she was. The minutes seemed like hours. Trip's shout, "Ah'm in!" brought me running to the back with a grateful sigh. "Catheter in place, Jon. Ah'll sew it in after we've expressed the bladder completely. Ah want to flush the bladder first. Tell Wendy to rest easy, Persh's signs are gettin' better by the second. It looks as though he's goin' to come around just fine."

Wendy had been just as intent to listen to those words from Trip as she leaned out from her chair in anticipation. As I returned smiling, she knew she had heard correctly. We both breathed deeply and settled back to unwind from the intensity of the moment. Our repose was brief however, when we were taken aback by the imposing uniformed figure of Officer Holtby in the doorway.

"Does anyone here own an '86 Volvo Wagon?" he asked.

"Why yes, it's mine," said Wendy with great concern and confusion. "It's right outside," she said as she pointed to the window where her car used to be.

"Not right outside," said the Officer. "If you look out there a little further you'll see that it's sitting right in the middle of the highway. It looks as though you forgot to put the car into park and it has rolled down the slight slope from the clinic lot, to stop right onto the road. As you can see, the traffic can't get by from either direction because it is perpendicular to the road."

Like the urinary calculus recently plugging the penis of a now contented feline, we looked out to see a Volvo wagon blocking commuters for several yards to the east and west. Rather than a catheter, an embarrassed Wendy Flitz and a set of keys extricated this blockage. Wendy didn't stop to apologize. She simply squealed away to her husband's office to fax the promised documents, very likely including a report on Pershing's ordeal, though not likely an account of her latest autoventure.

FLUTD...

....What's all the FUS about?

Let's talk...At the back of my mind during my disastrous examination of Puddy Tat Pardan was the possibility of Feline Lower Urinary Tract Disorder (FLUTD), often also referred to as Feline Urologic Syndrome (FUS). Pershing survived the problem and was resting comfortably. He could have died. This condition, although not common in the large population of cats, is one that deserves special attention because veterinarians see enough serious cases each year to make us cognizant of the critical nature of the disease. Pershing showed some initial signs that warranted concern. His abdomen was distended and it was reasonably painful to touch. Puddy Tat, despite being female —- blockage is less frequent in female cats —- could still have been suffering from the disease. But it is the male cat that suffers most from the syndrome.

There are several predisposing causes to the condition and it seems that not all of the questions about FLUTD are yet answered. In fact, every time I attend a lecture on the condition, something new is revealed.

What it is

Fundamentally FLUTD is an inflammation of the lower urinary tract of the male or female cat. There may be infection present. In many cases there is none. In a few instances crystals form in the bladder as a result of the chemical composition of the urine. If you think of salt crystals and basic chemistry you can envision that in particular solutions, crystals are formed. Urine is a concentrated solution of waste products eliminated by the body in fluid forms after filtration through the kidneys and deposited into the bladder. It is composed mainly of chemicals that can form crystals.

If the urine is not acidic enough, those ingredients join to crystallize. As the crystals aggregate they can form 'stones' that can reach a size and number adequate to block the urethra of the cat (the tube that leaves the bladder to the vulva of the female, penis of the male). Males suffer more from blockage since the urethra is narrower and longer than that of a female. It may also have less elasticity than a female's urethra.

This is especially a disease of cats from one to four years of age, rare in cats under a year old. Fortunately, fewer cases seem to be reported than ten years ago, likely thanks to specially formulated diets.

The ensuing backup of urine causes the disastrous effects on the body as evidenced by the unfortunate Pershing Gimps. Affected cats become uremic (poisoned by the backup of waste products in the blood that can no longer be emptied into the bladder since the plug effectively stops elimination) and this causes them to vomit. Dehydration and depression follow quickly, usually within 48 hours. Death can result within three days of onset.

And what to do...

Prevention of this condition can be accomplished by feeding cat food with a formulation that provides a continuous acid pH to the urine. Not all cats need such a diet. Determining who does and who doesn't however, is next to impossible. Certainly any cat that has experienced the problem could be a candidate for the special diet. Male cats that are neutered (especially if done at less than six months of age) seem to be more predisposed so they deserve careful observation of their litter box habits.

It is also important to minimize stresses in a cat's environment as some stressors have been implicated as contributing to the problem. Too frequent changes in the diet, not cleaning the litter regularly, feeding only dry cat foods, may be harmful. Changing litter often, in order to ensure that the cat does not hold back on any voiding is just as important as the diet.

Availability of fresh water and feeding canned food to cats are helpful. Pet feeding has been made much more convenient with the advent of many brands of excellent dry dog and cat foods. Canned food has also been unnecessarily blamed for poor dental hygiene. The reality is that pets can and should (in my view) be fed both canned and dry food. Canned food in particular because it can consist of up to 75% water. Body water turn-over (ingestion of water, use of water in metabolism, and subsequent excretion of water through sweat, respiration and urine) is a critical component of healthy digestion and metabolism. Feeding canned food as well as setting out fresh milk or water are essential to the process. Cats who suffer from this disease should perhaps eat only the canned diets specifically formulated to control this disease.

Most veterinary clinics carry these special foods that help treat and prevent FLUTD. Some retail brands are available as well in some areas. At the very least cat owners should discuss the condition with their veterinarian for an assessment of risk. Advice as to whether such preventative diets are indicated for your cat, and direction as to which brands to consider, could also be discussed.

I may never get to see Puddy Tat Pardan again given that Elwood and Mabel think seriously that this veterinary profession is out to lunch without a bucket. Pershing Gimps however will be a steady client. He's already a ravenous consumer of the veterinary diet that we carry. Trip offered him a bite to eat in the kennel room. Persh loved the morsel and we were relieved to see him accept it, a clear sign of recovery.

CHAPTER SEVEN

Ark and Bark

Animal Clinic

CHAPTER SEVEN
Ark & Bark Animal Clinic
Tuesday July 18, 1989

Morning Emergencies:
Bob Dickerson - calving
Jack and Doris Petersen - Hamlet attacked the mail-man

Morning Farm Calls:
Kasper Button - pig ruptured
Norty Glip - check horse, yawning all the time

Morning Surgeries:
Mrs. Mack Fandel - Mitzie, amputate leg
Mrs. Jerome - spay dog and cat

Morning Appointments:
10:00 *Mrs. Tothe - dog will not eat, or anything*
10:15 Mr. Rolfe - vaccinate 2 kittens
10:30 T. Currelle - bitch lost a litter
10:45 Vicky Calaman - doberman - vomiting and diarrhea
11:00 *Claire Shelby - Barney - coughing and not eating*
11:15
11:30 Mary McLee - Scottie's coat is matted
11:45 Rex Jimp - Taffy due for vaccines
12:00

Afternoon Farm Calls:
Doug Spenser - drop by to check coughing chickens

Afternoon Appointments:
2:00 Gloria Logel - chinchilla not eating, smells bad
2:15 Agnes Huskins - cat attacked by a bird
2:30 H. Dockerty - recheck ears
2:45
3:00 Bert Single - dog shaking
3:15 Mrs. E. Druist - check bird's beak, may be broken
3:30 Bob & Gail Spanish - recheck Mork, still not eating well
3:45 Cary Caruther - poodle may have miscarried
4:00 *Mark Haley - house call, Smokey is failing*

Evening Emergencies:
Nathan Biddle - Winston wrapped up in barbed wire
Jim Judd - cow with milk fever

Wednesday October 11   Morning Farm Call...

...Lucky's Loss

A rural vet benefits from the pleasures of the outdoors. This fall in particular, the panorama of flaxen, crimson and hues of green, make an early morning drive to a calving worth the effort. Bob Dickerson's heifer is straining to bring an addition to the herd into the crisp autumn air. I was looking forward to the call, lost in reverie brought on by the psychedelic streams of light through the trees, when my foot fell off of the gas peddle as I passed by the Tothe farm. Reality of life dimmed and dulled the colors of the day as I drove past a lonely dog lying flat on it's abdomen at the end of the laneway, eyes as mournful as death itself.

Lucky was young Patrick Tothe's dog. Patrick had lived in Heron Point until the family moved to a new house on the family farm. Lucky was a new puppy acquired as a companion for Patty when he was no more than eight years old. The pup was primarily a black water spaniel although certainly not a pure-bred — as though that would ever have mattered to Patrick. Young Pat and Lucky were inseparable from day one. Patty could be seen skipping stones at the stream, sending Lucky out after sticks, exploring the back streets of town or chasing the birds and rabbits in the bush along the tracks.

Lucky was the friendliest dog one could find — to Patrick. But Lucky was so attached to his master that he became overly protective. No one could touch Pat let alone approach him for fear of attack by Lucky. Patrick could do anything to the dog with full impunity. No one else could encounter the duo without risk of vicious snaps of defence.

Two years ago, after months of attempting to tolerate this aggressive behavior, the Tothes brought Lucky and Patrick into my office, ostensibly to see if there was anything I could do to remedy the problem. In reality, the parents were determined to put the dog down. There was nothing physically wrong with Lucky. He had simply imprinted on a single master. Patrick was his world (and vice versa). He was merely protecting the friend that he loved dearly. Looking into Patrick and Lucky's eyes that day I would never have been able to live with myself if I had agreed to euthanize a dog because it loved its master.

"How about a compromise?" I had suggested. I knew that Patrick's grandfather farmed on the other side of the river. I went on to recommend that Lucky be moved to the farm so that he would be kept away from people. The grandfather no longer kept up the farm other than renting out the land so that the only visitors would be Patrick and his family. Lucky could be a companion for Grandpa and Patrick could visit as often as possible to keep Lucky content. Grandpa Peterson knew dogs well enough to avoid the beast in Lucky and would be more than able to feed and house him.

The Tothes were gladdened with the suggestion, Patrick certainly, but his parents seemed as relieved with the idea. They didn't want Lucky to hurt anyone and could not envision a solution other than euthanasia even though the answer was waiting for them across the river.

Apparently, the solution back-fired initially. Lucky was not to be outdone. On the designated weekend for Lucky's exile, the family piled into the car, Lucky and Patrick in the back seat. Their home was just across the river from the grandfather's but the bridge to get there was three miles south. They drove the three miles south, the mile east across the causeway and bridge and three miles north to the farm. After a picnic on the lawn, good-byes to Lucky and Grandpa, they drove leisurely home for the evening. When they drove up to their house who was sitting waiting patiently, panting and dripping wet? Lucky!

Somehow, never having been to Grandpa Petersons before, certainly determined to figure out how quickly to return to his master, Lucky deduced that the shortest distance between two points was a straight line and headed right out to the marsh, swam the river and rushed immediately to the porch in time for Patrick's arrival. Patrick was overjoyed, his parents were devastated. Did this mean they would still have to put him down?

They made another attempt, this time tying Lucky up until he could realize that Patrick would be coming back to see him. Lucky got the message. He became content to sit at the end of the lane to wait.

Fate twisted the string connecting the Tothe family once again though, when Grandpa died last year. Fortunately for Lucky and Patrick the Tothes decided to move onto the farm. Patrick and Lucky were once again joined forever. Until destiny ripped the string apart.

Patrick became quite ill during a meningitis outbreak that afflicted the local school-children this September. It was only after a few days of extremely high fever that Patrick died.

The last time Lucky saw Patrick he was getting onto the bus at the end of the lane. As was his custom, Lucky knew when the bus would return at 4:45 every day. Patrick had been rushed to hospital straight from the school on that day and died a few days later. He would never get off the bus again. Lucky did not understand. He waited and stayed at the end of the lane day after day. He would not eat, rarely slept. Ears would perk up when the sound of the school bus roared in the distance. His heart would sink when the bus would not stop.

My truck had come to a rest as I could not take my eyes from this melancholy animal. I walked over to Lucky, cognizant of his penchant for snapping but certain that there was no danger from the dejected and lonely look in his eyes. "Hallo Lucky my friend," I said as I caressed his black fur. A sombre pair of eyes looked up towards me as if to say, "Have you seen Patrick?"

I could only drive away to make my call, certain now that Mr and Mrs. Tothe would likely be in soon to discuss what to do with Lucky...

Tragedy Strikes Jack and Doris Petersen ...

...Hamlet the Great Dane

Jack and Doris Peterson were friends and clients. They were animal lovers. When they first moved to town they brought a two year old Great Dane, named Hamlet, into the clinic for his annual vaccination. There had been some discrepancy about this pup's heritage as his mother had 'slept around'. Yet he had a regal bearing, even as a puppy and they were fairly certain that his father was the grand champion of the Dane world who had unfortunately, recently died, under suspicious circumstance. Apparently, Claude-Elsinore Baykennels, the littermate of the pup's father, had become the new reigning champion.

The Petersons doted on Hamlet like a son. It was the coddling that obfuscated the pup's true problems, as initially their questions seemed to be referring to a different dog. Hamlet's behavior would always come into question with every visit to the clinic. Yet with each examination there never appeared to be any physical evidence of disease or disorder.

Last year Hamlet was brought in for vaccinations and Doris recounted that for several nights he would run to the door barking frantically to get outside. Once into the darkness he would chase the shadows from the streetlamps for hours, barking and growling as if to be addressing invisible ghosts in the night mist.

Whenever Hamlet was taken to the classes for obedience training, where he would meet his relatives and neighborhood pals, the pup would lash out at Claude-Elsinore, his uncle, as if in revenge for secretive and mysterious shame. Hamlet was friendly, though not impassioned, towards his mother Gertrude. He enjoyed dallying with Horace the Basset with the floppy ears. But he was often difficult to train as a result of such erratic behavior — once attacking Claude, then to be rubbing up against Gertrude, then bounding off to frolic with Horace.

It was Sophie, the Bouvier de Flandres, that brought Hamlet to his knees. She was an imposing beauty with black frizzy hair, deep brown eyes that penetrated whomever she chose to watch, from her stance in the middle of the obedience ring. Her stares at Hamlet caused him to stop dead, trapped in her spell.

But it was Rosie the poodle and Gilda the Dachshund, nipping at Hamlet's heels that caused the furor at that fateful training session. Hamlet went mad with anger at being harassed by such diminutive and impudent animals. He lashed out at them — - and Sophie. Jack and Doris were banned from the obedience lessons.

Jack brought him in to the clinic after the first real 'incident'. They had a dinner party and Hamlet snapped at one of the guests who simply reached down to pat him on the head. There seemed to be no apparent reason for such an outburst. Jack couldn't understand why a dog that was so gentle with them, could have done such a thing. Jim Poloner, the victim, loved animals and Hamlet had bitten right through his napkin.

We decided that we would give Hamlet a reprieve given that the napkin ensured that there was no blood drawn and the dog was fully vaccinated. It wasn't until today that we realized that there was nothing left to do but to euthanize.

"Last night he dug up half the yard," Jack said as he described the recent events. "There were a couple of other dogs helping him. They seemed to be looking for something but all that Hamlet brought out of a completely destroyed back garden, was a jaw bone of some dead animal. Alas. It was the poor Yorkie that the previous owners of the house had buried back there. I think Hamlet knew him, but why dig him up? Anyway, from that moment on he seemed to distrust anybody and everything in the neighborhood. He raced after every cat, bird and dog that happened to impinge on the space of our yard."

"Finally this morning," Jack continued regretfully, his eyes dropping to his side where Hamlet sat indifferent to the tragic situation. "No sooner had Larry Fortina, the mailman gotten to the top step of the porch, when Hamlet burst through the screen door. He almost knocked Doris over. She had opened the storm door to greet Larry and get the mail from him when Hamlet saw him through the screen and bolted after him. It should have been a storm door but we hadn't gotten around to replacing the screen with glass. Now the entire outside door is in splinters and man-

The ghost of Hamlet...

gled mesh. What is worse, Larry has had to have 13 stitches."

Not everything we do and see can be explained away through science. The sixth, seventh or eighth senses some people seem to have are made plausible if and when you experience them yourself. I have looked into many an animal's eyes to witness an ethereal communication. Perhaps the years of treating dogs and cats gave me this sense about animal behavior, especially those about to bite. Perhaps subconscious signals emanate from subtle body language. Perhaps it has simply been a learned skill. But after several bites in my early years of practice I have managed to avoid most of the attacks. Hamlet transmitted his messages loud and clear, at least as I perceived them.

"There is definitely something going on here," I said as I made a careful and calculated examination. "He has no medical problem that I can see, but he does seem to be developing an attitude. Since you've been bringing him in for these outbursts we've tried every kind of behavior modification technique that I know of. I've consulted with behavioral specialists and you've both applied all of their recommendations faithfully."

"Doctor, what are we to do? If he attacks a young child we could never live with ourselves. We love him dearly but we can't let this go on." They stood on each side of Hamlet in grim acceptance of the expected solution. Unfortunately, I couldn't give them any other recourse. Dogs that become unreliable as pets are truly dangerous. Euthanasia is the unpleasant remedy for some of these cases. Hamlet seemed to have a death wish.

"It has to be done," said Jack, finally, resignedly. "Will you......put him down, please?"

There was nothing to do but prepare for the termination. "Do you want to be with him?" I asked. Many can't bear to see the end of their pet. Jack and Doris wanted to stay with Hamlet. Such a large dog could not be lifted onto the examination table so I merely dropped to one knee to face this regal chestnut face. With the tourniquet tightened and the syringe ready, I was too intent on the procedure to worry about him attacking me. But Jack and Doris were as much concerned over another incident as they were with the dismissal of their best friend.

Hamlet embarrassed his family no further. He looked into my face seeming to know that this was the moment of decision. His princely countenance and magnificent soul inflated before me as if to say, "I am Hamlet! do your worst, I am prepared!" The barbiturate knifed through his veins slowly and assuredly. Hamlet ended his torment with quiet dignity. The three of us knelt beside him with tears in our eyes. He was a beautiful dog gone bad, or mad. As a result, he was not to be...

10: AM Mrs Tothe wants to euthanize Lucky...

...not really

A disconsolate Linda Tothe walked into the examination room alone, head down and weary. I could barely imagine her pain. I knew what her visit was for, but neither of us could find the words to begin.

"Lucky is in the car, Dr. Runcibal," she said finally. "He's not eating, not moving around...he just lays at the end of the lane waiting for..." Tears welled in her exhausted eyes, Lucky was not the only one losing sleep. "I hate to have to do this. Patrick would never forgive me. But the poor dog is suffering. Is there anything else we could do?"

"Perhaps there is," I thought out loud, surprising myself as well as Mrs. Tothe. It had never occured to me earlier in the day when I stopped to pat Lucky, but I knew that euthanizing this keeper of their son's heart would make matters worse rather than better. "You know Lucky has had reprieve's before, thanks to Patrick. Patty would prefer us to continue to be innovative I'm sure."

Mrs. Tothe, biting her lower lip and anxiously twisting a handkerchief looked at me in disbelief. "What can we possibly do? The dog will die of starvation."

"We can never replace the companionship that is gone, but we might be able to get Lucky to take on the role of guardian once again," I suggested.

I have always been an advocate of people owning more than one pet. Cats may be solitary hunters but they can and should enjoy the company of other felines. Dogs are pack animals and establish a pecking order amongst their mates whenever there are more dogs in a household. Having a companion for a dog or cat is healthy. It minimizes behavior problems seen with single pets (although other problems arise if the pecking order results in conflicts for dominance). A second pet stimulates exercise, often neglected or unavailable from the owner; and more than once I've seen a surviving pet provide it's owner a unique bond of understanding and friendship to allay the grief the owner felt for one that had died.

"I would like to suggest that you get a new puppy," I said. "Lucky is a care-giver. He protected Patrick with all his heart. Perhaps a dependent puppy will stimulate his instincts to be concerned for the new dog rather than his own loss. It would be worth a try."

Mrs. Tothe could say nothing and I didn't expect her to. She did ask on the way out where she could find a dog on such short notice given that this had to be tested immediately. Fortunately, Peterson's mongrel bitch had a litter seven weeks ago and I had seen the pups this morning. Linda set out to pick one out.

The strategy worked. The puppy pestered Lucky enough to stimulate the dog to start to eat. His innate sense of guardianship forced him to follow the pup around, show him how to stay out of trouble, even drag him away from the road when he wandered off.

But every evening after school has been let out, whenever I happen to drive by the Tothe laneway, Lucky stands waiting. Looking desperately for his master to return.

11: AM *Claire Shelby...*

...Barney's last visit

Some days offer a run of blocked cats, puppies with worms or dogs with impacted anal glands. Today's special was the loss of dear friends. I knew just as well as Claire Shelby, what the outcome of her visit today would entail. If there was any way to turn back the clock at this moment I would gladly do so.

Claire's diminutive presence suffused the corner where she sat, Barney lying motionless at her feet. No longer were the blissful sounds of Mr. Shelby bellowing 'Baaarrny, Baarrney, my old pal' emanating from the waiting room. Gerald had passed away last month. He had been on medication for congestive heart failure for the past six months and had been getting along relatively well. His walks with Claire and Barney seemed to be recuperative and rejuvenating. But the ebbs and flows of degenerative disease oft show little mercy. In July, Gerald suffered from a serious heart attack. His vigor allowed him to rebound, temporarily. He had no stamina to sustain the second assault.

I cringed and my heart sank as Claire coaxed a sad and weary Basset to his feet to come into the examination room. Barney no longer howled in glee...his sounds were now productive rales from deep within his chest.

"He's doing a lot of coughing Doctor. I think he's got himself quite a cold," she offered as a hopeful suggestion.

Listening to Barney's chest my eyes closed despondently. This was not just a cold. Barney too had been suffering from Congestive Heart Failure, just like Mr. Shelby. I had taken radiographs and an electrocardiogram to confirm my suspicions and with all of the tests completed there was no doubt. Gerald Shelby was 84 when he died. Barney was 14 years old, perhaps the same relative age as his master and friend. Had this loss of a best friend contributed to a lack of will to live, to give up the battle for life?

My thoughts sped past a procession of affable images. Claire, Gerald and Barney, three spry senior citizens, playfully coming into the clinic for the regular nail clip. Three youthful geriatrics walking the path through the park laughing and smiling at one another as Barney crystallized the unconditional love they shared. "Now don't you pull on your collar young man, or you'll pull me right over. I'm not as young as I used to be you know so you be a good dog!" Claire would admonish Barney for bouncing like an elongated imp at her feet. His ears would flop with every bounce and he would talk back with yips and yelps anticipating that when they got home he was certain to get some tasty treats. Gerald's long arm would extend down to comfort and steady Mrs. Shelby, as he bent his grand stature to become one with two friends shorter than him, but equal in the unconditional love they all shared. "Baarn, yes Baaarney..." rang in my ears.

"I'm afraid....Barney is not getting any better," I said hesitatingly, knowing the impact of those words. Barney and Claire had been in for a checkup three months ago, while Gerald was in the hospital with his first seizure. I had diagnosed the heart condition and will remember forever Claire's expression of sudden perception...she would lose them both to the same affliction! She muddled through the shock of the moment as I dispensed medications to strengthen the heart, diminish fluid build-up and enhance blood pressure. "These are the same medicines that Gerald takes," she had said.

I had assured her than that we've been able to keep dogs comfortable for quite some time. I prescribed a special diet so that Barney would not be eating foods that could contribute to the heart failure. Mrs. Shelby was faithful with the nursing care needed by Barney and Gerald, taking husband to the hospital, Barney to the vet. But every time they left our door there was no more friendly banter. Barney didn't hop and skip around their legs, Claire and Gerald stepped cautiously, more fearful of tripping...or of stressing two weakening hearts.

Until today. Claire said nothing but looked up at me with searching eyes, her head shaking slightly with age that suddenly had come to nest in this previously sprightly body. Barney had reached the end of his time. The medication now made little difference. He was becoming a terrible burden to Mrs. Shelby though she would have cared for him regardless, but she knew that he was suffering. He was having great difficulty breathing and his legs were swelling with the fluid that his body could neither distribute nor eliminate.

"I'm afraid there's just one alternative left for the good of both of you," I said. "Barney has been a great dog...but his time has come." She acknowledged the decision with a nod of her head.

"I don't think I can bury him," she said with concern, still worried about care Barney would need in the end.

"Don't worry about that, we'll take care of everything," I said to reassure her.

"What do I owe you?" she asked fighting the tears in her eyes.

"Nothing," was all I could say. This was not the first time that I forgave the cost for a euthanasia. I owed this to them and Barney.

Mrs. Shelby hesitated for a moment. She knew that the decision had been made, yet she somehow didn't realize that this time she would be leaving without Barney. She turned to leave somewhat confused and bothered. Then she came to her senses and walked over to the table to caress Barney for the last time.

Barney looked up at her and made a feeble attempt to wag his tail. It thumped a few

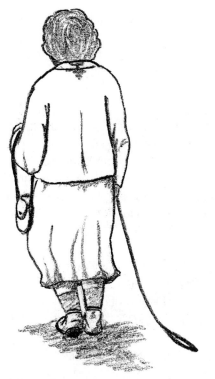

Claire's lonely walk home...

times on the stainless steel table. "Now you be a good dog for the doctor," she admonished with a last motherly banter to her last link to her husband. Barney showed a glimmer of recognition in his eyes, then he watched her walk away. She would not be able to stay with Barney for the final injection.

I helped her out of the door and down the steps. "Are you going to be okay?" I asked. "Is there anyone to stay with you?"

"I'll be all right. Thank you Doctor. My niece is coming to see me this week-end. We've been talking about the old folks home. I guess I'm about ready now that Barney's gone."

I watched her wend her way down the street...alone, an empty leash suspended from her hands.

4: PM House Call to Mark Haley's

Good-bye Smokey, my friend...

Mark Haley would say later, "I never thought I could cry like a baby until that old lab....That dog meant the world to me. It was like murdering your own kid. And she was such a good dog. You were her only doctor. They say that you only ever have one in your lifetime — one good dog."

There are words and deeds that haunt. As much as there are comedic and tragic moments in the life of a veterinary practice, euthanasia remains the most haunting. If you practice long enough you will end up having to euthanize an animal for 'old age' that you would know throughout its entire life. Veterinarians seek their profession largely due to deeply felt empathy for the animal world. When we meet the owners of the animals we realize that there is mutual sentiment. So it becomes very natural to form a bond, not just with the patient but also with the person.

When Mark first brought Smokey for puppy shots, I met two new friends. Smokey was a jet black lab pup. She was clearly a queen of the breed with her stream-lined face and intelligent eyes. Mark was proud of this new addition to the family. "Feel that bump on the back of her head Doc. They say that's the 'bump of knowledge."

Smokey certainly had a prominent bump, and her telling eyes led me to believe that this would be a smart dog. I watched her grow and prove just that. Hardly a sick day in her life, I rarely had to tend to her medically other than her annual vaccinations and occasional stitches.

But the years rolled by and a dog's biological clock is wound tighter than ours. Today, when Mark came into the clinic, I knew right away what was on his mind. He was always a man who could look you straight in the eye. He usually always had a smile on his face and a story on his lips. But today, he couldn't make eye contact, nor find the words.

"Smokey's gettin' pretty frail Jon," he said falteringly. "I'm afraid..." He hadn't brought her with him. "Is there any way you could come out to my place to put her down. I've dug a grave under the maple tree for her." Having the same respect for Smokey as for Mark, I agreed. I followed him on what seemed the longest 'short' drive to his home at the outskirts of town.

Smokey was lying by the back door and made several attempts to get up before she walked, stiff and sore, to greet us. This once proud and sleek black hunting dog was now grizzled and grey. She winced with every step even though I had prescribed considerably high doses of pain killers. Now she was both incontinent and had lost control of her bowels. She ate very poorly and was visibly losing weight day by day. I had no words to help rationalize this terrible moment. I knew that Mark had made up his mind. He had seen Smokey suffer for too long. It still wasn't easy.

We walked over to the red maple. There was already a grave dug on this little knoll overlooking the meadow. "She'll be able to watch over the goings-on from here." Mark's voice quivered.

I sat Smokey down facing me. Her knowing and loving eyes penetrated my soul. I quickly put the tourniquet on her arm to raise a vein. I soaked the upper forearm with alcohol to make the vessel stand out. Then Mark, standing behind me, gave her a final pat, "Bye old girl".

Sleep was instantaneous. Smokey simply fell into a deep slumber. I held her head to lay her gently onto the grass. In seconds her heart had stopped and she was gone. I stayed where I was, kneeling beside her. She embodied the many dogs that I've had to euthanize. I wasn't bothered by having to 'put her to sleep' because this was, in the end, the right thing to do. But I too felt her loss.

Mark's tears were suppressed as much as he could for the moment. I knew he would cry later. He somehow had to talk about her to me now, to remember her, and to justify this act of compassion.

A winter funeral for an old friend...

"Smokey was a loving dog," he began softly. "If the cat cut it's paw she would lick it, if we had baby ducks she would cuddle them, completely surround them with her paws and let them snuggle with their heads into her fur. She would lay right there, nice and still, and never disturb them.

She would hunt and retrieve ducks, dead or alive, but never had the urge to kill anything in the barnyard. If you took her hunting, she went hunting — that was her job, and she knew that. Many times here on the farm, I would have a duckling separated from a farm duck. I could send Smoke out, into the pond. She would take that baby duck in her mouth, bring it back to me so that I could carry it over to the mother.

She was so gentle in the mouth, that I could show her off at the July celebrations down at the pier. I would blow up a balloon, throw it out on the water and set her off after it She would retrieve that balloon in one piece — never break it!

And most farm dogs would kill a ground hog if they caught it. Well not her. She came home one day with a live baby ground hog dangling from her lips. The ground hog was just a-chewin' on Smokey's lip but she wasn't gonna hurt it....Why one day..."

Finally Mark became silent. He hadn't realized that he had been going on for such a long time. It was as though he had been seeing Smokey's life passing before his eyes. Were they the visions Smokey finally shared with her master as she passed into the next world?

I didn't have any more words of comfort but I knew my empathy was felt. I could only quietly pack my kit and walk to the car. I looked back to see Mark leaning on the shovel, gazing down at the grave of a dear old friend.

The final doorstep...

....Good Grief

Let's talk...How long will my dog or cat live? The answer lies within the animal and/or the environment. There are two schools of thought as to longevity. One school feels that there is a genetic timer within each and every soul. It's alarm is set. No matter how much dieting, miles we jog or mantras we incant, when the read-out reaches 5..4..3..2..1 we depart. Clearly we can ensure that the alarm is set to go off as late in life as possible by healthful living —- or speed it up with tobacco and other abuses. But the clock is ticking regardless.

Others debunk this idea to say that we can not only extend longevity, perhaps one day we can even cut the yellow wire to become immortal or at least stretch it to become Methusalan. So new-age-sapiens embrace crystals, nutrition, meganutrition, and extreme exercise.

The truth is likely somewhere in the middle. Evidence is in the animals around us. Every species does seem to be running on its own biological timer. The Galapagos tortoises outlive generations of humans. Parrots live as long as, or longer than, people. Dogs and cats live shorter lives than ours. In fact breeds within a species have distinct life spans. This is particularly true in dogs.

At other times, with animals, perhaps sooner or later with humans, we recognize the disparity between quality of life and quantity. A noble racehorse, Secretariat, the 1973 Triple Crown winner, had just been put down last week. He suffered from painful foot disease. Compassion from his owners, I'm certain, was replaced by grief.

The eternal truth, though, is death. It waits for every living being. As pet owners and care givers, we must accept this postulate and find the positive opportunity that death brings. But first we must learn to deal with the demon of grief. We must transform this spirit into an angel.

Can there be such a thing as good grief?

Anyone who has lost a parent, sibling or friend knows the depths that grief can take you. If you love animals you will be faced with loss more than once in your lifetime. Grief follows a well traveled road. The only way to deal with it, is to stay the course and meet the stations along the way.

Counselors in grief propose the existence of stages through which we must pass successfully in order to resolve our grief, come to grips with reality of the loss, and emerge to a normality of existence. Having had my share of pets, friends and relatives leave my world, and having to deal with the necessity of taking lives from the world as a euthanist, I propose some axioms of my own that may help.

Is it right to grieve for a pet?

Can grief from the loss of a pet be as intense as that for the loss of a human? Absolutely! Further, the unconditional love we've received from a pet can often make the loss more austere. Loss of this form of love is deeply missed. Our pets grieve when they lose their masters. The depth of Lucky's grief led him to the brink of death. Barney's loss of one of his best friends likely contributed to his weakened condition. It should be a mission of pet owners to recognize death and grief as inevitable consequences of pet ownership. They simply come with the territory. Our objective is to demonstrate and endure good grief!

At the outset, I recommend professional resources if and when you feel that these words and text cannot raise you from your well of despair. Grief can be health-threatening if you and your immediate support system are not coping. There are several professionals currently involved with dealing with the loss of a pet. Veterinarians are becoming much better trained as first level grief counselors. If further help is needed they often know where to find it for you.

Separation is loss...is grief:

Grief comes from sudden death, planned euthanasia, protracted death from disease, even from the separation from the beloved pet. Patrick Tothe was spared the emotion of grief when we found a solution for Lucky. Lucky suffered the loss of his friend who would never get off the bus again...and grieved for him.

Pet loss and children:

It is especially important that we do not ignore the grief experienced by a child. The death of a pet they have loved can cause deep despair. They may never have experienced a crisis of this magnitude in their short span of existence. While it may be difficult for an adult to relate to and cope with death, even given the ammunition life gives us with each succeeding year. A child has none of the learned life-skills but this moment is an excellent time to teach them. Use the loss of a pet as the opportunity to share one of life's bitter, real lessons.

The younger the child the simpler the explanation. Most important, they must know that they are not responsible in any way for the fact that Fluffy isn't going to be returning home. Otherwise, guilt is the undeserved token the very young might carry with them for a long time. The older the child, the more the explanation can and should be provided. I believe in honesty with children, about everything. But six year olds should not be given a detailed discourse on the meaning of life and death. Tell the child what they can relate to at their age and level of maturity. If they seem to be suffering from sleeping or eating disorders around the time of the pet's death it may be a sign that they are not coping, that they need more honesty, even professional intervention.

Stages, phases, feelings:

Most of us have had a share of losses. So what stage are you at? In my view, referring simply to stages of grief belies what is really happening emotionally. 'Stage' suggests that there is a logical sequence of feelings. Having dealt with many animal deaths at the end of a syringe or across an examining table, I've seen a multitude of emotions, unpredictable and without sequence rather than foreshadowed. We may feel shock, denial, sadness, despair, guilt, anger, in that order or jumbled together as a state of confused numbness.

Rather than distinct stages I feel that we flood our world with shifting feelings. We try to well them back like a dam until it has bursts with a flood of memories that courses unchecked. We are swept down one stream for a time, only to be grabbed suddenly towards another when the trigger word or memory enters from the world around us.

There is no time limit to the feeling, nor to the duration of grief. You could learn to become resolved within hours or days, or think you are. It could take weeks or months. Your role, always, is to strive for good grief.

The goal is to find acceptance. In order to reach that door, open it and walk through, we must deal with each emotion, as it arises.

It's okay to feel confused. Grief floods the grey matter with images of our lost friend that would otherwise give us joy. Thoughts of loss collide with those reflections to elicit every emotion imaginable trying to take over your intellect. Confusion in the midst of conflicting feelings reigns.

It's okay to deny. We didn't want this to take place. So deny the fact for a moment. You will quickly realize, yes, it has happened.

It's okay to feel anger. How could this have happened? Who is responsible? Why did this life have to end? Answers are moot. Nothing can change the reality. But rage clears the deck for the next emotion.

It's okay to feel short-term guilt. What did I do wrong? What could I have done to prevent this? The feeling is real. The logic is usually displaced. Perhaps the animal's clock came to the final count —- you couldn't stop that. Maybe the injury was beyond repair —- even if it had lived there would be no hope for quality or quantity of life.

It's okay to cry. Some of us can shed tears outwardly, others who let them flow silently, internally, feel them nonetheless. Don't worry if others say, "It's only a dog!" or, "It was just a cat!" An animal can be as close a friend as any human. Tears are appropriate.

The final phase...

Remember that there is a final phase of life that is inevitable no matter how health conscious we are with ourselves or our pets. That final phase I refer to here and in the appendices is memory. Veterinarians know that many clients who have lost an animal at their clinic will not return to them —- despite overwhelming compassion the clinic staff showed towards the pet and the owner. The pain associated with the clinic is simply too much to bear. This is unfair to the vet. By enduring and ratifying grief you can reach the station, get off with your fond memories of a good friend intact. When comfortable you can find a new pet. Not a replacement —- a new pet. Take it to the same veterinarian. He or she endured a piece of your grief and has also, a memory of your friend.

Good Heavens...

...Nathan Biddle goes for a ride

Feeling rather dispirited from a day full of loss I resolved to get home as soon as possible. I felt a tremendous need to sit down with Pud on my lap and Cody at my feet while dealing with my own sense of grief towards the loss of Barney, Smokey and Hamlet. Yes, veterinarians and many of the staff suffer their share of grief for each patient that succumbs to life's final rung. My deep thought was interrupted by Mary's attempt to get my attention.

"Jonathan...Jon..." she prodded with a hand gently shaking me from my reveries. "Sorry, Jon, but I just got a call from Nathan Biddle. Thackery broke into the neighbors field and is down. He's wrapped up in barbed wire and Nathan is beside himself."

My restive moment would have to wait. I let my daydreams thrash with the angers, sadness, guilts and fears as my truck sped off to Biddle's farm seemingly steered by someone or something else other than me.

I drove into Nathan's driveway. The professor was waiting patiently with a bucket of steaming water, towels and rope in anticipation of needs. He climbed into the cab sprightly and with a sense of urgency and concern. "I'm so thankful that you were able to come right away, Jonathan," he began. "We can get to the spot quickly if you cut across this field. The fence is down where Thackery transgressed to the neighbors land. Unfortunately, he walked right into a nest of barbed wire that Mr. Pertl had been accumulating. Rather than extricating himself, he became completely ensnared and enveloped in the wire. I'm so afraid of the consequences..." The water sloshed at his feet with every roll of the land, the four by four sped across the field to the victim, and we were silent in desperate anticipation.

Daylight was waning, as it was just after five on this October evening when the call came in. The sun was setting on a crisp evening. I could see the clump of hay that had attracted Thackery from his domain. Bob Pertl and Garth Kitchens were both sitting on Thackery's head and neck keeping him laterally recumbent so as to minimize further thrashing that would only tighten the strands of wire. Lanterns that they had brought, correctly assuming a protracted evening, swayed with each attempt that the horse made to rise from his predicament. As long as a horse's head can be held to the ground it cannot get up. I was thankful that Bob and Garth were well aware of that.

"You've got a few cuts to thread together Jon," shouted Bob Pertl as Nathan and I walked from the truck to survey the damage. Nathan gasped at the scene. Thackery moaned angrily and soulfully. This salvaged Standardbred had become a gentle field friend for Nathan. His blackish coat now bled from several sites where strands of wire had lacerated or penetrated. Bob and Garth had snipped the majority of the strands so as to eliminate further wounds and prevent those pieces embedded into the flesh from becoming more deeply imbedded.

"Looks like you've taken care to prevent serious damage, fellas," I said acknowledging their common sense preparations. "Let's settle down for an evening's work." My task appeared to be the removal of multiple coils of wire, cleaning, dressing and suturing the many wounds inflicted. This would have to be field surgery as the coils effectively tied legs and neck to the torso. Trying to move the horse would only make it worse.   After a sedative intravenously and antibiotics intramuscularly, I crouched between my patient's four legs to begin reparations to the abdomen and flank. Bob and Garth leaned over me to inspect and monitor my sewmanship.

Clearly confident that Thackery was finally in good hands, Nathan planted himself on a large rock to begin the evening's lecture...

"This brings to mind the conditions of the surgeons during the American civil war," he began. "Although, in most cases any injured horses were simply shot, the medical officers had to perform much of their surgery on soldiers in the field...." Bob, Garth and I, intent on the task at hand, listened bemused but interested in the drone of Nathan's voice. It was as though as a radio program played in the background as work ensued — like the times when you only half listen while reading, studying or working around the house, every once in a while breaking from intended focus to hear more distinctly a portion of the broadcast. The three of us provided all the impetus Nathan needed to prolong his discourse, as each of us raised an eye from time to time to Nathan's podium, to ratify a point of interest.

The civil war discourse led to the war of 1812, which eventually brought us to the mid-nineteenth century. I had reached stitch number 92 and wound number 17. Thackery was asleep, perhaps sent to slumber by Nathan's voice more than the mild sedation I had injected. "You know, I named Thackery for the author, William Makepeace Thackery, who was a sometimes illustrator for Dickens Pickwick serial, author and lecturer. In 1856, Thackery came to America to conduct a series of lectures on The Four Georges...Dickens, my other horse, obviously named for one of my favorite authors of that era...you know Dickens.." Each of us looked up from the hulk of the horse to determine whether he was referring to the author or the horse...the essay that ensued affirmed the former."...Was as popular in his day as those other British stars, the Beatles, are today." A topic more current provoked a pause from each of us. We all looked to the sermon on the rock for edification.

"Yes," continued Nathan, content with his stratagem for ensuring interest in his current ode. "You see when Charles Dickens came to America in 1842, January I believe it was...Boston Harbor the first stop in a journey to several American cities. His popularity was immense. Hundreds of people came to the dockyards to greet his ship. Dozens of the populace lined the streets to wave at the cavalcade of carriages as he passed by. Given the slowness of communication in those times, not to mention the literacy rate of the masses, his repute could be considered at a par with those musical British exports that followed more than a century later..."

The final stitches in the black of night were punctuated by a discourse on Luther whose real contribution to change was not just the content of his thought but the translation of otherwise forbidden fruits from academically-owned Latin to publicly-consumed German. After a final inspection of Thackery's body, having had to roll the beast onto his opposite side, we four beasts, Bob, Garth, Thackery and I creaked our cramped muscles to a standing position. A pass of the lanterns, since darkness was now upon us, over every line and crevice assured us of a now intact beast. Nathan, tone indicating contentment, rather than concern, continued his oration. Mr. Kitchens walked a slightly slumbering Thackery towards the barn. Bob Pertl smiled and waved us away, picking up any debris and supplies he had carried to the site. Nathan climbed into the cab beside me as I drove slowly towards his house.

Mrs. Biddle hurried to meet the truck as we drove up to the front door of the farmhouse. Concerned for the lateness of the day, she had to advise me that I had yet another call. Jim Judd had a cow down with milk fever and since this was my evening on call, Mary had traced me to Biddles' place. Agnes Biddle handed me some sandwiches, kindly anticipating the need for sustenance. Nathan at my side in the truck was lost in his dissertation — that had now led to the printing press, and it's impact on literacy, spread of thought, knowledge and ideas. I smiled at my personal professor and realized I could not push him from the truck. I placed the meal between us, took a bite of my share and drove off to the next call. Nathan, secure in his love of words, added more to his repertoire. His train of thought, spurred by an evening of authors and their words, could only lead to one of the finest word magicians, Shakespeare. Turning onto the sideroad that led to Judd's farm, Nathan began to talk of his favorite tragedy, Hamlet.

As we drove towards my next patient, my thoughts drifted, remembering friends I would miss...Hamlet...Barney...and Smokey...

Nathan's lecture becomes a road show...

CHAPTER EIGHT

Ark and Bark

Animal Clinic

CHAPTER EIGHT

Ark & Bark Animal Clinic
Monday December 18, 1989

Morning Emergencies:
3:00 am - Mrs. Troy, Muffin can't sleep
7:00 am - Wendy Flitz - cat caught in fan belt

Morning Farm Calls:
Fred Folter - horse with infected cuts
Closter Brothers - herd health

Morning Surgeries:
Marjorie Kim - eye ablation
Toby Bilt - neuter 2 cats

Morning Appointments:
10:00 Mrs. Tranney - vaccinate Tinkle
10:15 Milt O'Grady - cat is very thin
10:30 Harold Apel - dog coughing
10:45 Jai Chen - check new puppy
11:00 Kay Wallace - anal glands and check stool
11:15 Nancy Noone - vaccinate Nooner
11:30 Walker - vaccinate two antique shoppe cats
11:45 Jim Pilsen - recheck dog and paying on account
12:00 *Stephany Runcibal and dad - take clinic cats to Lake Haven*

Afternoon Farm Calls:
Rocklin's - mare is sick
Stokely Harper - herd health

Afternoon Appointments:
2:00 Mrs. Kutter - vaccinate Kramer
2:15 Mr. Birdsall - Moose
2:30 Mrs. Mabel Pointer - Pandy, pedicure
2:45 Bob Decker - Charlie's check-up
3:00 Mike Griff's friend - crow
3:15 Mrs. Tupperman - Sylvester
3:30 Lucy Cartwright - Cody's needles
3:45 Mark Haley - first needles for a new black lab puppy
4:00 *Al Latimer - bringing in Bounce*

Evening Emergencies:
Christmas shopping

...In Defense of Anthropomorphism

Monday December 18, 1989

Let's talk...There are several ways to look at illness and disease. One approach is to despair at the callous nature of ill health. A more positive perspective would admire the amazing resourcefulness of the body's defense mechanisms. Anthropomorphism is defined as the assignment of human characteristics to animate creatures or inanimate objects. Some see this as unworthy. I suggest that we would understand these other worlds better if we instilled an anthropomorphic relevance. Take the world of disease for example. Many medical professionals see disease as a war, being waged in or on the animal. Our role as practitioners is to arm the flesh with ammunition to fight, hopefully to defeat, the enemy.

The Invaders: There's a fungus among us...

Illness comes in many forms. It can be caused by visible creatures like the internal and external parasites that crawl through the coat, skin or bowels — or microscopic enemies, larvae or microlarvae, either as fully grown aggressors or intermediate stages of the beasts. Size of the assailant relative to the body may diminish but the antagonist's terror remains the same or increases. Bacteria, fungi and fungi-like creatures, more miniature but able to replicate their battalion of spores or cells more rapidly, can infect the animal with far more generalized devastation. Certainly, they can cause local havoc such as infecting a cut, but their capabilities for whole-body infestation is the greatest concern.

Viruses and virus-like organisms are only detected with an electron microscope that magnifies otherwise invisible microarmies that can disperse their forces through corridors of vessels or penetrate cell walls to destroy from within.

The Weakened Defense

Other disease mechanisms have nothing to do with invaders from the outside (or inside). Through no fault of its own, flaws in the body's makeup can lead to ill health. This can be the result of inherited defects in defense mechanisms leaving the host subject susceptible to the particular disorder. Or the system can simply become impaired. An immune system that cannot fight as well as it should, will leave the animal weakened, unable to sustain assaults from secondary invaders.

As humankind persists on the planet, the animal's body —- animals are just as much the victim of human foibles as is the human species —- is assaulted by the pollutants of the environment. Accidental poisonings and incidental exposure to long-term environmental toxins contribute to diseases of the twentieth century. Second hand smoke is just as harmful to pets as to humans, perhaps more since the heavy fumes concentrate near the floor where the pet resides.

Cancer —- the Atomic Bomb of Disease

Cancer can incorporate many of these principles of destruction. What is cancer? It is actually a catch-all term for a multitude of different diseases with a somewhat common thread. The diseases refer to the organ or organs afflicted and/or the cell type of the cancer. The theme that connects these cancers is the modus operandi of the culprits inflicting the disease. Somehow, the cells of a specific area of the body become inconsistent with their normal role in life. Replication of these aberrant cells results in growth of something the body cannot eliminate, thus a lump or bump suddenly appears, grows and blights. Depending on the location, such growths can destroy normal tissue and impair the function they would otherwise provide for the body. In critical locations such as the liver, lungs or brain, the pressure of the tumor on surrounding tissue further diminishes the organ's functions. Some cancers send an army of cells to other sites in the body or diffuse throughout the blood or lymphatic system (metastasis). These neoplasias kill more rapidly.

Defense Mechanisms

Yet the body does come with significant ammunition to fend off these internal or external hordes. First line of defense is the blanket of skin that covers the outside of the body. Cells along the gut and lungs protect the innards much like a lining of skin. These are barriers so that every invader might die at the castle wall before ever gaining access. At a cellular level, the white blood cells in various uniforms, become a mass-produced instant army that marches to any and every breach in the fortress wall.

The critical organs of the body for elimination and dilution of toxins include the gut, the liver, lungs and kidneys. Only overwhelming or persistent attack can defeat or diminish their power. Within the animal a vigilant immune system that includes the spleen and lymphatic circulation, is constantly producing chemicals to counter-poison or neutralize the enemy's counterparts.

Responsible Owners and Pet Fortification

We can contribute to the defeat of these enemies by equipping the body's defense mechanisms. Adequate diet, exercise, vaccination, love...can result in an animal being much more immune to disease. Deficiency of these munitions can lead to a shortened life, or a painful end to a life of poor quality. These armies can attack at any time of an animal's life, from the womb to death's doorstep. They have no mercy.

We can even prevent some of the common cancers. The easiest procedure is the spay and neuter that effectively eliminate ovarian and testicular cancers respectively and minimize mammary and prostate cancers.

Is this simplistic analogy too superficial? Is giving the invaders an anthropomorphic personality naive? Perhaps. But after all, those organisms are simply striving to survive just like any other living creature. They just happen to be causing damage to their host. And at least some of the power to fight illness lies within our grasp. We may not be able to contend with every genetic disease, but we will succeed with many in time. We may not be able to rid the world of every disease organism, but we have eliminated a few viruses from the face of the earth. Some, at least, from regions of the earth and in time, perhaps more.

At the complete opposite end of the scale of anthropomorphic application, author James Lovelock epitomized mother earth as Gaia, a living being. Humankind could be seen as a symbiotic caretaker or parasite depending on your state of twentieth century optimism or cynicism. If we lose our host, our fate is sealed. Personifying this globe certainly helps establish critical perspectives.

Responsible pet ownership requires collaborative care. Working with the staff of a veterinary hospital and their extended family of specialists, we can minimize the incidence of disease and maximize quality of life for those afflicted. Realism must always be present. Veterinarians are human. They make human mistakes. Medicine is a dynamic science. What we knew yesterday has changed. What we will know tomorrow will change. It is the daily battle that demands that all forces be working together —- veterinarian and hospital staff allied with the pet owner, using every aspect of the animal's innate defenses and the power of modern medicine and nutrition....

7: AM emeRgency...

...caT on a colô Tin Roof

It was a cold December morning at 3: AM as my boots crunched through the snow to get to the truck like I was walking on the corn flakes that I wasn't going to get for breakfast —- again. Muffin Troy couldn't sleep so neither would I. Thankfully, otherwise I would have appreciated the call even less, Muffin's distress was justified, and rectified quickly. A bone had become lodged between the molars of the upper palate. Muffin, a mop of fur covering a Pekinese dog, had been racing through the house for most of the evening swatting at what seemed like imaginary ghosts. She had actually been pawing as close to her face as possible but could not reach the back of her throat with her stubby legs.

After removing the obstruction and admonishing Mrs. Troy for feeding bones, I sent them home to reflect on my lecture, and emergency fee. Perhaps I was somewhat harsh, but pets can too readily break a bone into shards that can lodge in the throat or the bowel. I simply cannot condone feeding bones to pets.

It was 4:30 AM when I finally fell back to sleep in the comfort of my bed. It was scarcely two hours later, I was just beginning to benefit from rem-slumber when Mary urged me out of reverie with disturbing pushes on my shoulder. "Jon, Jonathan! You have an emergency!"

"Wha'? Huh?...never mind...mmmm, let's do that again Christy..." I muttered, not to Mary but to...someone in my dreams —- to which there was an immediate termination by a swat to the back of my head.

"Get up and get to work!" Mary barked. "Leave 'Christy' alone!"

Sheepish, not remembering the fantasy but accepting guilt nonetheless, I massaged the welt on my cranium as I rushed to slip on my clothes that were still cold from the earlier mid-morning jaunt.

The message from the answering service described a frantic Wendy Flitz. She let Calicat and Pershing out for a romp in the snow while preparing breakfast for the Flitz crew. John Flitz had driven through the night and arrived home at 5: AM from yesterday's sales trip so the motor in his Toyota was still warm. Wendy went out to warm it up for the trip to school with the kids as John slept. The car started readily. Unfortunately, it was the warmth and sudden crank of the engine that created the explosive emergency today.

Calicat, not as keen on the outdoors in winter as Pershing, perhaps because of a shorter haircoat, had crawled into the engine near the fan-belt, attracted by the inviting lingering warmth or the reclusive refuge from the winds. As soon as the engine revved and the blades of the fan spun into action, Calicat was sliced by several revolutions of the vicarious guillotine. Unearthly screams wailed with each repetitive thud and thump. Wendy grasped her face with trembling hands attempting to think of what could be causing the clamor. It was almost too late when she realized that the one sound was her cat, and that all of the noise emanated from the engine of the car.

Immediately, though, she turned the key to stop the engine. She rushed to the front of the car — but held back an instant to raise the hood, anticipating what she would find. The gruesome scene weakened her knees but not her resolve. Calicat lay draped between the radiator and fan belt. At first she was certain the cat was dead. Sanguine tissue lay exposed as folds of skin were clearly torn away from the torso. Blood specks spattered the hood and motor. Calicat finally gave a faint moan.

Wendy scooped up the mangled feline as soon as she recognized the glimmer of life. She raced to the car door ready to place the cat into the vehicle. Thinking faster than thoughts could come she decided to have the kids alert the clinic. Calicat was dumped, gently but abruptly onto the roof of the car. Wendy rushed to the door to yell at the kids, "Call the vet! Cali is hurt! Tell him I'm on my way! Be there!"

She ran to the car, winter jacket partly covering her bedclothes and housecoat. The hood was unceremoniously slammed shut. She looked back to the front door as Willie and Wanda called after her to see what was wrong. "There's no time!" she screamed. "I'm on my way to the vet! Call him right away!" She jumped into the car and sped off for another Wendy Flitz autoventure.

I recognized the urgency in Carla's voice, the normally cool and assuring owner of the local answering service. Neither of us could understand the cryptic frantic refrain Wanda made to punctuate the call: "She's gonna kill Cali!"

My drive to the clinic was a mere five minutes, so I felt assured that I would beat Wendy to the hospital this time. Her trip from further outside of town would normally take about 20 minutes. As I creaked my weary body from the truck I stopped to listen to what I thought was a police siren. There also seemed to be a racing motor. The siren was one that I didn't recognize as it was more like a demon's howl.

The engine and alarm increased in intensity and was clearly emanating from down this very road. I looked towards the banshee cries to see Wendy's wagon screaming towards the clinic at breakneck speed. On top of the vehicle, not in it, was Calicat, front limbs spread wide across the roof, claws dug deep into the metal. Cali was the siren, her mouth wide and vehement with cries of horror. Wendy could now be seen pressed towards the steering wheel, intent on reaching the clinic faster than a speeding bullet, oblivious to the cat on the cold tin roof.

The wagon skidded into the parking lot sliding to a halt beside me, spraying stones and snow at my feet. Wendy acknowledged my presence as she looked over to tell me the predicament, extricating Calicat's embedded nails from the roof. "Cali's been caught in the fan belt!..." She began as she dashed over to place the cat into my arms. She stopped half-way between me and the car looking back to the claw marks. Staring down at her precious package who was wide-eyed and trembling, she realized what she had done. "Oh my! Oh my! Oh my!" she could only say repeatedly and fadingly.

There was nothing else to do but to get Wendy into a chair in the warm clinic and Cali into the surgery. At least two of Calicat's lives were spent this morning but I was determined, for Wendy's sake, that the remaining souls would remain intact. I sutured the hide back to the frame wherever the fan belt had ripped it away. Fortunately, there were no broken bones, as is often the case with fan-belt disease. Wendy waited in the chair, vacant stares directed into oblivion, not believing, yet believing what she had just done.

Cat on a cold tin roof...

"Come on back to see Cali," I urged Wendy, once the pieces had been put back together. I knew that she needed to see an intact and vibrant pet after this December morning crisis. I had also called her home to let the family know that everything went well, and that Cali had survived both the pounding of the fan belt and the buffeting of the open-air ride.

Wendy thawed from her frigid stare and state as soon as she could see Calicat sleeping leisurely, sutured and content.

It seemed fitting to lighten the moment and reassure her at the same time. Wendy nodded and gave me an abashed smile as I mocked, "You might consider adding a few more seconds to your next trip to the clinic by putting the cat in the car."

12: noon - vet and daughter...

...visit the waiting place

Several years ago when my daughter Stephany was seven, my uncle was a resident in the local retirement home. Although he has since passed away, it was a visit to his room and residence that led to an important application of benefits animals bring to humankind.

On that July afternoon, Mary, Stephany, and I drove into town on a vet's day off to visit Uncle Don. A war veteran who had never married, this grizzled and spry character delighted everyone who visited, with stories of the 'old days' when great-grandpa John ran a saw mill in the bush of Northern Ontario, and the ten kids would ski to school, swim in the cold northern streams, or ride horse-drawn sleighs to church with cloth wrapped bricks from the wood stove placed at their feet to keep their toes from freezing.

Outside the residence, was a busied, world of abundance. Inside, time and events stood idle — or time-traveled backwards. I hadn't recognized these opposing environments, perhaps because of the perverse 'wisdom' that comes with age. To me, the nursing home was a part of my realm, a fixture with a purpose. But on that summer day as Stephany walked behind us, down the hall to Uncle Don's room, her eyes roamed from person to person sitting inactive and silent in chairs, couches, wheelchairs, or standing reflectively supported by a walker or the bar along the wall.

"What are all these sad people waiting for?" came the innocent accurate question.

There could be no valid explanation or correction to her observation. These latter-day pioneers, factory workers, teachers, business executives, mothers and fathers, were waiting, sadly. They were waiting for the children and grandchildren to visit. Waiting for the next meal. Waiting for the next day. Waiting for the end. There was no joy in waiting. Their eyes told you so.

After feeble attempts to explain what this place was and that the people here get the best medical care possible, there was still the undeniable truth. There seemed little for them to do but wait. We explained that they had exercise, bingo, television, movies, crafts, many things on which to spend their time. Looking around rebuked these arguments.

"Well, what do you think could be done to cheer them up?" I had asked.

Stephany's eyes blazed bright with innocence and common sense. "They must love animals! Everyone loves animals. Let's bring the clinic cats in to play with them!"

Ever since that day, on Friday afternoons for the past four years, someone from the clinic or a friend or relative, when our schedule permitted, carried Harley and Chatter, later Fester and Tinker, to the Lake Haven Nursing Home. Several other local agencies got into the act taking dogs and cats from the pound, or pets from home, so that there were regular visitations of furred friends for the seniors to enjoy. Oh, they were still waiting. But their anticipation and attitudes were gladdened.

Today Fester, a black and white domestic short-hair purred and pawed at Jacob

Stickley's buttons. Jacob, bespectacled and wearing a weathered fishing cap that nevermore went fishing, was at first uncertain as how to accommodate this inquisitive cat, finally relented to it's playful jabs and played back. "Whoa, kitty! Your going to tear the buttons right off my shirt..."

It was particularly heartwarming when Stephany placed Chatter, our lop-eared Persian, on Claire Shelby's lap. "Chatter, yes I know...you're such a pretty little cat..." her smile and tearful glint as Chatter swatted at her blouse made the entire enterprise worthwhile. Humane societies and veterinary clinics around the country provide this kind of pet visitation service to retirement homes and other peoples who could benefit from the moments of cuddling. If your community doesn't, think about it.

The Human-Animal Bond...

...In Defense of Anthropomorphism

And so it goes at the Ark and Bark Animal Clinic. The clinicians and staff are given extraordinary experiences with people and their animals. Yet in an instant there can be heart-breaking moments. We've met some interesting animals. From the 400 pound tiger with a cut on it's paw, during the circus last summer, to the 400 gram hamster brought in with overgrown incisor teeth —a broad spectrum of patients in a typical veterinary practice.

Clients have been equally stimulating. We've seen dog and cat owners take on the appearances of their pets. There was Mrs. White who was owned by the ice frost Persian cat with long, soft, white fur. Mrs. White transformed her gray hair to bleached fuzzy white. She even puffed her face with white powder and most of her clothing was white. They were a living, breathing, self-fulfilling prophecy of symbiotic-dependent white creatures.

The staff has inherited a menagerie of pets, a work-related benefit. Typical clinic staff cannot live with themselves if they let animals be put away that could otherwise live a healthy happy life. Leslie's ginger cat, Hobo, had been cruelly thrown out of a car window. Only three weeks old, Hobo was paralyzed when brought in by an angry animal lover who had seen this atrocity and reported the perpetrator to the police. It looked as though the kitten would be quadriplegic but one or more of her lives kicked in, along with the generous and rapid development of young bones and tissue. She not only survived with all locomotor ability but she lived to be 20 years young.

We were able to save a few of the rejects brought to the clinic. We couldn't save all

Creature comfort comes to the waiting place.

of them though, and there were legitimate reasons for many of the animals to have been euthanized. But the weight of loss was carried poorly by most of us on those sad days.

The good days kept us going. The humor of human nature and the wonder of the animal mind and spirit made us want to keep doing what we were doing. Most importantly it was the bond that was clearly manifest between human and creature.

Dogs were initially the predominant pet that we saw in practice during the 60's and 70's but as soon as the baby boomers moved into the working world the cat came into its own. Here was a pet for the 80's and 90's that did not have to be taken for a walk — in fact it could be left inside for days at a time, if forever. It generally required less attention than a dog (unless it was a 'dog-cat'). And it usually never made a mess on the carpet. Note that I do say "usually".

Pets have become members of the family. If you own a dog, you have been lucky enough to buy or inherit something that humans crave, but often find hard to get — - unconditional love. A dog will forgive all your sins. A dog will remain steadfast and loyal no matter what you do — to yourself, others and them.

Cats on the other hand, offer a new set of parameters to pet ownership. The rule is, feed me, house me, and keep my litter clean and I will grace your home with my presence. If I am a Cat-cat then you may touch me at your peril. If I am a Dog-cat then you will never get the hairs off your slacks. Unconditional love from cats is provided by their graciousness.

For the veterinarian, the cat presents a different set of diagnostic problems. Their diseases are different from the dog. Their response to disease is different. A dog will come to the clinic with a specific set of symptoms. That allows us to follow a certain path of tests and treatments to diagnose and make it better. But a sick cat is a sick cat. It is often just "not eating and lethargic". And when a cat doesn't eat it is difficult to get them to start eating again. Despite our best efforts they seem to say, "I'm sick and I'm not going to eat no matter what you do! Just as I ruled my so-called owner's house, I shall rule this hospital."

Now the reader might be assuming by my dissertations on cats and dogs that I like dogs more than cats. Not so. I have always had at least one cat and one dog as cohabitant pets. It is the distinctiveness of each creature that I enjoy. Dogs have a dependence on us that is endearing. Cats have an independence that is just as endearing. A cat slumbering in a window warms the heart as much as a dog snoring by the hearth. Certainly there are cat people and dog people who prefer one to the other. I simply cannot discriminate that readily. I cherish the companionship of my dog and am compelled to worship my cat.

Like most veterinarians these affections for furred creatures extend to those in the home, woods, zoos or farms.

Farm practice may have changed. Where we used to visit several farms a day to treat individual cows or horses, we now spend the entire morning or even a day on one farm operation. It is no longer economical for a dairyman or swine producer to call a veterinarian to treat just one animal. The cost of the medicine, call fee and time to treat one pig could be more than the value of that pig. So the veterinarian has had, once again, to learn a new facet of veterinary medicine — herd medicine, or more specifically today, production medicine.

Practitioners that go to the farm today look at several animals, pour over the production and health print-outs from the farmer's computer, and advise on the nutritional changes necessary to get more milk, meatier pigs and beef.

But the basic love for animals that the farmer had in years past is still there. It might be one cow out of many in the herd, but she usually has a name besides the computer number. And if anything were to make Daisy sick, the farmer would still be willing to spend a little extra to try to save her, even if the costs were more than her "book value".

The pet owner, the farmer, the veterinarian and the veterinary clinic staff are still there to ensure comfort and care for those other creatures with which we share this world. We suffer pain and grief from time to time but our lives are enriched so much by living and caring for animals that give so much in return.

Unconditional love, for humans, is the accomplishment we feel for having cared for another creature, by fixing a broken bone, or providing a loving home. The animal, in turn, nurtures our need for creature comfort by returning what we interpret to be their unconditional love for us.

And they've made life's adventure that much more enjoyable....

There are many who reject any and all attempts to ascribe human traits to animals, as though we are debasing our own species. They suggest that it is almost sacrilegious to even imagine lower life forms thinking and talking like the master species, human-kind. So, Disney characters are contraventions to the 'real' world. And the pandering our society is placing on pets today is proof of this depravity through anthropomorphism.

I don't buy that. A human being is an imperfect animal. Foibles, faults and mistakes litter their road to success. If I were to be so arrogant as to believe that I was superior to my dog, cat — or the whale and porpoise — I believe that I would be discounting too much of the wonderment of life. And so the veterinary practice continues to admit and care for new friends, with characteristics unique and human-like...

Look who's sitting in the clinic waiting room this afternoon...

Consider Pandy Pointer. Pandy is a Standard poodle cared for extensively by Mrs. Mabel Pointer. Pandy and Mabel always come to the clinic with matching outfits. In cold weather like this it's a chartreuse woolen-knit sweater with four matching booties, and bows on her head and tail — that's Pandy's outfit, Mabel wears matching materials and only two booties. Pandy looks indignantly at Charlie Decker who comes in to the waiting room wearing only a red checkered scarf around his neck. Charlie is a mixed breed who had his lineage crossed with every imaginable pedigree. He has a Spaniel's head, Retriever's ears, Collie's nose and Shepherd's tail. Bob Decker just got off work at the construction site and he has clomped over in his heavy ice and clay-encrusted work boots to plomp down beside Mrs. Pointer. Mabel and Pandy raise their noses and point them to the far wall. Charlie snorts at the snub and lays down at Bob's feet.

There's a strange looking man in one corner with a large black crow on his shoulder. He is a young chap, quite frail-looking, with a mustache and goatee. They both (bird and boy) stare straight ahead with glazed eyes. It would turn out when they come into the exam room that this pet crow has gotten into the young man's hash and they are both on a trip, more than to the vet's.

In the first exam room sits Kramer the Wire-Haired Terrier on the cold stainless steel table. Kramer's owner is discussing several home-care options with Dr. Tripper. Kramer has just undergone extensive orthodontic work and Trip is showing his owner how to brush his teeth.

At the counter stands Mr. Snider who is here to discuss the computer print-out of the ration analysis for his dairy herd. We have been able to eliminate several metabolic diseases that his cows had suffered previously including milk fever, ketosis, udder edema, and retained placentas. Beside him is Officer Holtby who has dropped by to pick up the prescription food that we have recommended for Spooky, his German Shepherd.

Standing well up against the wall, holding Sylvester, the black and white Ragdoll cat, is Mrs. Tupperman. She is very active in the community, driving for Meals-on-Wheels, and helps spearhead the Pet Visit Program. Sylvester is just one of the animals that make trips on Friday afternoons to the retirement home.

With a princely bearing, Cody, the Golden Retriever sits in his harness beside Lucy Cartright. Lucy is legally blind but because of Cody, not sightless. Cody is not just a tool for getting around. Lucy and Cody are very close friends. On other days, Hearing dogs for the deaf and dogs that provide the arms and hands for people confined to wheel-chairs come in for shots or treatment. In every case, the friendship between dog and person is self-evident.

Waiting for me in exam room two, is Knowlton Brice. He actually had a dog prescribed for him as an effective medical treatment for high blood pressure. He is sitting beside Moose, a two year old Lab-Shepherd cross that he saved from destruction at the dog pound. Moose rests his immense head on Mr. Brice's lap to be gently and continuously stroked, giving Moose infinite pleasure — and reducing Knowlton's blood pressure.

Gratefully, sitting on Mark Haley's lap, is a lump of black coal with endearing brown eyes. Babe, a new Black Labrador puppy surveys the creatures around him and snuggles back further into Mark's chest with every woof and wail. A new friend. Not the same stream-lined face culminating in that bump of knowledge, this pup has a wider bolder face and head. She would never replace Smokey. But she will become a lifetime companion.

What do these people have in common?

Certainly they all care for animals. But it's also very likely that they all enjoyed watching Bambi, Dumbo and Lassie movies and books when they were young. They laughed at Thumper's shyness and wryness, cried when Dumbo was separated from his mother and marveled yet understood the artificial intelligence of that beautiful Collie, Lassie.

What harm did these anthropomorphic exhibitions do?

Very few of us have succumbed to a pathological patronization of our pets. Rather, we have found a critical outlet for our feelings. The unconditional affection animals give us and apparent forgiveness for transgressions makes them the perfect receptacle for our sentiment.

Most animal lovers are not addicted to their pet. These extremes of the psyche that make cat ladies codependent on multitudes of cats, to the immoderate advocate of vegetarianism, to the militant animal rights person who would boycott tuna in order to save the dolphins, are all based on a fundamental desire to equalize the rewards animals give to humans. The pet owner is just the grass roots caregiver.

Ever since that first wild dog crawled into a cave from a past millennium there evolved a growing kinship between man and beast.

Towards the next millennium we could experience an era of disassociation. Cold numbers and computers will run our daily lives. Entertainment and communication media will attract more and more of our available hours at work or at home. It would be easy to see the pet becoming expendable because they 'cost so much' or an animal on the farm simply a 'production unit' that will be culled if the output is not greater than the input.

We are here because nature is here. When nature is gone, so are we. Though one species amongst millions on the planet, we seem to be competing with Mother Nature to see which of us can eliminate the most species.

Are we so vain to think that the only animal that can communicate is Homo sapiens? As research continues, it is becoming clear that other species communicate with one another. And we are now bridging the gap between animals and humans with sign language. Elephants can communicate across miles with one another. Gorillas, chimpanzees and dolphins seem to be talking back to us.

And that's the defense of anthropomorphism. We are not alone. We are not the only creature with feelings and intelligence. As the century turns the corner and the technologies grab more and more of our attention let's not lose this precious link to the animal world from which we rose.

What's the greatest gift we receive from the care we give to our pets? It's the unconditional love permeating these stories! Pets show an affection for the human master regardless of the good or bad characteristics we might exhibit. They love us for who we are. They give us creature comfort. Let's continue to give creatures comfort just as they give us unconditional love in return...

4: PM Al Latimer...

...Bounce comes home

It appeared as though the day's medical cares and crises would end on a positive note, and early enough for me to get downtown for a last minute, first attack, at Christmas shopping. I had some concern though when Al Latimer came to the waiting room door with what seemed like a frown. I dried my hands with paper towels preparing for the next patient. I did not want anything to have happened to Bounce. The dog was not in the waiting room and his absence gave me cause to worry.

"Doc," Al said with no explanation. "I'm afraid I'm going to be moving away."

"No!" I said with surprise and disappointment. "What's happened?"

"Well," explained Al, leaning against the doorframe casually chewing on a stick of straw. "Our feed-lot really never made any money. Nothin' worth callin' home about anyways. And the land is right out to the west where housing has been movin'. Anyways, a developer came by three months ago and made me an offer I couldn't refuse. So now I'm out of a job and a home. The good news is that I can afford to be. I'm headed out to Calgary to work with my brother. He's always wanted me to work with him in his printin' business." He straightened up to finish what seemed to be just a farewell visit. "Anyways, we're headed out this weekend so's to be there for Christmas."

"I'm sorry to see you go, Al," I said, with the subliminal message that he knew who else I would miss.

Al flashed that frown once again, this time somewhat devilishly. "You remember, when Bounce first came in to you all mangled and broken up by that train? You said that if I didn't want to keep him, that you would?" I nodded, anticipating where Al was leading. "Well, we're going to be living in the city, and Bounce has always been a country dog. We're driving out to Calgary so it would be awful hard to have a wife, two kids and a dog, for that long a trip. And I know you live out north of town on what's left of the old Snider farm," Al continued. "Anyways, I was wondering whether you were still interested in having this dog Doc? I know how much he likes you. He's friendly to everybody, but he always gets excited when he sees you come to the farm. Why he even seems to know the sound of your truck above everyone else's."

"I would be happy to give Bounce a home Al," I smiled and said without hesitation.

"I knew you would," Al replied with a wave of his hand towards the clinic door. With the door only slightly ajar Bounce bounced in. He jumped up to greet me putting his front paws on my chest as he stood there panting and smiling, almost knocking me down.

"Don't ask me how he knew, but this dog must've reckoned that he was yours from the beginnin'. Anyways, his mother Sherpa will always be my dog, even though she's gone. Bounce was always yours." Al concluded with a warm grasp of my hand as I struggled under the licks and woofs of Bounce's weight and presence. "So long Doc, bye Bounce," he said with a gentle pat on the surrogate friend's head.

"Take care Al. Enjoy your new career," I said as Bounce and I followed him to the door. Bounce, instinctively glued to the side of my leg, made no attempt to go with Allen Latimer. "Give my regards to Elizabeth and the kids. Have a great Christmas! You've made mine a perfect one."

With a reticent nod Al waved good-bye to us both. He would miss Bounce nonetheless.

"Well, Bounce," I said, stooping over to look past the locks of hair covering the playful eyes of a contented sheepdog. "You're going to make a household happy this Christmas." His tongue dropped to the side of his mouth as he smiled at me, his body bouncing from head to foot though sitting in one spot.

Leslie, Trip and Samantha had already left for the day. I locked the front door and turned towards the counter, Bounce following me with each step. I gazed down at the appointment book full of almost a year's worth of crises, successes and defeats. Too many emotions flooded my thoughts so I closed the book, tapped it gently and went out the side door to the truck.

I drove away with Bounce in the passenger's seat, off to do some Christmas shopping, knowing that beside me sat a friendship that would endure for many years...

Creature comfort is a friend by your side...

Coda I - PetSpan

Pet Age Chart for New Age Pet Owners

The old wives' axiom that a year in a dog's life is equal to seven human years simply doesn't stand up for every dog that I've known. The reality is that an animal's biological clock is significantly different from the Homo sapiens. Perhaps some of the ape species, birds and a few other animals have body timers in sync with ours — parrots for example can live as long as humans — but every other animal seems to have distinct timers. In fact, breeds within species have different life spans.

What follows is a chart that attempts to give, to the dog and cat owner at least, a sense of measure for a pet's life span. This chart is to be used in the subsequent appendices on Life-Phases to determine what preventive care is best at your pet's time of life.

In this chart I compare the seven intervals of a pet's life that demand attention by the owner and have distinct requirements medically, nutritionally and physically. I like to compare the size of dogs to the automobile. Subcompact cars like toy dogs have to work a lot harder at keeping their motor/metabolism running. They tend to rust and die off at an earlier age. Compact vehicles and dogs the size of Bassets, Schnauzers, Poodles and Dachshunds come with particular body designs to suit some aesthetic desire of their owner. They burn energy at a fast rate, but not as bad as the shoe-box car or Chihuahua dog. 'Standard' sized cars and dogs like the Retrievers, Dalmatians and Collies tend to consume moderate amounts of fuel so they wear out at a more moderate rate. Limo's and Giant Dogs like the Great Dane, St. Bernard and Great Pyranee are gas guzzlers. Their engines fatigue rapidly with subsequent deterioration of body parts.

Why bother? Why compare pet lifespan to humans?

We have embraced the dog and cat as integral to our lives. Many pet owners feel passionately that their pet is a member of their family. Anthropomorphizing the dog or cat with human 'qualities' has come with the passion. We must learn to accept the realities that come with such humanization. Those truths include the shortened life span to which your companion is tied. If we are going to humanize our furred friends let's include a rational approach to the preventive health care necessary to keep them living as long as their clock allows. Let's also learn to accept their demise so as to maintain sobriety and common sense. It is easier to understand another creature's needs when there is evident relevance to our own.

It is critically important to recognize the lifetime schedule of the dog or cat in order to make time for preventive care. There is much less time in a dog or cat's life to institute prudent measures that ensure good health. These guidelines —- and that's all that they are —- provide estimations for the pet owner to follow.

PetSpan Periods

In order to use this chart, I suggest we first, consider the phases that take place throughout the animal's lifetime. Shakespeare spoke of these phases in less than cryptic language: 'Mewling and puking...' being one of them. Here is Dr. Runcibal's theorem of dog and cat life ages:

PetSpan I - Birth to Babyhood (mewling to terrible two's)

Ever wonder why human babies are so vulnerable and helpless at birth while a new-born puppy or kitten can stand and walk within minutes? It's because animals are higher in a particular evolutionary scale —- the one that measures survivability through independence.

PetSpan II - Childhood (pre-teen in human terms)

This is when the infant pet is most vulnerable. It's spirit can be broken by harsh words and cruelty which would make it distrust the human with supposedly more intelligence. It would become an untrustworthy dog or cat that will bite the human hand that feeds it. If nurtured with love and kindness it will become a human's best friend for life.

PetSpan III - Adolescence (the human parent's nightmare years)

This is a time critical to the development of self-discipline. Tough Love and education are fundamental needs during this phase. Otherwise you'll have a pet that knows no rules — and breaks all of yours. (Sound similar to your kids?)

PetSpan IV - Adulthood (the 20 to 30-something malleable human)

Pets need attention during this life phase but they tend to be more resilient than their human counterparts. They often have to wait hours or days for their busy human to play with them or even take them for a walk. Pets can get bored too. Think of this during this phase in your pet's life — would you want to receive only ten minutes of excitement per day?

PetSpan V - Middle Age (humans' era of enlightenment)

If you haven't tended to preventive care by now there is a lot of work to be done. For if the pet's clock has not been serviced regularly its springs can be weak and worn. Now is the time that you and your pet can truly become close friends.

PetSpan VI - Senior Citizens (Human Geriatrics)

The clock ticks more slowly...only if you let it. Your pet will die younger than it's predestined time if allowed to wither. Given reasonable health care, nutritional support, and moderate physical activity your pet has a reasonable chance to surpass it's age equivalent demise.

PetSpan VII - Memory (we all become a memory, sooner or later)

It is likely that the pets we own will die during our lifetime. In fact, if you love animals, you will see several furred friends pass away. I have my own memories of Rusty, Teddy, Lucky, Spook, Lollipop, Bounce, Jiggs and Mr Chips. I hope this book helped you to realize how valued these memories are, and allowed you to cry for your 'Rusty' along with Mark Haley's loss of Smokey. That's normal. But then we need to move on with our memories and rekindle the gift that a pet brings to our lives by buying that new puppy or kitten.

Age Equivalency

As I have said, the rule of one pet year equaling seven human years, does not hold for all dogs and cats. In fact it is very difficult to truly extrapolate a human equivalent. As dogs and cats go through breeding cycles, and as research discovers life-extending nutrition and preventive medicine, we continue to enjoy longer and longer associations with our four-legged companions. This increase in longevity has been going on for generations. Humans in the Middle Ages lasted no more than an average of 30 to 40 years before they died from disease or were skewered by the sword. Their pets likely had a life span of a couple of years before death by skewered stew.

There have been several attempts to chart age equivalents for dogs and cats. Most ignore the relevance of the baby years to the development of the independent child-pet. Others class all dogs into only one or two columns. I believe that such a chart, at least for dogs, needs to incorporate a proportional equation. A definitive study comparing pet size to the age of demise, may prove or disprove the chart that follows. And there are individual animals in a breed, or breeds within a size category that defy this chart. So use the following attempt to equate your dog's age to human years, with a grain or two of sodium chloride.

There are three components to this age equivalent chart for dogs and cats:

1. **Babyhood:** Most puppies and kittens are babies until they are eight weeks of age compared to humans who take up to two years to achieve the same life skills.

2. **Range:** Since size of dog and breeds of dogs and cats vary significantly and since it is difficult to assess an accurate cut-off point in size of dogs, I propose a range of human equivalent ages.

3. **Average:** In order to give the pet owner a singular multiplier, I suggest that an average number is applied.

Age Equivalent Chart for Dogs
Age Equivalent to the Human Animal

Auto-reference:	Sub Compact	Compact	Regular-Sized	Lincoln-Cadillac	Limo-Sized
Body weight:	under 9 lb.	10 to 20 lb.	21 to 55 lb.	56 to 99 lb.	over 100 lb.
Breed Type:	toy breeds	standard	Labrador, etc.	Rottweiller sized	Danes & Newfies
Babyhood:	in puppyhood, in all dogs, 1 puppy day equals approximately 13 human days				
PetSpan: Age Range:	1 year = 9 to 10 human years	1 year = 4 to 7 human years	1 year = 5 to 8 human years	1 year = 6 to 9 human years	1 year = 7 to 11 human years
Average Age Factor:	1:9	1:6	1:6.5	1:7.5	1:9

Did you notice a pattern?

Clearly the toy and giant breeds have inherent differences in their makeup. As a result of refined breeding in order to develop the tiniest or the grandest of dogs, the resulting breeds have tended to inherit a compressed life span. This doesn't make them any less the dog, they simply have to cram a lot more enjoyment and companionship into a shorter span of time.

One could also classify dogs into far more categories than just the five listed above. The reality is that every breed of dog (and cat) could, and perhaps some day will, have it's own age equivalent chart. There are more factors than just the dimensions of the animal and it's weight. Proclivity for longevity may someday became a heritable trait.

How do you use the chart?

Consider for example that you have a Golden Retriever. You've had her for four years. Goldens generally reach an adult weight of 60 to 80 pounds. Such a weight could place the dog into two possible columns: Regular Sized to Large Sized Dogs. The chart suggests then that you could use a multiplier of 6.5 or 7.5 in order to calculate the human equivalent years. So your four-year old Golden could be compared to a 26 to 30 year old person. I do not suggest that you factor in the puppy-baby weeks. These are only used to indicate the rapid progression from birth to childhood in a dog, and to emphasize the limited time available for the specific care necessary for the infant years.

Taking this a step further, if your Golden is now 26 to 30 in human terms, you should look at PetSpan IV, the Young Adult Years in the following Coda. Following this chart will help you to determine the preventive care necessary for your dog at this period of its life.

Do this for your own dog(s) or cat(s) to set them onto a path of effective and specific health care.

Age Equivalent Formula For Cats

Fortunately for felines, the species has proven difficult to genetically alter, at least in regard to size. I guess that's just as propitious for the pet owner for if we had Great Dane-sized cats inhabiting apartments we would be reading more obituaries of cat-owner deaths ('Mr and Mrs. Jones were found as semi-formed fur balls under their beds last night...'). Cats have learned to survive well in the human world. Their longevity has evolved in some ways despite us, rather than thanks to us. Cats can live to at least twenty years of age, although some breeds show some minor variants. I'm using the new age theosophy that humans can and should live to the ripe age of one hundred (or more depending on how 'new age' you are) . So after kittendom, if we pamper our feline friends with good preventive maintenance, we can enjoy our feline friend for a couple of decades.

New findings on animal nutrition, breed differences and feline diseases are contributing greatly however. Perhaps we will be able to add one or two more lives to the nine.

Age Equivalency Chart for Cats

PetSpan I: As with dogs, cats are babies till they are eight weeks of age then they become playful kids. So one could say that
One kitten day equals 13 human days.

Range: *One cat year equals approximately 6 to 9 human years.*

Average: *One cat year would be equivalent to 7 human years.*

Thankfully and regrettably there are exceptions to the rule. Just as some people die young and Andaluthian farmers in Transylvania who smoke and imbibe regularly, live to be one hundred and forty three, some dogs and cats have a biological clock wound so tightly that they seem to die shortly after teendom. Others live on, and on, and on. The oldest cat in the Guinness tome was clocked at 36 years of age.

Now You are ready to use the PetSpan Guide

What follows in Codas II and III are the specific health management strategies necessary to provide optimum health for any dog or cat at that particular stage in their life. Use these charts for age equivalency and designated care according to the 'PetSpan' of your dog or cat.

Coda IV provides a list of symptoms for those unfortunate times when disease or disorder knocks on your door. It will help give you insight into seriousness of the problem according to severity and significance of symptoms.

You are what you eat - Your pet is what you feed it!

While I discuss nutrition with general recommendations, I caution that there is at least another books' worth of information that could be written. If you have a muffin-bodied, toast-and-jam-legged, pizza-headed dog with a tail on the end, there is a distinct possibility that you may be feeding the wrong diet. Fortunately, pets can be fed balanced meals-in-a-can that deliver every nutrient at the prescribed level of need. Your veterinarian can direct you to them.

CODA II: HealthStyle for Dogs
FastTrack to your Dog's PetSpan HealthStyle

PetSpan I: Birth to Puppyhood

Recommended Preventive Care (up to the age of eight weeks).

Weaning Puppies thrive on mother's milk in the early days of life. They can accept bowls of milk or formula by the time they are four weeks of age. I would not recommend weaning until they are able to be self-sustained with puppy food, water and milk by approximately eight weeks of age.

Teeth Teething (eruption of permanent teeth, pushing out the baby teeth) occurs generally up to six months of age. In the first few weeks there is little concern for the pups but increasing distress on the mother. Helping mom at meal-time by the time the pups are four weeks old minimizes the painful nips at the teats.

Immunity Puppies have secured passive immunity through placental blood from their mother and suckled milk. They benefit from protective antibodies from the bitch who had to fight disease. The levels of these antibodies will ebb gradually but certainly by the time the puppy is eight weeks of age. It is important then at six to eight weeks, to launch the dog onto an artificial immunity platform for the first 'puppy shot': Canine Distemper, Hepatitis, Parvovirus and Kennel Cough

Nutrition Mother's milk should continue for as long as the bitch can handle the brood. With a large litter, and if the pups are extremely aggressive, wean them from her completely if she tells you to —- she will do this by trying to escape them. Other clues include the drying up and reduction in the size of the mammary tissues, the pups may become more restless and cry for the diminishing sustenance —- it's time to supplement. After a few days add pabulum for substance, then by the time the pups are five to six weeks old a dry or canned puppy food can be placed in front of them. Initially they will just play with it and get their muzzles messy but they will quickly learn that the smudge just licked off the nose is rather tasty, and soon seek food instead of nipple.

Parasites Puppy may have acquired any number of worms from it's environment or regrettably, from it's mother. These squirming lecherous

creatures suck the puppies blood as they grasp their jaws onto the lining of the gut, or they feed off the nutrients passing along the digestive tract, weakening their unsuspecting host. It is imperative that a stool sample be examined by your veterinary clinic on or before a puppy's eighth week of age, ideally one at six weeks and one at eight. Some worm medicines can be given at ten days of age.

PetSpan II : Childhood

Recommended Preventive Care (up to the dog-age of six months).

Teeth Teething dictates chewing. Chewing will consecrate holey socks and slippers unless you substitute chew toys. Stockings and shoes are aromatic attractions to the nose and teeth at the ground-level world of the puppy. Puppy-proof the house by raising or hiding such items for the duration of the teething process. If you own a retriever breed, you may be wise in building a permanently secure place for shoes and boots. Start rubbing your fingers along the teeth and gum line to prepare the pup for a future tooth brush.

Immunity 9 - 12 weeks of age: Canine Distemper, Hepatitis, Parvovirus, Kennel cough

16 weeks: Canine Distemper, Hepatitis, Parvovirus, Kennel Cough and the first Rabies Inoculation. Your veterinarian may be on a schedule of 6, 9, and 12 weeks or 8, 12 and 16, depending on choice of vaccine.

20 Weeks: Parvovirus Booster*
In addition: many veterinarians vaccinate for Coronavirus. If endemic to your area ask about vaccination against Lyme Disease
*If you own a young Labrador Retriever, Doberman, Rottweiler, German Shepherd, Springer Spaniel, Pit Bull, or Yorkshire Terrier seek your veterinarian's advice as to the incidence of Parvovirus in the area. These breeds, and a few others seem predisposed to the disease and regrettably seem to develop poorer immunity despite routine vaccinations.

The MicroChip Inoculation: Technology has now provided us with a new way to find lost animals. A small microchip about the size of a grain of rice that stores numbers and letters in a code can be injected under the skin (into the pectoral muscle of birds, in the neck ligament of horses. These codes can be read by a scanner much like that used to determine the price of your groceries. A lost animal, picked up by the local pound, humane group or veterinarian can then display its owner and home phone onto a computer screen.

Tattoo's and nose prints are usually unintelligible and dog tags fall off or go out of date. The microchip is an excellent way to ensure the pet gets returned.

Nutrition All puppies need a pet food designed for growth and energy. Veterinarians, Breeders and Trainers are good sources of advice on diets that perform well for the growing dog. It is important though, to get medical advice. Too many large breed dogs are overfed for rapid growth to subsequently develop musculoskeletal disease that can become debilitating. I can tolerate a somewhat plump body condition on a puppy but by the time they reach six months of age their silhouette should be becoming lean and slim.

Training House training is first on the list unless you wish to wear boots around the house. To do so, place puppy in a closed area like a collapsible kennel, large box, or small room such as the bathroom. Cover the bottom or floor with newspapers (so you can easily wrap the certain treasures). Puppies dislike soiling in or near their bed so they will nose around for a place to deposit hesitatingly. By observing this activity be ready to scoop up the puppy before the deposit. Run it outside and wait for nature. Reward the good deed with praise. Eventually the pup will catch on and bark its desire to be carried outside. You can then widen the box to a larger room (with cautionary papers) then the house —- and you can catch up on the news of the day without crawling across the floor. Try to 'house-train' rather than 'paper-train'—- in other words, use the crate/confined system to get the pup to tell you when it needs to go out rather than confusing it by allowing it to soil on the papers. This requires vigilance during the first few days of pethood.

Hair-Coat Long or short, get into the habit of brushing. You'll minimize the complaint "That damn dog is shedding all over the couch!" improve spousal harmony, and acclimatize the dog to regular grooming. Use a stiff brush, a stainless steel comb for long fur. Brush at least once a week, ideally, once a day. All the while, check for bumps, bugs and burrs. If you can't find time to do so, pay for a groomer to do it for you! Think about it. How long would it take for your hair to become matted, infected, infested if you stopped brushing and combing every day? Notice an itchiness in your scalp at the thought?

Parasites At eight weeks of age a fecal sample has hopefully been checked. If the clinic has found eggs of worms they would have given you some pills or syrup to administer. At six months of age I would recommend a second stool analysis to ensure that the course of treatment was effective and there are no new freeloaders present. The course of treatment recommended may include a second or third dose of the worm medicine; give it strictly according to the label. The first round may have only killed adult worms. Immature worms or eggs still in the gut can grow rapidly (within days or weeks) to begin the worm's life cycle anew. Only repeated doses of the medication will kill all stages.

Exercise Puppy has a lot of energy and likely a bit of puppy fat from its mother and the high energy puppy food. Don't let that wad of puppy fat remain to make puppy a fat waddling dog. Get off the couch, turn off the damn TV and walk the dog —- hell, run! You likely need to lose a few pounds anyway. Play toys for inside and outside can help keep it amused when you are away. Enlist everyone in the family to take turns burning the pup's fuels and developing locomotor skills. It will be foolish and clumsy in its playfulness. The rolls and romps are teaching balance and social skills. If the pup were in a dog pack in the wild, the elders of the group would all be helping to teach the young'un. You and your family are the substitute pack members and the socialization and playskills are your responsibilities now.

PetSpan III : Adolescence

Recommended Preventive Care (six months to 18 months of age)

Teeth By six months of age most of the permanent teeth should have arrived. Occasionally the baby teeth have refused to fall out. See your veterinarian if this seems to be the case. Otherwise the permanent teeth can be forced to become crooked and/or periodontal disease can develop. Continue to acclimatize the dog to handling the mouth and teeth. Whether you like it or not we now recommend that every pet owner brush their dog's teeth. The consequences of not doing so are pain, infection, early loss of teeth and diminished ability to live a longer healthier life. See your veterinarian for diets and chews that are best for dental hygiene.

Immunity Some breeds, as mentioned above, have less ability to generate immunity against some diseases. Parvovirus, a deadly enteric disease, seems to more readily attack specific breeds as listed above, perhaps other breeds as well. It may be prudent to booster such breeds against Parvovirus at six months —- perhaps every six months, at least once a year. Over-vaccination though, may be just as bad —- so consult with your veterinarian to determine individual programs.

Nutrition Essentially most breeds of dogs are still growing until they reach 18 months of age to complete their teenage years. I recommend a growth-type puppy food throughout this period. Again, large breeds should be fed with care so as to prevent too rapid growth. Since every dog is different, feed according to the diet's recommendation but use body condition as your monitor. As long as you are able to feel and see ribs without the impression of 'slimness, not thin-ness nor fat', the dog is eating enough. If the ribs become predominate or unidentifiable then increase the diet or cut back respectively. Mixed feeding of canned and dry food is best. Water, freshened daily, is essential. Table scraps, occasionally, are okay, provided you ask yourself, would I eat this? Should I eat this? Rather than dump the chicken skins, fat, gravy, and icing into the dog dish —- throw it out! If you have some leftover spinach, green beans, lean meat, and you can't finish it, give it to the dog. Remember though, whenever table scraps, or pet treats are given, to cut back on the dog food for the day accordingly. Ideally, no table scraps and only dog foods that are formulated for the age and activity of the pet is best. But I know how hard it is for you to resist those pleading eyes and whimpers!

Training The teen years can be productive learning years for the dog. A distinct vocabulary can be learned. If you have little or no experience in training dogs seek the advice of professionals. Obedience Schools for Dogs are available at veterinary clinics and by professional dog trainers. A veterinarian or

breeder can help recommend reputable and effective schools for your dog. Discipline is as important to a healthy socialized life for a teenage dog as for a teenage human. It would be nice if your teenager thanks you some day for their discipline. You will thank yourself that you trained and raised a disciplined dog.

HairCoat Daily brushing as described above, ideally against the grain of the coat to remove the dead hair more readily, then with the grain to groom the coat. Regular inspection for flea dirt, ticks, lumps and bumps can produce evidence of things to bring to the vet's attention sooner rather than too late. Dogs have become primarily house guests so that regular brushing will help reduce a clogged vacuum cleaner. Dogs left in dog houses still need daily brushing, perhaps more attention to external parasites because of the breeding ground that a dog-house environment provides.

Parasites Assuming that fecal examination and worming medication have already been done the only concern for worms comes from environmental reinfestation. If the dog has fields nearby where mice and moles can readily be caught and eaten (or if the family cat is catching mice to feed the dog) — - then rechecks of the stool is in order. Actual visual inspection of the feces in addition to a sample to the vet is indicated. Tapeworm segments are rarely seen in fecal analysis and usually seen as white squirming grains of rice in or on a section of stool. Worms can also be picked up by exposure to other dogs and beasts. Hunting dogs, especially if they hunt with other dogs, should have regular stool checks. External parasites include fleas, ticks and lice. Fleas, if allowed can suck enough blood from an animal to make it anemic. Tickscan carry diseases such as Lyme Disease, a threat to dogs and humans. Lice, both sucking and biting, can also climb onto human hosts to create multiple welts along the belt-line, back, neck, anywhere where they can migrate over the human torso. Dogs can readily scoop ear mites from the grass. These bugs live only in the ear but cause severe pain and itchiness. Imagine having 30 to 100 eight-legged miniature insects crawling around in your ear, biting and chewing at the sensitive tissue lining. If there is evidence of these creatures (perhaps only itching and scratching) see your veterinarian for medication to kill the beasts, and ask about new control remedies.

Exercise Teenagers must have regular, energetic exercise. Fetching, swimming, jogging, long hikes are all worthwhile. Every breed has its own tolerance and predisposition to exercise. A ten-mile hike will wear a Chihuahua's pads to the flesh. But try to keep a Labrador Retriever out of a pond or stream! Fit the exercise plan to the breed of dog. But make a plan! Incorporate your own exercise needs into the regime. If and when you go on vacation and have to board your dog, especially for an extended period of time, ensure that the boarding facility has adequate room and strategies for exercise. It doesn't take long for joints to become stiff, sore, even damaged from inactivity.

Spay/Neuter Teenagers become sexually active during this period of time.

They become sexually attracted to one another. Left to nature we would end up with dozens of dogs and cats in every household. As it is, stray dogs running the neighborhood consummate enough relationships to add to the existing surplus. Dog pounds are full of unneeded puppies and adult dogs that will never find a home. Neutering a male dog will, in my opinion, secure a more stable personality, prevent testicular cancer, and ensure a longer contented life. Spaying a female dog will prevent life-threatening mammary cancer and pyometra (pus-filled, infected uterus) that is brought on by years of estrus cycles and pregnancies. It may also lengthen her life and protect her from attacks from stray males. Both procedures are mandatory for the pet owner, essential for the breeding dog when their breeding days are over.

PetSpan IV : Young Adult

Preventive Care (18 months, dog years, human-equivalent: the early 30s)

Teeth Regular daily brushing. Alternatives may include some of the new oral hygiene products or hard chew biscuits. Regular examination of the gum line for evidence of plaque build-up, tartar, gingivitis or periodontal disease is essential. Early detection and dental prophylaxis will ensure that the dog will not lose teeth. Halitosis is a good indicator. If your neighbor bends down to pet your dog and keels over, succumbed by the potency of Rover's bad breath, you're probably too late. Call the vet for a dental checkup.

Immunity Annual Vaccinations: Canine Distemper, Hepatitis, Parvovirus, Coronavirus Kennel Cough Complex Rabies*

Rabies In endemic areas (where rabies predominates as a disease in skunk, fox, raccoons and other animals in the wild, as well as significant incidence of the disease in the pet population) get the dog vaccinated annually. In areas where the disease is less prevalent, ask for the three-year vaccine against rabies. Check with local regulations as well. Islands, great (like the British Isles) and small, have strict regulations for rabies vaccination, particularly if the disease has been eradicated from the island.

Nutrition Dogs are omnivores by nature so that a well-balanced maintenance diet that provides adequate protein levels but a properly balanced vitamin-mineral content is essential. Canned and dry food feeding is better than only one or the other. Crunching dry foods helps clean away oral bacteria from the teeth that could contribute to dental problems. Dogs this age could be fed once a day. It is important however, to feed according to lifestyle. If the dog is relatively active throughout the day, two or three feedings are still better. If the dog extends most of its energy in the evening when the family returns home from school and work, an evening feeding may be all that is needed, (although a bowl of dry food to snack on during the long day could be appreciated).

Training Expanding the vocabulary and the repertoire is well worth the effort. After establishing a healthy discipline in the dog's early years you can now concentrate on communication training. Instead of shouting "Down!" every time the dog jumps up on people, teach the dog to respond to a more pleasant, firm statement: 'Please get down.' If the dog is standing at the front door with muddy feet, teach him to go to the mud room by setting the door ajar and saying, "Would you go to the back door please?" Such refinements in pet communication training can make pet ownership a great pleasure, especially when you can say, "Would you open the fridge and get me a beer, Cody?"

Hair-Coat Keep brushing!

Parasites Fecals should be checked if rodents are in the diet, or social habits include exposure to other dogs or cats. Checking for external parasites should be a life-long hunt.

Exercise This is an age where exercise may be neglected. If feeding guidelines are also ignored the dog can become a fat young adult. Keep up the daily exercise routines, share them amongst the family.

PetSpan V : Middle Age

Recommended Preventive Care (Human equivalent of 40s to 50s).

Annual Exam I cannot overstress the importance of an annual physical

examination by your local veterinarian. Given that a dog ages more rapidly than a human, then you are actually taking them in for a five to nine year recheck with just an annual visit to the vet. A lot can happen that your dog cannot tell you, but your practitioner can determine with a regular physical.

Teeth The mouth is aging and the wear and tear on teeth and gums along with the number of times that you have shamefully neglected to brush have now led to some form of periodontal disease. See your veterinarian for advice as to the veterinary dentistry needed. It is very important to do so in order to save teeth from extraction and permanent damage to the gingiva. Get back to the routine of brushing!

Immunity Most veterinarians advise annual vaccinations throughout the life of a dog. I would suggest that vaccination now be tailored to the diseases endemic to the area and the type of breed you have. Healthy humans benefit from a vigorous immune system. A dog should be no different. Repeated annual vaccinations with multiple vaccines could be a considerable affront to the immune system. Perhaps a compromise is a two-year schedule for the 'booster' or selective immunization of endemic diseases such as Parvovirus, rabies and kennel cough. No hard and fast recommendations of this type have been established as yet, but consultation with your veterinarian as to the best vaccination regime for your pet in your environment would seem most sensible.

Nutrition Consider this common scenario. Parents buy a new puppy for the kids (ages 6 and 7). Children and family enjoy playing with the dog until high school years. The dog is now 6 or 7 dog years of age and the family has other priorities (school, work, new friends, both for the children and the adults). The dog is 'middle aged', has its feeding guidelines ignored, and is exercised less. The dog starts to gain weight. No one notices the excess because no one is paying as much attention. The dog becomes lethargic, having to carry around the extra pounds. If this has happened already see your veterinarian for a weight loss diet! If it hasn't happened yet, don't let it! Follow the diet's feeding instructions, watch the rib cage. A middle-aged paunch on a dog is just as dangerous as on the couch potato human.

Training Keep adding to the vocabulary and the communication training. This dog will happily become a useful member of the family. How about, "Where are my slippers?"

Hair-Coat Keep brushing!

Parasites Keep checking!

Exercise Keep jogging!

PetSpan VI : Senior Citizens

Recommended Preventive Care (human equivalent of over-the-hill).

Annual Exam Critical! Perhaps twice a year.

Teeth It is extremely important now to go to the veterinarian for regular dental checkups. This is likely covered in the annual physical examination. I would recommend annual dental visits if you are brushing faithfully, semi-annual if you are not. Loss of teeth from poor dental hygiene is a common contributor to an earlier demise. Infected gums and excessive tartar can cause considerable pain, even too painful to eat.

Immunity While the immune system may have vigorously maintained high titres of vaccinated antigens during PetSpan IV and V, it's vigor is diminished with age. A geriatric body has battled with so many antigens and germs over the years that it has spent much of its' arsenal. Annual vaccinations for the elderly dog, in my view are paramount. I recommend annual: Canine Distemper, Hepatitis, Parvovirus, Coronavirus and where indicated, Rabies and Kennel Cough. Until veterinary hospitals can economically test titres of disease immunities, this and the above recommendations are considered today's minimal requirements.

Nutrition As we age, human and beast, we lose our senses of taste and smell (some humans lose common sense as well, although that doesn't appear to be at all related to age!). Dogs and cats thrive and survive through common sense. Dogs will become disinterested in food, not because of a lack of need, but because their enjoyment of the food is diminished by the loss of sensations. Ask your veterinarian for diets that are designed for the senior citizen of the canine world. Such diets incorporate enhanced tastes, aromatic additives, increased B-Complex vitamins and adjusted water soluble vitamins.

Training You can so teach an old dog new tricks! In fact, maintaining life-long learning for the dog will make its' life longer and happier. Dogs live to please their master. If there are new ways to do so throughout its' life it will stay vital and young.

Hair-Coat Keep brushing!

Parasites Keep checking!

Exercise That scenario of the kids going off to high school is worsened when they go off to College, eventually to marry and move away. The dog's pack (his extended family) has deteriorated. Worse, we have geriatric humans caring for geriatric pets. The risk is for everyone to sit around and vegetate. Exercise for the empty nesters, including the dog, is critical to healthy older bodies. Walking, distance adjusted to the breed, is the best form of mobility. Get out and do it!

PetSpan VII : Memory

There are two concerns with the final phase of a pet's existence. The first is the time of termination and the second is the ability to cope with the loss. A veterinarian is by nature and extension, concerned with both.

Death Loss of life from disease or accident can occur at any point in the continuum of the PetSpan. Adherence to the preventive procedures can minimize the risk of premature death but longevity is not an automatic guarantee for any creature's existence. Death is one of the stops along the way. Whether there is another series of stops for human or beast beyond this is up to individual belief, or faith. Memory though, should be the goal of pet ownership. Our pets are likely to die before we do so let's accept that and strive for responsible and loving care while we've got them and enjoy the memories we'll gain from their companionship.

Euthanasia We have accepted euthanasia as a solution to suffering of animals. It is still a difficult time for both the owner and the veterinarian. There are specific criteria to consider should the decision be placed before you and your veterinarian:

1. *Quality of Life*
Will the course of treatment, that could prolong this dog's life, also prolong the pain and suffering?

2. *Objectivity*
Are we keeping this dog alive out of selfishness? Is it because we can't cope with the loss that we are blind to the pain it is suffering? Step back literally and figuratively to look at the situation from as distant a view as you can.

3. *Quantity of Life*
Is the course of treatment going to maintain the dog for a reasonable length of time? Determine how much time is reasonable.

4. *Economics*
Veterinary Care, particularly intensive care, nursing, drugs and monitoring can add up. Can you afford the price and are you willing to extend every effort at any cost within your budget?

Coping with Grief Your dog's death is your opportunity to begin a lifetime of reflection on the joys and friendship conferred by this companion over the years. If you need grief counseling, get it. If not, walk yourself through the process towards a goal of happy memories. Many veterinarians today have some training in Grief counseling. If not, they at least have an innate sense of empathy that can go a long way to help you through your loss. They may also know professionals to whom they could refer you if it seemed necessary.

Resources for getting through your grief:

In addition to talking with your veterinarian you may wish to find other sources of information or counsel. There are numerous books available, Internet Web Sites (see appendix 6) and several places for you to call:

1. *The Closest Veterinary College in your area:* Many Veterinary Schools have a resident resource. Cindy Adams is a researcher at the University of Guelph for example, whose expertise includes Grief Counseling. Other

Veterinary Teaching Colleges would either have someone who could help or be able to direct you to more local resources.

2. *Local Pet Loss Support Groups:* Contact your local Chamber of Commerce, Minister, Rabbi or Pastor who may be able to direct you to a local support group. In Ontario for example, there are the following groups:

Hamilton Pet Loss Support Group - 905-547-1257

London Pet Loss Support Group - 519-652-2348

Metro Toronto Animal Loss Group - 416-742-2596

Oakville Pet Loss Support Group - 905-845-1551

Ottawa Saying Goodbye to our Animal Friends - 613-760-0848

In addition there are likely paid professional grief therapists listed in the phone book who may be able to help.

Coda III : FastTrack to your Cat's PetSpan HealthStyle

PetSpan I: Kittenhood

Recommended Preventive Care (up to the age of eight weeks).

Weaning Kittens thrive on mother's milk in the early days of life. They can accept bowls of milk or formula by the time they are four weeks of age. I would not recommend weaning until they have been able to be self-sustained with kitten food, water and milk by approximately six to eight weeks of age.

Teeth Teething (eruption of permanent teeth, pushing out the baby teeth) occurs up to six months of age. In the first few weeks there is little concern for the kids but the sharp teeth put increasing distress on mom. Help her at meal-times by the time the kittens are four weeks of age with supplemented milk or pabulum.

Immunity Kittens have secured preventive vaccination through placental blood from their mother and suckled milk. They benefit from protective antibodies that fight disease. The levels of these antibodies will ebb gradually and certainly by the time the kitten is eight weeks of age. It is important at least by nine weeks of age to launch the kitten onto an artificial immunity platform. The new pet owner, or breeder should see the veterinarian for the first 'kitten shot' that incorporates: Panleukopenia (distemper) Feline Viral Rhinotracheitis (the 'colds & flu') Calicivirus Chlamydia

Nutrition Mother's formula should continue for as long as the queen can handle the brood. With a large litter, and if the kittens are extremely aggressive, wean them from her completely if mom tells you to. Her innate sense of when to wean should be evident. Give milk first, then after a few days add some pabulum for substance. By the time the kittens are five to six weeks old a dry or canned kitten food can be placed in front of them. Some kittens (or puppies) can be allergic to lactose (milk sugar) and suffer from profound vomiting and diarrhea. If this is evident take them off the milk and call the veterinarian.

Parasites It is imperative that a stool sample be examined by your veterinary clinic on or before a kitten's eighth week of age. Some medications from your veterinarian can be given as young as ten days of age.

Training Litter training can be initiated very early with kittens. A tray of kitty litter near the queen and her nest will allow the kids to watch and mimic Mommy. Cats are fastidious about their hygiene. Unlike the dog who may turn on the recently deposited stool to sniff, even taste it, the cat will immediately try to hide the waste by flicking dry litter over the deposit. It is imperative though that the litter provided be continually checked and changed whenever too wet, odorous or crowded with fecal logs.

PetSpan II : Childhood

Teeth

Teeth Teething in kittens may not seem to demand the same replacement strategy as needed for puppies. Kittens won't be carrying around old socks and new shoes to carve holes and chewed segments. But they will suffer teething pains nonetheless. Dry crunchy food will help. Look at the size of the kernels. They must be small enough for the minuscule kitty teeth to handle, otherwise the kitten will ignore the food and teething will not be aided. Teething toys could also be provided even though the kitten may not seem to be chewing them as much as a puppy would.

Immunity 'Boosters' and inoculations for additional diseases are needed as close as possible to these ages:

12 Weeks of age: * Panleukopenia, Rhinotracheitis, Calicivirus, Chlamydia booster * First Feline Leukemia vaccination. Note that this may be provided with only one injection. The distemper, colds and flu viruses could be incorporated as a liquid in one small vial while the Leukemia vaccine may be a dry compound in another vial. By adding the liquid vaccine to the desiccated vaccine each and every component is activated. The kitten need only suffer the indignity of one needle yet become protected from five diseases.

16 Weeks of age: * Panleukopenia, Rhinotracheitis, Calicivirus, Chlamydia booster * Feline Leukemia booster * Rabies vaccination In this case the two boosters are likely to be combined into one needle and the Rabies in a second injection.

FIP (Feline Infectious Peritonitis) is now available as an intra-nasal vaccine.

In other words your veterinarian can squirt the vaccine into the nostrils and the vaccine is absorbed by the nasal blood supply. Not many cats enjoy this procedure however. Be prepared for stress and sneezes if recommended by your vet. This vaccine should only be given to kittens over sixteen weeks of age.

Nutrition All kittens need a pet food designed for growth and energy. By the time cats reach six months of age their silhouette should be becoming lean and slim. Pet owners often ignore the feeding guidelines suggested on the package and opt for the quick and easy dump of dry food to fill the bowl or the glob of canned food that the kitten cleans up. There is too much danger of overfeeding with this technique. Read the label and follow the instructions as to amount of food to feed for the age of the animal.

Training Litter training should have been accomplished by now. If not, and if you are the happy owner of a new kitten, make sure you take litter box precautions or you may get an unwelcome surprise when you slip on your shoes tomorrow morning. These strategies include putting the new kitten into a small room, decorated with newspapers on the floor, a litter box with fresh dry kitty litter in one corner, and bowls for food and fluid at the farthest wall from the litter. Feed the kitten in the room several times a day and close the door so as to encourage evacuation shortly after the repast. The kitten, even if not litter-trained, will be attracted to the box and the consistency of the granules. It will do no good to congratulate the kitten as you would a puppy, they will begin to ignore you from this moment onwards. If they are comfortable with the toilet that you provided, they will use it. If not, check your shoes regularly!

Hair-Coat Long or short, get into the habit of brushing. You'll minimize the complaint "That damn cat is shedding all over the couch!" improve spousal harmony, and acclimatize the cat to regular grooming. Use a stiff brush, a stainless steel comb for long fur. Brush at least once a week, ideally, once a day. All the while, check for bumps, bugs and burrs. If you can't find time to do so, pay for a groomer to do it for you!

Parasites At eight weeks of age a fecal sample has hopefully been checked. If the clinic has found eggs of worms they would have given you some pills or syrup to administer. At six months of age I would recommend a second stool analysis to ensure that the course of treatment was effective. Cats that are good mousers may need regular repeated deworming particularly for tape-worms.

Exercise Kitty has a lot of energy, from a bit of kitten fat from its mother's rich milk and the high energy kitten food. Don't let that wad of kitty fat remain to make kitty a fat waddling cat. Play toys help keep it amused. So will strings, ribbons, shoelaces, curtain cords, electrical cords, yarn, fur, lint...anything that rolls or flutters past the inquisitive flashing eyes of the kit-ten. Kitty will romp, run, jump, dash everywhere. It will swat, bite, pounce and jump at every shadow, shoe, even its own tail. Encourage every bounce, every jump. Kitty is curious, discovering its world, enjoying being a cat! This is your time to be entertained by its antics!

PetSpan III : Adolescence Concern Recommended Preventive Care (six months to eighteen months of age)

Teeth By six months of age most of the permanent teeth should have arrived. Occasionally the baby teeth have refused to fall out. See your veterinarian if this seems to be the case. Otherwise the permanent teeth can be forced to become crooked and/or periodontal disease can develop. Now is the time to acclimatize the cat to handling the mouth and teeth. Rub your fingers across the teeth from time to time. If this is too icky, buy some disposable plastic gloves.

Immunity Kitten vaccination should have been completed by now. If you've inherited or saved a cat from the pound and it has not gotten its complement of the vaccines indicated earlier, discuss the regime needed now with your veterinarian.

Nutrition Essentially, most breeds of cats are still growing until they reach 18 months of age to complete their teenage years. At this point I would rec-ommend a growth-type food throughout this period. Feed according to the diet's recommendation but use body condition as your monitor. As long as you are able to feel and see ribs without the impression of 'thinness', the cat is eating enough. If the ribs become predominate or unidentifiable then increase the diet or cut back respectively. Mixed feeding of canned and dry food is best. Water, freshened daily, is essential. Provided the kitten does not produce diarrhea as a result, give fresh milk regularly. Some cats are not good drinkers. They ignore fresh milk or water at their peril. If you have a cat that snubs the water dish, feed primarily canned food. Canned cat food, perhaps with 75% or more water content, will provide the water intake necessary for metabolic, digestive, kidney and eliminative functions. At this age your cat is training you as to it's likes and dislikes. Try to remain objective to be at least a little bit judgmental. Treats may be rewarded by purrs and rubs along your leg but as with dogs, cut back on the cat food for the day according to the number of calories in the treats you are giving.

Training The cat's teen years can be a productive training period — training the so-called cat 'owner' that is. The cat 'owner' will develop a distinct vocabulary such as: You don't like that? Sorry Kitty! Want some Milky Poo? No? Not Now? Sorry Kitty! Now don't bite, don't bite, Owww! Stop scratching on the couch...oh no, another patch coming up.

The cat will begin a series of obedience training programs designed for the owner. Ultimately the owner will become subservient to the real master. The owner can be trained later to take your older body for a walk if you accept wearing a collar and leash.

But seriously, cat training involves behavior reading books that discuss normal and aberrant cat behavior as this is far too great a topic to cover superficially here. A list of books is included in a following appendix.

HairCoat Daily brushing as described above, from head to tail rather than against the grain as in dogs (some cats will tolerate it but most will chew your hand off if you brush 'the wrong way'). Regular inspection for flea dirt, ticks, lumps and bumps can produce evidence of things to bring to the vet's attention.

Parasites Assuming that fecal examination and eradication medication has already been done, the only concern for worms comes from environmental reinfestation. If the cat has fields nearby where mice and moles can readily be caught and eaten then rechecks of the stool is in order. Worms can also be picked up by exposure to other cats. External parasites include primarily fleas and ear mites. Fleas, if allowed can suck enough blood form an animal to make it anemic. Cats can readily scoop ear mites from grass. These bugs live only in the ear but cause severe pain and itchiness. If you see dark, dry granules in one or both ears and the cat is scratching frequently see your veterinarian. The clinic will need to examine a swab under a microscope to confirm that the bugs are present, then prescribe medication to kill the beasts.

Exercise Teenagers must have regular, energetic exercise. Cats at this age usually get their exercise from play. It is critically important to provide balls, toys, anything that will encourage running, jumping and playing. Your teen cat could become a plump adolescent if there is little to do to get them off the couch. Consider a second cat (or even a dog) as a companion for your cat. Dogs and cats are left alone for hours and hours. They may not feel inclined to exercise due to boredom. A second pet provides the mate to chase and play with. Pet owners often neglect walking their dog or cat even when they do get home from work. That companion pet helps stimulate both the owner and the two or more pets to get active, play and exercise. This is especially important at and during the later phases in life when the body slows down. Cats and dogs can keep their youth, keep old age at bay, if they have companions to keep them active.

Spay/Neuter Teenagers become sexually active during this period of time. They become sexually attracted to one another. Left to nature we would end up with dozens of dogs and cats in every household. As it is, stray cats roaming the neighborhood consummate enough relationships to add to the existing surplus. Animal shelters are full of unwanted kittens and adult cats that will never find a home. Neutering a male cat will secure a more stable personality and ensure a longer contented life. More importantly, neutering will prevent or stop a male cat's proclivity for 'marking'. Male cats particularly, delineate their territory by spraying urine around its boundaries. Since the household may be the entire territory, or a part of it, if the cat also goes outside, they will spray urine on the curtains, bedsheets, laundry and behind the couch. You may not notice the smell as much when you live in the same environment but visiting friends and family will immediately detect the sharp pungent bite of cat pee as soon as they cross your threshold. Neuter!

Spaying a female cat will lengthen her life and protect her from attacks of stray males. Mammary Cancer is greatly reduced and Pyometra, where the lining of the uterus becomes severely infected, though less common in the female cat, is also eliminated as a risk.

PetSpan IV : Young Adult

Preventive Care (18 months in cat years - equivalent to the early 30s)

Teeth Regular examination of the gum line for evidence of plaque build-up, tartar, gingivitis or periodontal disease is essential. Early detection and dental prophylaxis will ensure that the cat will not lose teeth. Halitosis is a good indicator. Sometimes a cat will refuse to eat dry food because it simply is too sore in the mouth to chew. Your veterinarian is your cat's dentist - make an appointment.

Immunity Annual Vaccinations: * Panleukopenia, Rhinotracheitis, Calicivirus, Chlamydia * Leukemia * Rabies: In endemic areas (where rabies predominates as a disease in skunk, fox, raccoons and other animals in the wild, as well as significant incidence of the disease in the pet population) get the cat vaccinated annually. In areas where the disease is less prevalent, ask for the three-year vaccine. Check with local regulations as well. Islands, great (like the British Isles) and small, have strict regulations for rabies vaccination, particularly if the disease has been eradicated from the island.

Nutrition Cats are carnivores by nature so that a well-balanced maintenance diet that provides higher protein levels with a properly balanced vitamin-mineral content is essential. Canned and dry food feeding is better than only one or the other. Crunching dry foods helps clean away oral bacteria from the teeth that could contribute to dental problems. Cats may be fed once a day. It is important however, to feed according to lifestyle. If the cat is relatively active throughout the day, two or three feedings are still better.

Training Expanding the vocabulary for the human takes place at this age. After establishing a healthy discipline in the owner's early years, the cat can now concentrate on communication training. Advice to the owner is often futile, the cat will remain in control. Do you really think the Egyptians built the pyramids for pharaohs?

Hair-Coat Keep brushing!

Parasites Fecals should be checked if mice are still on the diet, or social habits include exposure to other cats. Checking for external parasites should be a life-long hunt.

Exercise This is an age where exercise cannot be neglected. If feeding guidelines are ignored the cat can become a proverbial, literal, fat cat. Encourage playfulness.

PetSpan V : Middle Age

Recommended Preventive Care (human equivalent of 40s to 50s)

Annual Exam Preventive measures can be instituted with early diagnosis. An annual physical examination helps to find disorders before they become problems.

Teeth The mouth is aging and the wear and tear on the teeth and gums may have led to some form of periodontal disease by now. See your veterinarian for advice as to the veterinary dentistry needed. It is very important to do so in order to save teeth from extraction and permanent damage to the gingiva.

Immunity Most veterinarians advise annual vaccinations throughout the life of a cat. Repeated annual vaccinations with multiple vaccines seems a considerable affront to the immune system. Perhaps a compromise is a two-year schedule for the 'booster' or selective immunization of endemic diseases such as Panleukopenia, Rhinotracheitis, Calicivirus and Chlamydia. However, if the cat goes outdoors or is boarded in a kennel often, then I still recommend annual vaccination for these distemper, cold and flu viruses. Feline Leukemia should be boostered annually as well as Rabies if the cat is an outdoor cat (every three years with the appropriate vaccine if an indoor cat). Consultation with your veterinarian as to the best vaccination regime for your pet in your environment would seem most sensible.

Nutrition A middle-age paunch on a cat will drag along the floor. Middle-aged cats often feel that their humans have reached the apogee of their intelligence so no longer try to teach them further tricks. As a result they begin to loll around the house, just eating, sleeping, eating sleeping —- just like the human couch potato. Now more than ever the human servant must observe the rib cage. Feed at the low end of the feeding guidelines or even a calorie reduced diet. Seek medical advice if the cat is obviously obese.

Training Unless you enjoy subservience, read those books on Cat Behavior!

Hair-Coat Keep brushing!

Parasites Keep checking!

Exercise Middle aged cats become complacent about play-time. Humans around the world can be seen on all fours (elbows and knees), trying to rekindle that whimsical feline swat at a ball of wool or thread of ribbon only to be ignored categorically by that stare —- the look deep into your eyes that says, "See how low you've become, I've accomplished my mission!" Cat owners do not despair! Do not give up! When you are not around, Tabby might be seen playfully pouncing on that thread —- never however, in your presence. Keep supplying Kitty with play toys otherwise exercise is diminished to the occasional swat at the dog's nose. As mentioned above a companion cat added earlier in life would have prevented your need to crawl around the floor to get kitty to exercise. You could consider another cat now but remember that a new pet at this stage in life could cause cat number one to have behavior problems —- it may not accept an adult cat for example, may even not accept a new kitten. It is still a good solution to diminished activity but consult your veterinarian for advice on behavioral issues.

PetSpan VI : Senior Citizens

Recommended Preventive Care (human equivalent of over-the-hill).

Annual Exam Even more important for the geriatric cat, perhaps even bi-annual check-ups. Remember that a cat's year could be seven human years sobody systems could need a much more frequent checkup.

Teeth It is ever so important now to go to the veterinarian for regular dental check ups. I would recommend semi-annual visits unless your cat has permitted you to brush their teeth, in which case an annual dental exam is sufficient. Taking tabby to the vet for bi-annual exams as indicated above will include examination of the teeth. Old cats do not like to gum their food, healthy teeth are critical to prolonging health and longevity. And veterinary medicine has not yet developed dentures for cats and dogs. Careful attention to early signs of dental disease will prevent early loss of teeth, and Tabby will live longer!

Immunity While the immune system may have vigorously maintained high titres of vaccinated antigens during PetSpan IV and V it's vigor is diminished with age. A geriatric body has battled with so many antigens and germs over the years that it has spent much of it's arsenal. Annual vaccinations for the elderly cat, in my view, are paramount. I recommend annual: * Panleukopenia, Rhinotracheitis, Calicivirus and Chlamydia * Feline Leukemia * Rabies

Nutrition As with dogs and humans, age brings diminished senses of smell and taste. Diets that are designed for the aged cat have not only made adjustments to the changes in metabolic rates, they are often more aromatic and flavored. As a result the cat will be more interested in eating. Eating an adequate diet balanced for the older cat helps them to live longer. Common sense suggests that you find a good geriatric diet. Ask your veterinarian for options as thereare several on the market.

Training You can teach an old cat owner new tricks! In fact, maintaining lifelong learning will make the cat owner's life longer and happier. Cat's live to train their owner. Never stop learning from your cat.

Hair-Coat Keep brushing!

Parasites Keep checking!

Exercise Old cats will lay about all day long if allowed. Don't allow it. Keep offering play toys. If your cat will let you (especially if you've introduced a collar and leash at a younger age), take Tabby for a walk. Consider introducing a new kitten to the household (Tabby will be indignant, but the kitten will force it to get up from wherever it waddles to for a nap). Exercise is important to the dying day —- and that's another important reason to consider another pet to be a companion for the older pet —- because when your precious cat dies, the surviving pet will continue to be your companion. Both you and your other pet will miss the deceased animal. But you will still have that treasured invaluable fur to stroke and the love from a gifted companion in your time of need.

PetSpan VII : Memory

There are two concerns with the final phase of a pet's existence. When do we put the cat to sleep? and how do we cope with the loss? As mentioned above in the section on dog care, your veterinarian is by nature and extension, concerned with both.

Euthanasia Veterinarians are faced with putting an animal to sleep all too often. It can be just as difficult for them as it is for you. Yet we have accepted euthanasia as a sensible alternative to suffering.

As with the dog, good memories will come with the deed if we address the key issues:

1. **Quality of Life** Is the course of treatment, that could prolong this cat's life going to prolong pain and suffering? Remember that I discussed 'sick cats' as being somewhat different than dogs. The sick cat syndrome is a difficult one for veterinarians to contend with.

I have seen cats at death's door —-- no, halfway through the door —- and return from the other side to become vibrant and alive again. Perhaps they really do have nine lives!

Assessing the likelihood of survival is difficult. You must trust your veterinarian's judgment.

2. **Objectivity** Are we keeping this cat alive out of selfishness? Is it because we can't cope with the loss that we are blind to the pain it is suffering? Step back literally and figuratively to look at the situation from as distant a view as you can.

3. **Quantity of Life** Is the course of treatment going to maintain the cat for a reasonable length of time? Determine how much time is reasonable. Your practitioner can help immensely with this.

4. **Economics** Veterinary Care, particularly intensive care, nursing, drugs and monitoring can add up.

Can you afford the price and are you willing to extend every effort at any cost within your budget?

Death Loss of life from disease or accident can occur at any point in the continuum of the PetSpan. Adherence to the preventive procedures can minimize the risk of premature death but longevity is not an automatic guarantee for any creature's existence. Death is one of the stops along the road of life, perhaps the last exit ramp, perhaps a door to another place. Whether there is another series of stops for human or beast is up to individual belief, or faith.

Coping with Grief Your cat's death is your opportunity to begin a lifetime of reflection on the joys and friendship conferred by this companion over the years. If you need grief counseling, get it. If not, walk yourself through the process towards a goal of happy memories.

Resources for Grief Counseling Check with the closest veterinary college as most if not all of them have trained staff who can help. Local clergy, especially pet lovers can also be helpful. As indicated in the canine section above there are resources at nearby veterinary colleges. Michigan State University's College of Veterinary Medicine has a pet loss hot line for example, (517-336-2696) provided for people who are having trouble coping with the loss of a pet. These resources are often only available during specified times so check with the institutions for details.

The greatest resource is your own conviction. Give yourself permission to grieve for your pet. Avoid comparing your grief with anyone else's. Simply accept your own feelings about the loss and find healthy ways to express them. Seek professional counsel if the need is there for someone to help you through.

Coda IV - PetSpeak

Fastrack to Signs that Say, "Take me the the Vet!"

Will Rogers, the whimsical American humorist, talked about the fact that a veterinarian must be a good doctor, since their patients can't tell them what's ailin' them. This apparent lack of communication between human and beast could make diagnosis, treatment and prognosis difficult. Yet there is communication. The science of veterinary practice incorporates a knowledge and application of millions of facts. The art of veterinary medicine is the practice of intuition. Intuition can only be achieved through years of academic study, experience, and a lifelong dedication to learning. It must also integrate an intangible capacity to detect a level of wordless dialogue.

Despite this innate skill, education and experience, the veterinarian cannot provide effective care without the help of the pet owner. This book has been written with two goals. One, to entertain with stories about veterinary experience. The objective has been to reinforce the bond between human and pet. Second, to give the dog and cat owner the 'need to know' information about pet care, with an objective to help ensure that readers have the ammunition necessary to work with their veterinarian towards a long and healthful life for their pet.

The pet owner can help by taking an active role in preventive care. Regular 'wellness' visits to the vet according to the PetSpan HealthStyle Plan has the potential for optimum health, and a longer life. If and when the pet needs medical intervention, the pet owner can help the veterinarian with two essential sets of observations: an accurate history and recognition of symptoms.

History

Precise medical history is indispensable to a veterinarian at the outset of the medical examination. A diagnosis can be missed if the pet owner cannot give exact descriptions of timeliness and intensity. It can set the train of thought down the wrong track. What if your dog was presented to a veterinarian with diarrhea. There are approximately 199 possible causes. The practitioner cannot sift through that many conditions to tell you what is causing your dog's diarrhea without correct historical facts. If you say, "I think he's had it since this morning," when in fact the runny stools have been evident for four days, the possible diagnoses could be completely different —- and your practitioner could be sadly misled towards an empty train of thought.

Pet Owners' Role Regarding Medical History:

Make a point to keep a pet log book to write down times, dates and symptoms. Perhaps the book will never be used. If it ever has to be, it could be worth a life. Since your pet cannot speak, give the data to your practitioner as a modicum of translation. Pay particular attention to time, intensity and environment.

Timeliness
1. When did the symptoms begin?
2. Were they sporadic or continuous?
3. Has this happened gradually or rapidly?
4. Has this ever happened before? When?
5. How long has each symptom been evident?
6. What was the exact sequence of events and symptoms?
7. What time of day has this happened? (only in the morning, night, evening, right after eating, all day long...)

Intensity
1. Has the frequency (of breathing, coughing, eating, bowel movements, urinating etc. etc.) increased, decreased, stopped?
2. Has the (cough, urine, feces etc.) increased, decreased in volume?
3. Has the (lump, bump, sore...) remained the same, gotten larger, smaller?
4. What is the character of the symptom? (is the stool dark, normal or tarry? Is there blood in it? Is there a different, stronger odor?) Consider color and consistency changes of the stool, urine, vomitus. It would even help bringing in the deposit to show the vet.
5. What are the conditions that don't appear normal? (is there blood or mucous in the stool? Blood in the urine? Is the dog or cat straining to pass urine or stool?) (is there swelling, discoloration?)

Environment

1. Have you changed anything? When? (new food, moved, new rugs, plants, family members)
2. Has there been something special done to the environment? (disinfectants, lawn treatments, weed spraying, pest exterminator...)
3. Has any treatment been given at home? What? When?
4. Has this ever been treated by another veterinarian? When? What treatment was provided and to what effect?

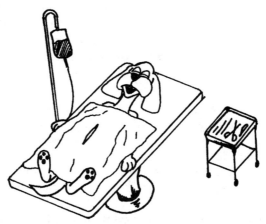

A Word about Compliance

One of the of the most frustrating things that concerns practitioners is 'compliance'. Compliance refers to the best case scenario where the pet owner gives all of the medication prescribed at the correct times. Yet it may well be that the majority of clients fail to follow directions. Veterinarians are called several days after they had correctly diagnosed and treated a case, only to have an irate client berate them for the animal's poor response.

The fault could very well lie in the court of the owner. If each and every pill or ounce of fluid is not given for the period prescribed on the label — - and especially if the pet owner stops giving the medication at a quarter to half way through the treatment process, there are two possible consequences: the pet may get better in spite of the cessation of medicine, perhaps due to the medicine's assistance, but largely due to the pet's constitution. More often than not however, the pet is likely to get worse! It may very well develop secondary problems, if not resistance to the medication.

Every veterinarian has had a client come to them to say, "The treatment didn't work at the last vet!" only to find (provided the pet owner is honest about the negligence which is not always the case) that the correct treatment was prescribed but only a portion was given. I thought it was getting better and didn't need any more pills!"

I urge you to comply. Whenever a prescription is given to treat your pet, give it all and give it according to the times recommended. There are distinct reasons for the schedule. The drugs have been clinically tested to work based on the dosages suggested and the length of time directed. Anything less is begging for failure.

If the medication does not seem to be working, call the veterinarian back to discuss it. It may be that a little more time is needed, perhaps a refill of the same medication. It could also be that the medicine simply cannot work against that particular organism. Many germs of the 90s have evolved with an acquired taste for antibiotics. It could be just a fine white wine to them rather than a toxic dose. In that case the veterinarian will only be too glad to shift thinking and prescribe a more deadly potion.

Don't consider changing veterinarians just because a particular course of treatment isn't working. Work with your practitioner as a team towards the resolution of the problem. The only times you should need to change veterinarians include:
* moving to a new location too far from your previous practitioner
* unable to communicate with your veterinary clinician (or staff)

Compliance with recommended treatment, and keeping in touch with your veterinarian will ensure better service for you and more certain resolution of problems for your pet.

If you truly feel that your practitioner is mistaken with his or her diagnosis or treatment —- tell them! If you feel that you would like them to refer the case to a specialist —- tell them! Your veterinarian is often thinking of the rising costs of the case and may hesitate to refer because of the significant expense that could bring. Veterinarians are human. They are caregivers. They empathize with the pet owner as much sometimes as they are fond of the animal.

Compliance need not be a problem. A responsible pet owner who follows directions to the letter eliminates the issue. But if the 'letter' is impossible to follow, call the vet and tell them. "Doctor, if I follow these directions I'm going to have to get up at three every morning for two weeks to give this damn medicine. I'm not sure I like this dog that much!" Your veterinarian will likely change the medicine or the dosage/schedule. After all we don't want our pet owners to resent their pets...

Symptoms

As your pet's guardian you really only need to observe the norm in your friend's daily routine. If and when the following signs come in to play, your role is not to interpret, diagnose and treat. Certainly minor ailments can be tended to at home. As more symptoms are added to the condition the complexity of diagnosis increases. In other words, if your dog is simply coughing, a particular list of possibilities might be considered. If it is coughing and has diarrhea, there are at least two body systems affected, and many more possibilities. Add vomiting and it may narrow the differentials down or make it even more complicated to figure out. Use the chart below as another guideline, but remember that more often than not, several symptoms coexist in a sick animal. Let your dog or cat tell you when to call for advice.

Translation of Dogeze and Cateze

Dogs and cats can talk, rather overtly in fact, particularly when it comes to the symptoms that they show as a result of a disease process. I have translated the messages such signs tell the pet owner. Use the chart and the descriptors to understand when your pet is telling you, "Take me to the Vet!"

Symptoms Categorized	Dogeze	Cateze	Translation
	Wf	Mu	Watch this. If it doesn't go away, ask the vet for an opinion on our next visit.
	Wuf	Mew	Give Doc a call to see what he/she thinks about this.
	Woof!	Meow!	Something's wrong, make an appointment as soon as you can.
	Wrroof!	Meoww!	Call the damn vet! Right now!
Thin	Wuf	Mew	**Note** Thinness can be in the genes in some breeds but it can also be due to endocrine disease, early illness, poor nutrition.
Emaciated	Wrroof!	Meoww!	Evidenced by sunken eyes, prominent ribs - very serious.
Obese	Woof!	Meow!	Over-eating is only one possibility, a thyroid or pituitary problem could be present --- you need the vet!

Symptoms Categorized	Dogeze	Cateze	Translation
Dull Hair/Coat	Wuf	Mew	A premium diet may be all that is needed, but it could indicate parasitism or disease. Take in a stool sample at least.
Not Grooming	Huh?	Mew	Dogs lick themselves clean of burrs and debris from between the toes (and disgustingly the fur around the penis!) but not with the passion and consistency of the cat. If a cat stops grooming the coat can become dull and matted.
Loss of hair	Woof!	Meow!	There are many possibilities for alopecia (loss of hair in spots or whole body). The size and nature of the spot or spots are important.
Non-elastic Skin	Wrroof!	Meoww!	Loss of stretchiness of the skin can indicate dehydration. Lift a fold of skin from the neck. If it doesn't bounce back immediately upon release get the pet to the vet!
Black Skin	Wuf	Mew	Some animals inherit dark pigmented skin. This symptom refers to blackened skin that wasn't there before. It tells the vet of possible causes.
Blue Skin	Wrroof!	Meoww!	Bluish discoloration indicates venous blood in the capillaries. If generalized, distress from disease such as pneumonia could be present. If localized to an appendage it could be poor circulation.
Yellow Skin	Wrroof!	Meoww!	If non-pigmented skin seems abnormally yellowish in tint check the mucous membranes of the lips and the conjunctiva (red area, normally, around the eyes). If these are yellowish there could be jaundice. Get attention immediately!

Symptoms Categorized	Dogeze	Cateze	Translation
Skin Sores	Wuf	Mew	Note the size of the sore, if there is more than one or several. Where is it/are they on the body, is it /are they level with the skin, raised, devoid of fur, scaly, moist, reddened, bleeding, oozing, is the pet licking at it/them, scratching at it/them? Adding any of these parameters to the equation and the animal is telling you to call for an appointment!
Lumps & Bumps	Wuf	Mew	Again note the size, number, location. Watch the pet to see if they are bothered by it/them by licking or scratching. If you decide to watch it as your pet has indicated here, note any change (larger, smaller, oozing, irritating the pet more). Now the animal is telling you to look up the vet's number! This is especially true of swellings of the mammary tissue of female dogs and cats. They can succumb to several types of breast cancer, preventable by early surgical mastectomies.
Bug & Bites	Wuf	Mew	You may never see the flea but you can follow the trail. Flea dirt is the excreta of the flea, mostly blood, from a bite. Drop some water on it and it will turn red. Some parasites on the skin are microscopic so you'll never see them. You will see tiny pustules where they've bitten and/or the self-mutilation the animal has inflicted by biting and scratching incessantly. Consider the redness you cause to your skin when you scratch at a mosquito bite. Imagine never putting lotion on the bite, nor having the sense to stop scratching.

Symptoms Categorized	Dogeze	Cateze	Translation
Swellings	Woof!	Meow!	Pets can have swollen joints that indicate injury, inflammation and/or infection of the affected joint. This may also be accompanied by fever, perhaps with loss of appetite. Call for an appointment. Other swellings can be due to abscesses under the skin. Cats are especially prone to Cat Fight Disease whereby a tooth or claw from an enemy cat has punctured the skin injecting bacteria through the hole. The bacteria grow and produce toxic substances. Both their presence and the toxins cause the body to pour white blood cells into the area. The result is a growing mass of pus under the skin. If the toxins or poisons enter the blood stream, blood poisoning occurs resulting in fever and pain, eventually damage to the heart, liver and kidneys. The swelling in either case may also be warm to the touch. In any case, call the vet!
Stink!	Wuf	Mew	Peeeuww! Dogs and cats can smell badly for several reasons, some of them distinct medical problems. Dogs love to roll around on dead, decayed fish and road-kill. The stench rubbee into their coat can be horrible. A bath, or two, is in order. Scented sprays or a few drops of Aniseed oil onto the coat can help (after the bath). But foul odor could also be a sign of impacted or infected anal glands; or, a rancid smell could indicate a cutaneous seborrhea; a smell of acetone could signal advanced diabetes; severe dermatitis causes a pungent, disagreeable smell. Your vet has smelled them all and you may need to test his/her nose with this one.

Symptoms Categorized	Dogeze	Cateze	Translation
Lame	Wuf	Mew	Call for advice if lameness persists, make and appointment if pain is evident. Swollen, painful or warm joints can indicate arthritic problems. Describe frequency, severity, number of limbs involved to your vet. Often the pet doesn't limp as badly at the clinic as the stress of going there makes them forget.
Worms in Stool	Woof!	Meow!	The vet would need to see them or get an accurate description in order to prescribe the correct remedy.
Itchy & Scratchy	Woof!	Meow!	One of the most common symptoms in dogs. A bit of scratching is normal. Constant scratching needs care. It may not be fleas or other parasites for it could be related to a food allergy or skin disease. Pets can lose sleep and become irritable if itchiness is not alleviated. Wouldn't you?
Bum Scooting	Woof!	Meow!	This is particularly characteristic of dogs although cats may be seen to rub their hind end along the floor as well. It is not necessarily a sign of worms as those old wives have decreed. Granted there could be some itchiness from tapeworm segments especially if the worm sections are still alive and wriggling around the rectum. Lift up the dog's tail to see if there is evidence of 'grains of rice' that indicate tapeworm segments. Otherwise call the vet if the scooting is persistent. The animal may have impacted anal glands. These are small scent glands on either side of the anus. Dogs and

Symptoms Categorized	Dogeze	Cateze	Translation
			attention to the teeth and gums, perhaps even checking for systemic problems.
Demeanor:			
Listless	Woof!	Meow!	It may just be sad, but could be feverish, toxic, or anemic.
Apathetic	Wrroof!	Meoww!	Pets generally live for the moment, if showing indifference, something's amiss.
Restlessness	Wuf	Mew	Unable to settle, sometimes looking at the abdomen. They're telling you that something's bothering them.
Frantic	Woof!	Meow!	If there is unusual frenzy take precaution not to be bitten and call the vet.
Whine and Cry	Wuf	Mew	If intense and unrelenting make an appointment. Maybe you forgot to feed them.
Eyes:			
Tears	Wf	Mu	Epiphora is the staining of tears on the face due to obstructed lachrymal (tear) ducts. Dogs and cats don't cry. If there is evidence of wetness or irritation around one or both eyes it can indicate several things. Trichiasis is a condition where the eyelashes are turned inwards and rub against the eyeball causing considerable soreness and tearing. These are correctable irritations by your veterinarian.
Swollen Eye(s)	Wuf	Mew	If one or both eyes seem to bulge beyond normal, see the vet. Some breeds of dogs have normally protruding eyes (Pugs, Pekes, etc.). Pets whose eyes bulge when they aren't supposed to, could be developing glaucoma.

Symptoms Categorized	Dogeze	Cateze	Translation
			Bluish discoloration of the eye, sometimes the entire eye, sometimes the lens, could signal an adverse response to Canine Adenovirus (rare), glaucoma, infection, cataract. Seek attention.
Blinking	Woof!	Meow!	Excessive blinking could indicate an ulcer or scratch on the cornea, perhaps a foreign body (something in the eye). You wouldn't want to leave this for long if it was your eye.

Ears:

Symptoms Categorized	Dogeze	Cateze	Translation
Smelly Ear(s)	Woof!	Meow!	If a dog or cat's ears smell badly, particularly if the pet is scratching excessively at one or both of them, there could be an infected ear or two. The infection could be secondary to ear mites. If a human had the pain and itchiness of some of the infected ears I've seen, they would have gone insane. Get attention right away.
Itchy Ear(s)	Woof!	Meow!	This too could indicate infection but often signals the presence of ear mites, microscopic parasites that live inside an animal's ear or ears. Think about it! Dozens of creatures scrambling around in your ear, biting and sucking at the flesh. Don't let the pet suffer, call for attention.
			If ear mites infestation and/or ear infection is left unchecked the violent shaking of the head can cause vessels between the folds of skin to burst. The result is a 'hematoma'-- where the ear flap has become a sack of blood and fluid. The remedy is drainage and surgery, necessary as soon as pos-

sible. At the same time the under-lying cause needs to be treated.

Nose:

| Warm Nose | Wf | Mu | The expression 'a warm nose means fever' is an old wives' tale that simply doesn't hold true. Certainly the nose of the dog and are normally cool and moist but if they've been rooting in the dirt or dust, and/or in an arid house, the nose can be dry and warm. |

| Sneezing | Wf | Mu | Occasional sneezing is normal. After all, if you had the keen sense of smell of a dog or cat and spent most of your life on the floor where dust and heavy odors from socks and shoes abound, you'd sneeze too! If the sniffling becomes too frequent though, check it out. There could be an upper respiratory infection or a foreign body up the nose. |

Symptoms Categorized	Dogeze	Cateze	Translation
Coughing	Woof!... cough	Meow!... cough	Here's where you could be help-ful. Think of Barry Berry and Trinity. Articulation of the cough may help the vet. Often the pet may feel stressed once at the clin-ic and will no longer cough. If you can describe or verbalize the cough it will help to localize. How often (frequent, infrequent), pro-ductive or non-productive; short or protracted (kof! or Coughghgghghghggh!); loud or soft; deep or shallow. Is it a wheeze, barking cough, tremulous cough or croaking?

Mouth:

Symptoms Categorized	Dogeze	Cateze	Translation
Dirty Teeth	Woof!	Meow!	Discolored teeth from plaque and tartar inevitably means there is also gingivitis and periodontal dis-ease. The pet needs the veterinary dentist!

Stomach/ Bowels

Symptoms Categorized	Dogeze	Cateze	Translation
Vomiting	Woof!	Mew?	Differing translations for the dog and cat. Cats may vomit from fur-balls with little or no need for concern. Dogs generally don't vomit as frequently. Occasional vomiting from both dogs and cats is common. Remember they are on the floor, they swallow many disgusting things that would make any respectable stomach retch. It's when vomiting persists, is accom-panied by other systems, that attention is needed.
Diarrhea	Woof!	Meow!	Emanations from the other end is just as serious. Simple digestive upsets happen to us all and simply need watching to see if the loose stool persists. But if any or all signs of fever, pain, vomiting, anorexia (not eating) are also pre-sent, then you need immediate

Symptoms Categorized	Dogeze	Cateze	Translation
			care. Be able to describe the diarrhea well. Take some with you if you can.
Constipation	Woof!	Meow!	Hard dry stool is not uncommon. Consumption of your favorite socks can slow the bowel down. It's when the cat or dog strains, won't eat, vomits, even sways uncontrollably on the hind legs that this constipation is serious. That missing sock may be causing an obstruction of the bowel; an x-ray and surgery could be urgently needed!
Straining	Wrroof!	Meoww!	This may not be constipation. Dogs and cats are known to get bones stuck in the lower bowel. Remedy: don't feed them bones that splinter.
Fart	Wfme?	Mme?	One might not hear a cat fart but they can and do. Dogs tend to 'pass gas' slowly, quietly, sonorously. In either case the fart can be odorous enough to clear a room. It is a normal process. Digestion of food results in gaseous production. Burps and farts erupt. Some foods are more causative than others but be prepared to tolerate occasional whiffs of normal bodily functions. If passing wind becomes too frequent perhaps the animal is eating too rapidly and swallowing too much air in the process. Perhaps the food, or ingredients in the food, disagree with the individual pet's digestive abilities. Feeding smaller quantities more often (or putting a large ball or hockey puck into the dish with the food)

Symptoms Categorized	Dogeze	Cateze	Translation
			may slow down the ravenous eating habits and cut down the gas. Otherwise you may need to change the diet.
Chest:			
Rapid Breathing	Woof!	Meow!	It is not uncommon for the dog to breathe irregularly, but thid should last a short time. If a dog or cat breathes rapidly, continously, there could be fever, lung or heart problem, perhaps it is a sign of pain.
Difficult Breathing	Wrroof!	Meoww!	'Dyspnea' is deep labored breathing. One of several serious chest problems (diaphragmatic hernia, fluid in the chest, stress, toxicity, lung disease) could be the cause. Sometimes dyspnea only occurs after exercise. In any case seek immediate attention.
Abdomen:			
Swollen Belly	Wrroof!	Meoww!	Especially with deep chested dogs like Jake Burtle's Rambo, a sudden distended abdomen, usually with a splayed stance and gasping for air, indicates a bloated or dilated stomach, or more seriously a twisted stomach (in the dog. Get help immediately! In a puppy or kitten just after eating, bloated tummy can be normal.) Kittens and puppies with swollen abdomens and thin, could be parasitized. In a female dog or cat that hasn't been spayed, call your friends - you've got a litter to get rid of. If you have a female dog with a swollen belly along with listlessness, vomiting, perhaps a discharge of pus from the vagina, call the vet right away, she could have pyometra (preventable if you spay!).

Symptoms Categorized	Dogeze	Cateze	Translation
Bladder and area:			
Peesalot	Wrroof!	Meoww!	It may be difficult to distinguish between frequent urination and whether there is an increase in urine volume but any increase in urinating frequency demands immediate attention. Both dogs and cats can suffer from diabetes. Cats, especially males are.subject to urethral blockage. Bladder stones, renal (kidney) infection or failure could be the problem. All are serious.
Painful Pee	Huh?	Meoww!	Although dogs can suffer from obstruction it is the male cat that commonly presents an acute lower urinary tract disease, usually seen as painfully attempting to urinate - call immediately, there is no time to lose! It is possible for dogs to seem to have painful urination when in fact they have an enlarged prostate. Don't ignore such symptoms in a dog.
Bloody urine	Woof!	Meow!	Bladder stones are more cmmon in dogs and blood in the urine could indicate their presence, often with no other sign. If a dog or cat has blood in the urine there could be a bladder infection, obstruction, tumor. Attention is needed.
Penis Licking	Wf	Mu	This vulgar habit of the male dog, even the male cat, is not uncommon, causing heads to turn in mixed company. Makes it difficult to reply to a child's question, "What's Rover doing mommy?" It's there and they can reach it - so it happens, okay? If however,

Symptoms Categorized	Dogeze	Cateze	Translation
			the licking becomes incessant and there is a purulent (pussy) discharge there could be an inflammation or infection of the preputial mucosa (folds of tissue around the penis). Call the vet if you see this.
Swollen Scrotum	Woof!	Huh?	Less common in cats, male dogs that are not neutered can suffer from testicular cancer or simple inflammation. See the vet as soon as you notice it. Better, neuter your male dog.
Male Erection	Wrroof!	Mu	Young dogs especially may exhibit erections, arousal, mount your auntie's leg during tea, even masturbate. Neutering dogs and cats at six months of age will prevent most of these social faux pas.

Nervous System:

Symptoms Categorized	Dogeze	Cateze	Translation
Seizure	Wrroof!	Meoww!	Dogs more commonly suffer from seizures. It is difficult but important not to panic. Turn down the lights and keep all other stimuli to a minimum. (In other words don't scream, "For God's Sake George Do Something!") The dog may be able to pick up surrounding stress and disturbance to worsen and lengthen the seizure. There are many possible causes from an epileptic cause to a brain tumor. See your veterinarian. Describe the intensity, duration, frequency, nature of the attack as the dog may not elicit the seizure in front of the vet.
Paralysis	Wrroof!	Meoww!	The opposite of seizure, paralysis is a lack of nervous stimulation. One limb, hind limbs or all four legs could be affected. There could be damage to the spinal cord. History is very important. Has there been

Symptoms Categorized	Dogeze	Cateze	Translation
			an accident? Has the pet been getting regular rabies vaccinations?
Ataxia	Wrroof!	Meoww!	If the pet doesn't seem to have control of the walking process, sways from side to side, perhaps falls on its hind legs, there could be minor damage to the spinal cord or central nervous system; effect from a poisonous substance; or it could be a middle ear problem.
Self-mutilation	Wrroof!	Meoww!	Severe itchiness of the skin caused by disease of the nervous system can cause frenzied attack of the tail or any site on the skin; the animal can lick, scratch or tear the flesh. The tail can be a special target. Get to the vet!
Fainting	Wrroof!	Meoww!	Sudden loss of consciousness can be caused by heart problems, oftenseen in pets with congestive heart failure ('heart block' is also a condition causing fainting, common in some Schnauzers) but could also be related to a cerebral hemorrhage or thrombosis.

Behavior Problems:

To properly describe symptoms related to problems with behavior —- and their significance —- would require at least another complete book in order to cover everything. Suffice to say, that any change in behavior deserves a call to the vet. It is even difficult at times to know whether your pet is exhibiting normal behavior. So call anyway, even if you think it may be nothing. The cause of the behavior in question could be a disorder of the nervous system, strictly aberrant behavior, or even healthy reactions to the pet's environment.

Healthy behavior can be problematical. For example, it is typical for a dog to sniff at crotches. Animals, including humans, have many more scent glands under the armpits and in the groin. Dogs identify and remember acquaintances by their smell. They would sniff at the armpits, tail and underbelly of any other dog. What's wrong with breathing in the odors of human visitors to the house? —- other than it's embarrassing for the home owner to be greeting the kid's teacher or the spouse's boss only to have them doubled over suddenly by a jab of a warm wet nose between the legs. This is especially stressful as you chase Kramer through the legs of a dozen or more houseguests, screaming, "Kramer stop that!" "Kramer, get down!" as you sheepishly wince an apology to your company who are wiping the drool from their pants and dresses.

Obedience training can be very helpful in minimizing such embarrassing moments but since much of what a dog or cat does is normal for its world, don't expect miracles. Recognize the realities and if you don't want the dog to spear your guests as a routine canine greeting, lock him up beforehand.

There are just too many behavioral symptoms to list here. Consult your veterinarian if the pet is acting in a way that you cannot understand. Such conditions can be classified as personality traits or changes in personality; eating orders or disorders; elimination habits or disorders. For example, if your dog makes a mistake in the house, or the cat starts missing the litter box, these could be signs of disease or behavioral problem. It could be as simple as not being able to hold it till you got home (and/or "You neglected to clean out my litterbox!") to jealousy because of the new baby in the house.

Although we cannot read an animal's mind, the science of animal behavior has given veterinarians significant insight into the rationale behind the actions. If the practitioner cannot help you they can readily find an animal behavior specialist who can help.

So you can see that although animals cannot speak the human language, their bodies speak to us nonetheless. Through observation of normal symptoms we can hear them speak to us when things go awry. We can talk to the animals if we listen with our senses.

Coda V - PetsRead
Recommended Reading

This book has been written as a narrative approach to pet ownership through the eyes and memories of a veterinarian. The format was chosen because there is a plethora of books that take an encyclopedic approach. There are also several authors that write animal stories with such panache that one cannot put the book down. Some of my favorites:

James Harriot
All Things Bright and Beautiful. St. Martin's Press, New York., 1972
All Creatures Great and Small. St. Martin's Press, New York, 1974

These are the first two of many editions and out-takes to follow. Alfred Wight, a veterinarian who practiced in the dales of Yorkshire England after the Second World War, wrote of his life as a rural practitioner under the pseudonym of James Herriot. His images mirror many of the experiences all veterinarians have faced. His evident empathy for animal and human inspired this writing.

Dr. Bruce Fogle

Dr. Fogle graduated from the Ontario Veterinary College near the same time as I. He has written several useful books of instruction for the pet owner including:
The Complete Dog Care Manual. Dorling Kindersley Ltd., London, 1993
This is a comprehensive guide to dog care and health with excellent charts, diagrams and pictures to fully illustrate each subject. The book covers most of the fundamentals of dog ownership including health care, breeding, and first-aid. There is also a chapter on dog shows.

Cat Owners Home Veterinary Handbook
Delbert G. Carlson DVM, and James M. Giffin MD
Howell House Books, New York., N.Y., 1995

The cat until recently, has been relegated to a few back pages of textbooks let alone entire books written specifically on cat health care. Now that the cat is overtaking the dog as the principal family pet there are some excellent books to consider. And, by the way, veterinarians now have textbooks dedicated to feline medicine and surgery. This book gives the cat owner some very good insight into care and feeding. It has an especially good section on emergencies with chart on Home Emergency and Medical Kit.

The Hidden Life of Dogs
Pocket Books, a division of Simon & Schuster, New York, N.Y., 1993
Elizabeth Marshall Thomas

It has taken an anthropologist to present a rationale for dog behavior. By observation of dogs, wild and domestic, Ms. Thomas has provided the reader with insight into the psyche of the canine companion. It makes us stop to think, I hope, of the hidden life of other beasts with which we share this earth.

Old Dogs, Old Friends
Enjoying Your Older Dog
Bonnie Wilcox DVM and Chris Walkowicz

Howell House Books
Our elderly pet deserves special attention. This book, through anecdotes and instructions, shows the physical and behavioral changes that old dogs experience and what the pet owner must do to accommodate them. There is a special section on bereavement counseling for the inevitable result of owning an old dog.

Pet Loss
A Thoughtful Guide for Adults and Children
Herbert A. Nieberg Ph.D. and Arlene Fischer
Harper Perenial

This is a particularly useful book to read or to use for children, if you or they, seem to be having a tough time coming to grips with the loss of your pet. It includes an excellent discussion of separation and the anxieties it brings, as well as covering the different ways in which we are separated from a beloved pet (sudden death, euthanasia, and losses unrelated to death that still elicit grief). The role of the veterinarian in the dynamics of pet loss is presented.

Dog Love
Marjorie Garber
Simon and Schuster, New York, N.Y., 1966

What I like about this book is that the author suggests that perhaps it is the love for dogs that makes us human. My sentiments that I extend to all animals - let's add the human·animal, all races, to the list as well and perhaps Homo sapiens will fit for once.

Dogs for Dummies
Gina Spadafori
IDG Books Worldwide Inc., Foster City, CA., 1996

Another comprehensive book on dog ownership from buying a puppy, training to all facets of dog care by the tongue-in-cheek makers of the Computer technology for Dummies people.

Ask the Vet
Questions and Answers for Cat Owners
Dr. Gary Norsworthy and Dr. Sharon Fooshee
Lifelearn Inc., Guelph, Ontario, Canada, 1997

This is a book for the cat owner who needs more information about the disease or condition the veterinarian has diagnosed. Practitioners simply don't have the time to describe the idiosyncricities of allergies, heart and lung disease, urinary problems, surgical procedures, individual parasites...and on and on. 'Ask the Vet' provides those details in an easy to read format — based on typical client's questions throughout the text. Relevant, easy to understand illustrations help the descriptions.

Ask the Vet
Questions and Answers for Dog Owners
Dr. Gary Norsworthy and Dr. Sharon Fooshee
Lifelearn Inc., Guelph, Ontario, Canada, 1997

The same format as the Cat text, this guide to canine diseases, parasites and common questions provides the dog owner with the answers to critical issues of patient care. Both of these books should be available through veterinary clinicians as well as directly from Lifelearn.

The Doctor's Book of Home Remedies for Dogs and Cats
Rodale Press Inc., Emmaus, Pennsylvania, 1996
Editor: Matthew Hoffman

Although I am normally not an advocate of home remedies because of the inherent danger that the pet owner might misdiagnose and mistreat (resulting in even worse complications), this book is a practical home remedy manual with some merit. There is a good overview of common conditions and their melioration. Topics have been categorized and a panel of experts polled. This provides balance of judgment. The result is an easy to read set of guidelines for home care with some very good preventative advice.

There are so many other authors and texts that it would be insulting to try to list more than a few of my personal favorites. I've probably insulted dozens of excellent authors by not including them here. Despite the wealth of printed volumes I reiterate what I have said before and say again in the following appendix on Internet sites. Speak to your veterinarian on any question you may have. Use books to supplement your understanding, rather than as a replacement for professional care.

CODA VI: PetsWeb

Recommended Web Sites on Animal Care

In the new Millennium I predict a revised axiom: "A lot of learning is a dangerous thing!"

We no longer inhabit a 'James Herriot' globe. Farm animals are production units. Pets are integral family members. The human-animal bond is still intact whether it is the farmer attending the needs of his livestock or the pet owner caring for the puppy or kitten. But the 90s have made us technopeasants or technomasters. It is this sophistication of the animal owner that will drive veterinary care in the future.

There are inherent dangers in these waters. 'A lot of learning is a dangerous thing' may be a more fitting epigraph for the coming information age. Humankind has never had so many media, resources, accesses to so much information in its brief history. There are magazines for virtually any self-interest, books for any and all quirks, and a world-wide-web of digital access to individuals, corporations, associations, and institutions. The world is literally and figuratively at your keyboard.

The risks are clear should one assume that the author at the end of the computer cable is a true authority; that the information is accurate beyond question; that the data received is the definitive essence of the subject. Yet if any or all of these assumptions is wrong, one can self-diagnose, self-treat in error. The pet of an assumed technomaster could be the recipient of incomplete care because of blind faith in the digital god.

How can a three minute data-bite address every intricacy of the subject being surfed?

I am an enthusiastic advocate of the Internet and the technologies for information access that evolve from it. Yet I caution the pet owner, take the data given with several grains of salt. Use the live experts, the ones with flesh on their bodies, to help in the interpretation of the information. Together, you and your veterinarian can provide optimum health for your pet. Divided, disassociated, you may bring danger to your pet's doorstep.

Technology can provide an enormous opportunity for everyone to learn more about the world around us. It is the management of this digital library that will result in technoenlightenment or technoharm.

Sites to Surf:

At the time of this writing the following Internet sites caught my eye. There are literally thousands of sites on the Internet that can be accessed by key words such as animals, pets, care, veterinary, health, nutrition, behavior, specific breeds of dogs and cats, diseases, and on and on. Some of these pages may no longer exist or they may change hands from time to time. If still available, and I hope they are, you can see some of the characteristics I prefer to see in an Internet site dedicated to animal care:

* Interactivity - the ability to do something within the site

* Freshness - something new each day you visit the site

* Valid Data - a group or individual with credentials involved in providing the data

* Connectivity - ability to ask questions - and get reasonably quick response time

The Pet Channel:

http://www.thepetchannel.com/
Created and maintained by Media Connection of New York, the comprehensive site
includes: Pet Links (to help the browser find a cat)
On-Line Pet Trainers
Find-a-Pet Service
Pet News (e.g. an article warning home owners about dog napping)
Pet Health (provided by the Mark Morris Foundation, a very credible resource)
Ask the Vet, Ask the Therapist
Featured Articles (e.g. Heat Stroke, Interview with a veterinarian on Iguana Care)
and
Pet Fun (a section that includes: Pet Stories, PetToons, Pet Gallery)

Waltham:

http://www.waltham.com
This is one of the better commercial sites on pet care maintained by Waltham, the
pet health and nutrition research division of the Mars Corporation. You can fill in
an on-line questionnaire to determine which breed of dog is appropriate for your
family dynamics and lifestyle. You can also ask questions on health, nutrition and
behavior, all subjects of Waltham research. Waltham has excellent ethics for animal
research in that they tolerate no invasiveness nor will they induce disease in order
to study it. They get my vote for support of their diets as a result.

Sherlock Bones:

http://www.sherlock.com
This site is especially helpful with articles on what actions to take if your pet goes
missing or if you've found a stray dog or cat.

Dog Fancy and Cat Fancy Magazines, both excellent resources for keeping
the pet owner up to date, have complimentary web sites:
http://www.dogfancy.com
http://www.catfancy.com
Both give a directory of breeders on-line links to one another as well as links to information on care of other species of animals (birds, fish, reptiles, horses).

NetVet - The Electronic Zoo

http://netvet.wustl.edu
Dr. Ken Boschert from Washington State has developed an excellent site for people
who want to have fun learning about animals on the Internet. Included in the site are:
Virtual Tours - great for kids to learn about life on the farm
On the MOOve - a games area for kids
Pick of the Litter - a selection of the best items for the week
Dairy Biz - an online magazine that would be of interest to dairy farmers

Pet-Vet
http://www.pet-vet.com/index.html
Dr. Lowell Ackerman, a colleague who graduated from the Ontario Veterinary College has developed this site as a resource for the pet owner. You can find out about recommended reading, breeds of pets to consider and information on which hotels allow pets if you take your pet on vacation with you. Another section worth the visit is the Virtual Pet Cemetery.

Canadian Animal Network
http://www.pawprints.com
Steven Sheils and Dr. Jeff Silver have developed an Internet Site for the Canadian Veterinarian and the Canadian Pet Owner. Especially for the pet owner, is the ability to go to the 'Ask the Vet' section with questions on pet care. You can also find out about Pet Insurance, other species of animals (fish, reptiles, amphibians, wildlife), look into a pet adoption section to help find an animal that needs a good home. If you've moved to a different part of the province or country you can look up a directory of veterinarians to find a new family vet. The network is developing sites for kids as well as adults.

Creature Comfort
http://www.petsweb.com
This author is also a strong advocate of the Internet as a resource for pet care information. You can access products that I would recommend for pet care that includes information on how to use them. I provide a forum for stories about life's experiences with pets and an ever-increasing review of books and Internet sites on pet care.

Postlude

Creature Comfort Found

Before hominid crept across the tundra
Reptiles and mammals attended this Gaia.
Nature kept balance through selection for food.
Species were reduced or eliminated
By the dominion or prevail of others.
Yet all was done according to plan.
By faiths, according to design.

Then Erect-One raised apposed-thumbed hand
And reflected on abundance with arrogant intellect.
And the decline began.
The hominid designed to dominate
To possess soil and species
To change nature so to inveigle whims.
Gaia began to cripple in anguish and despair.

Flora and fauna heretofore in balance were no more.
Waste and ravage built up in vapors and solids
Heaped deep where hominid endured.
What was once grassy plain, rain forest or treed valley
Became peopled, buildinged, carred, paved, scarred.
Animals were squeezed from habitat or made servant
According to greeds and needs of Hominid.

Gaia and her natural friends were being afflicted with a pathogen
Till compassionate hominids took note of the destruction
And cried out for this parasitism to end.
Others embraced domestic animals as kindred spirits
While spreading alarms for the cessation of wilderness slaughter.
Those who doctored every beast but the hominid,
Nurtured this renewed respect for Gaia's children
Only to cry at every turn of the modern page.

For thousands of years from the first erect steps
Hominid has sought only self-succor.
If this continues there will be no sustenance left.
For the Golden Rule applies to all of life.
In order to get creature comforts, unconditionally
One must give it, as unconditional love, to friend, foe, family
And Gaia and all her creatures.

RefeRences

Canadian Veterinary Journal
Volume 37, Ottawa. pp. 667-671. November 1996.

Johnson, Edgar.
Charles Dickens His Tragedy and Triumph.
New York, New York. Penguin Books. pp. 201-235. 1986.

Danel, Clifton (Ed. in Chief).
Chronicle of the Year 1989
Mount Kesco, New York. Elam Publications. pp. 183, 526, 529. 1989.

Tilley L. P. T., Atkins C., Goodwin John-Karl.
Companion Animal Cardiology
Series One, Modules 1, 2 & 3. Lifelearn Inc.,
Guelph, Ontario, Canada. 1996.
CD-i, CD-ROM.

Anthony, Emily, Gorrel, Harvey & Pook.
Companion Animal Dentistry
Series One, Modules 1, 2 & 3. Lifelearn Inc., Guelph, Ontario, Canada. 1994.
CD-i.

Compendium on Veterinary Continuing Education, The.
Trenton, New Jersey. February 1997. pp. 127.

Curtis, R., Barnett, K. C.
The 'Blue Eye' Phenomenon. **Veterinary Record**, Vol. 112. pp. 347-353.
United Kingdom. 1983,

Holmes, Jeffrey T. G. and Summerlee, Alastair, J. S.
Equine Foot, The. CD-ROM. Guelph, Ontario, Canada. 1995.

Norsworthy, G. & Fooshee, S.
Feline Medicine and Surgery. Lifelearn Inc.,
Modules 1, 2 & 3. CD-i, Guelph, Ontario, Canada. 1995.

Tilley, L. P. & Smith Jr., F. W. K..
Five Minute Veterinary Consult, Canine and Feline.
Baltimore, Maryland. Williams & Wilkins. 1997.

Lovelock, James. Gaia
A New Look at Life on Earth.
Oxford - New York. Oxford University Press 1979.

Greene, C. E (Ed.).
Infectious Diseases of the Dog and Cat.
Chapter 46, Lyme Borreliosis, Greene, R. T. pp. 513, 260-263.
Philadelphia, P.A.: W. B. Saunders Co. 1990

Chew, Dennis J., DVM, Dip ACVIM & Buffington, C.A. Tony, DVM, PhD, Dip ACVN.
Management of Male Cats with Urethral Obstruction.
The Ohio State Universtiy College of Veterinary Medicine, Columbus, Ohio.
Buffalo Academy of Veterinary Medicine. Buffalo, N.Y. November 7, 1996.

Chew, Dennis J., DVM, Dip ACVIM & Buffington, C.A. Tony, DVM, PhD, Dip ACVN.
Management of Non-Obstructive Lower Urinary Tract Disease in Cats.
The Ohio State University College of Veterinary Medicine. Columbus, Ohio.
Buffalo Academy of Veterinary Medicine. Buffalo, N.Y. November 7, 1996

Marotta S. M.
Seminars in Veterinary Medicine and Surgery
The common and uncommon clinical presentations and treatment of periodontal
disease in the dog and cat.
SVMS 2[4], pp 230-240. November 1987.

Georgi, J. R.
Parisitology for Veterinarians, 4th Edition.
Philadelphia, Pa.:W. B. Saunders Company. pp. 84, 155-173. 1985.

Pederson, N. C. Holzworth, J. (Ed.)
Diseases of the Cat, (Chapter 7-2).
Philadelphia, Pa.:W. B. Saunders Co. pp. 193-211. 1987.

Muller, G. H., Kirk, R. W. and Scott, D. W.
Small Animal Dermatology, 3rd Edition
Philadelphia, Pa.:W. B. Saunders Co. pp. 304-306. 1983

Etinger, S. J. (Ed.)
Textbook of Veterinary Internal Medicine – 1983.
Chapter 27: Bacterial, Viral et al, Farrow, B. R. H.; Lowe, L. N., pp. 269-273.
Chapter 58: Diseases of the Small Bowel, Sherding, R. W. pp. 1,316.
Philadellphia, Pa.:W. B. Saunders Company. 1983.

Anderson, N. V. (Ed.)
Veterinary Gastroenterology.
Philadelphia, Pa.:Lea & Febiger. pp 569. 1980.

Glossary

Ablation - Surgical removal of a part.

Abscess - A condition whereby bacteria get under the skin and become walled off by surrounding tissue. The result is a pus filled sac.

Acute - Sudden onset of a condition. Can also refer to the seriousness of the disease.

Adenovirus - One of many types of viruses that are being discovered and implicated in animal diseases. One if its family, adenovirus type 2 has been implicated in the upper respiratory disease of dogs commonly referred to as kennel cough.

Afterbirth - The placental materials that come out of the womb with the fetus.

AIDS - Auto- Immune Disease Syndrome, a disease described in humans. In cats a similar condition of compromised immune system is often given the acronym FAIDS for Feline Auto Immune Syndrome. The two are not related.

Alopecia - A term to describe loss of hair.

Amino Acid - A chemical component that makes up protein that is released on the digestion and breakdown of the protein. Specific types of amino acids are known to be essential to specific species of animals.

Anal Glands - Scent glands on either side of the anus.

Anemic, anemia - The condition of being depleted of blood through bleeding or disease. Without normal blood levels the animal is severely weakened.

Anesthetic - A drug that induces a state beyond sleep whereby no pain or recollection of surgical procedures is felt or recalled.

Antibody - A chemical made by the animal to fight off an invading chemical or antigen.

Antigen - A chemical component, usually protein in nature that can be foreign or harmful to the body. Too many antigens can trigger an allergic response for example.

Antiseptic - A chemical that destroys or minimizes bacterial contamination of a site.

Arthritis - Inflammation of a joint or joints with or without infection.

Auscultation - Listening to the heart and lungs especially with a stethoscope.

Barbiturate - A drug that induces sedation and the anesthetic state.

Bladder Stones - Hardened nodules of crystallized salts and chemicals that form inside the bladder in the urine. They must be removed surgically as they cause damage to the bladder wall.

Bordatella - Another organism that is implicated in the upper respiratory infection of dogs called kennel cough.

Borreliosis - A term that describes Lyme Disease, a condition caused by a bacteria discovered by French bacteriologist Amedee Borrel. The disease can affect both mammals and birds.

Calicivirus - This is another virus that has been detected to contribute to diseases of the cat.

Cesarean - The surgical removal of a fetus or newborn from the uterus. Usually as a result if impossible birth circumstances.

Calf Bed - a colloquial term to describe the protrusion of the uterus outside of the animalís body. Not an easy thing to put back.

Castration - Surgical removal of the two testicles of the male in order to minimize aggressive and sexual behavior thus reducing unwanted pregnancies.

Cataract - A condition whereby the lens of the eye becomes opaque.

Carnivore - A meat eating animal.

Catheter - A tube that is inserted into the bowel or to the bladder so as to remove fluids or administer medicine. Used in FLUTD to allow a male cat to pass urine if it has become blocked by urinary calculi (stones).

Cerebral - Pertaining to the cerebellum, the center that is responsible for movement.

Chlamydia - An organism that has recently been implicated in a number of disease processes of animals particularly in the cat in upper respiratory disease.

Colic - A condition, in veterinary practice particularly in horses, that refers to a severe abdominal pain which can have several causes or differentials.

Cryptorchid - A condition in the male whereby one or both testicles are retained inside the abdomen rather than descend into the scrotum which normally occurs at or shortly after birth.

Debride - Surgical removal of dead or diseased tissue from a site.

Dehydration - Loss of fluid from the body.

Demat - Removing matted fur from an animal through grooming and or shaving - sometimes under anesthesia if too severe.

Desiccans - Refers to dryness. In Osteochondritis Desiccans in the large breed dog for example, the joint affected is often lacking in the normal lubricating material making the joint very dry - thus especially painful.

Diaphragm - The flat muscle that separates the abdomen from the chest cavity.

Distemper - A term that is often used to describe specific infectious diseases of animals. It has been used extensively to define diseases in cats and dogs that are evidenced by runny nose and eyes, fever, loss of appetite, sometimes diarrhea. However, dog distemper and cat distemper are caused by different organisms. Dogs canít catch cat distemper and visa versa.

Downer Cow - a condition of cows whereby after giving birth they are unable to get up due to a multitude of contributing factors (pressure on the nerves to the legs, mineral deficiencies, difficult birth etc.).

Duck Dick - Penis. Actually birds do not have a penis. All they have is a small nipple shaped projection that can't really be described as an anatomical penis as seen in mammals. However, this nipple or papilla is much more developed in ducks and lím certain that this is what Bud Mullit saw dangling between Fredís webs.

Dysplasia - A term to describe abnormal development. In canine hip dysplasia for example the hip joint develops as a loose-fitting arthritic joint rather than the tight socket-in-joint that it is supposed to be.

Dyspnea - Difficulty breathing.

rasites, generally microscopic in size, that inhabit an animals ears.

Edema - The build up of fluid within tissue.

Electrocautery - An electrical scalpel that cuts through flesh by intense localized heat thus minimizing bleeding.

Encephalomyelitis - A term that describes inflammation of the brain and spinal cord.

Endemic - Describes the nature of a disease - whereby the disease is prevalent in a particular area e.g. Malaria is endemic in a number of tropical countries.

Endocarditis - Inflammation of the endocardium - which surrounds the heart.

Endocrine - Refers to organs in the body that secrete chemicals that have an effect on other organs or tissues. These are secreted into the blood or lymphatic system.

Epiphora - Excessive tearing. In dogs and cats especially evidenced by crusts of dried tears and dirt below the eye or eyes.

Euthanasia - Giving an overdose of an anesthetic in order to induce a quiet and gentle death. Primarily used in veterinary practice to terminate suffering of a sick or aged animal.

Eczema - A skin condition of animals that encompasses a number of parameters of size, pain, inflammation and infection.

Fad Pet - A pet that has become popular but often becomes neglected when the pet owner realizes the special needs of the animal. E.g. Pot-bellied pigs, hedgehogs.

Farrier - A person who trims horses hooves, fits horseshoes.

Febrile - Feverish.

Feces - Excrement, fecal material from the lower bowel.

Femur - The long bone of the leg that fits into the pelvis.

Foreign Body - A common problem in veterinary practice, something that shouldnít be there - such as a tennis ball in the stomach of a dog or a needle and thread in the throat of a cat.

Founder - In veterinary practice a term to describe a horse crippled with inflammation of its hooves.

FLUTD - Feline Lower Urinary Tract Disease. A condition in cats describing an inflammation with or without infection of the bladder. This occasionally also affecting the urethra.

Furball - Literally a ball (although usually irregular, matted and messy) of fur that a cat normally vomits if it is too large to pass through the bowel.

FUS - Feline Urologic Syndrome see FLUTD

Gaia - A term given to the planet earth by author James Lovelock whereby he posits that the earth could or should be equated to a living entity.

Geld - To castrate but a term used especially when referring to the procedure in horses.

Genetic - Referring to the genes or heritable characteristics of animals.

Gingiva - The tissue surrounding the base of the teeth.

Gingivitis - Inflammation of the gums or gingival tissue.

Glaucoma - A disease of the eye or eyes as evidenced by increased internal pressure hence bulging of the eyeball. Medical attention is necessary.

Granuloma - Describes a mass that is made of fibrous or scar tissue, generally not cancerous.

HBC - An acronym used in practice describing an animal Hit By Car.

Heartworm - A parasite that terminates itís adult life inside the chambers of the heart of an affected animal especially the canine family. In other species of animal the life cycle may not get to the heart but may end up in the liver.

Hematoma - A condition whereby a blood vessel bursts inside the outer and inner flaps of the ear causing the ear to swell sometimes to extraordinary size.

Hemobartonella - An organism that is not a virus, not a bacteria but somewhere in between and known to be a cause of a disease called Feline Infectious Anemia.

Hemorrhage - Bleeding.

Herd Health - A health management strategy developed in the mid sixties that is designed to prevent disease in herds of farm animals. The veterinarian visits the farm on a regular basis to check animals for early signs of disease, pregnancy and discusses preventive measures through vaccination and nutrition.

Hernia - Describes when a loop of tissue protrudes through an opening, commonly seen as an abdominal hernia or a testicular hernia.

Hip Dysplasia - A term to describe an arthritic condition particularly seen in large dogs. The socket that normally surrounds the ball of the large leg bone degenerates giving the dog instability and pain.

Holistic, holism - This is a term to describe a whole body and/or global approach to treatment of disease —- even the prevention of disease. Numerous interpretations and applications can and are applied to this practice (acupuncture, herbal remedies etc.).

Hookworm - A small parasite found in the bowel of infested animals. Their moth parts are hooks that allow them to attach to the lining of the gut so as to suck blood.

Immunity - The ability of the body to fight disease. This is achieved through the immune system made up of the lymphatic system, spleen, liver and other defense mechanisms.

Immunodeficiency - A term to describe an immune system that has been compromised and weakened.

Infectious - When a disease can spread readily from animal to animal.

Injection - Inserting a drug into the body by means of a syringe and needle.

Intramuscular - Into the muscle.

Intravenous - Into the blood.

Jaundice - A condition whereby bile pigments are deposited into the skin and mucous membranes. This gives the skin and tissue a yellowish coloration.

Ketosis - A condition in which an abnormally high level of ketones (a chemical produced by the breakdown of sugars) are present in the blood.

Laceration - A cut.

Lachrymal, lacrimal - Tears. Particularly important are the lacrimal ducts or tear ducts that often get plugged.

Laminitis - Inflammation of the laminae (thin layers that make up the hoof structure of the horse).

Larynx - Tissue made of muscle and cartilage at the base of the tongue at the back of the throat.

Leptospirosis - A disease caused by a microorganism that appears under the microscope as spiral worms with hooked ends. There are a number of species of the germ.

Leukemia - A disease of blood forming organs whereby there is a tremendous increase in leukocytes or white blood cells poured into the circulation. Complications of anemia, swelling of blood forming organs such as bone marrow and the spleen cause the animal to become debilitated.

LDA - Left Displaced Abomasum. The cow has four stomachs, the abomasum being the one that is supposed to be on the right side. This acronym is used in veterinary practice when a clinician finds the abomasum on the left side - usually this requires surgery to get it back and keep it there.

Lice - Small, usually microscopic parasites that bite the skin of an animal or suck blood.

Listeriosis - A disease caused by an organism called Listeria.

Lyme Disease - Borreliosis. This is a bacterial disease carried from animal to animal by ticks. It causes disease in animals and humans resulting signs that could include arthritis, lameness, pain, lethargy, anorexia, depression and fever.

Lymphosarcoma - A malignant cancer that has developed as a result of disease of a specific white blood cell called lymphocytes.

Metabolism - The process describing the breakdown of nutrients into components that can then be absorbed and digested by the body, then utilized by the various organs.

Metastasis - Spreading of a disease particularly cancer to other parts of the body.

Microfilaria - A stage in the life of a parasite that can only be seen under the microscope e.g. the microfilaria of the heartworm.

Meningitis - Inflammation of the tissue surrounding the brain.

Monday Morning Disease - In veterinary practice a term to describe a condition in horses whereby their muscles tie up and they may exhibit urinary difficulty. This is often seen in horses that get little exercise during the week but are ridden strenuously on the weekend. Hence the condition is common on Monday mornings.

Neoplasia - Cancer.

Neuron - A nerve cell.

Nose Twitch - A device that snares the nose of a horse. Much of the surgery performed on a horse can and should be done without general anesthetic. In order to keep the horse from kicking the veterinary surgeon someone assists by placing the nose twitch on the horse.

Obligate - Out of necessity.

Omnivore - An animal that can eat almost any type of food.

Ophthalmoscope - A hand-held instrument with special opticals that allow the practitioner to see almost every anatomical feature of the eye, from the front of the eye to the back.

Orthopedic - Referring to bones.

Osteochondritis - A term that describes inflammation of both the bone and cartilage.

Panleukopenia - A viral disease of cats that causes a reduction in the white blood cells. This causes lethargy, anorexia, vomiting and diarrhea. Usually fatal.

Parainfluenza - A term to describe the disease or the virus that cause a condition in animals called influenza - commonly referred to the flu in human terminology. More specifically in dogs for example this describes a virus implicated as one of the contributors of kennel cough.

pH - Measurement of any fluid that shows the acidity or alkalinity of the fluid. A pH of seven is neither; a number higher than seven is alkaline, lower than seven is acidic.

Periodontal - Referring to the area around the teeth.

Peritonitis - Inflammation of the peritoneum which is the tissue that lines the abdomen. This condition can cause abdominal pain, vomiting and/or constipation.

Pituitary - A gland at the base and central in the brain just behind the area of the eyes. The gland produces hormones that help regulate reproductive mechanisms.

Placenta - The sac that covers the fetus inside the womb. Placental.

Plaque - Dried, dead bacteria forming and sticking to the teeth if the teeth are not cleaned.

Plate - In surgical correction of fractures, veterinarians often place a plate across the two or more fragments. The plate has pre-drilled holes for screws so as to keep the pieces together.

Prep - Shortened term describing preparation of a site for surgery or cleansing of a wound.

Prophy - A shortened term used in practice to describe the prophylactic cleaning of a petís teeth.

Pharmaceutical - A drug that has been produced for a specific purpose e.g. an antibiotic to kill bacteria.

Post Partum - The period just after birth.

Preputial - Tissue ahead of and surrounding the prepuce (the foreskin).

Purulent - Pertaining to pus.

Pyometra - A condition of the female animal whereby the uterus becomes infected and filled with pus. Death can be rapid.

Rabies - An infectious disease of animals especially seen in dogs, foxes, wolves and other canine species as well as in skunks and raccoons. It can be transmitted to cats and other pets including humans through bites from the infected animal - even simply through the saliva coming into contact with the skin that may have a minor scratch or cut. Usually fatal.

Radiograph - An X-Ray.

Reagent - A chemical that is used in a laboratory test.

Renal - Pertaining to the kidney.

Retrovirus - A specific virus species.

Rhinotracheitis - An inflammation of the upper respiratory tract including the nasal sinuses and throat.

Root Canal - The process of filling a cavity of an affected tooth (for example with a fracture but you donít want to lose the tooth) with a material that will prevent bacteria and fluids from getting into the area thus assuring that the tooth will be stable.

Roundworm - A relatively common internal parasite of animals. It looks much like a slim version of the common earthworm but it lives in the bowel.

RP - Retained Placenta. Particularly in cows, occasionally in horses, the sac that covers the fetus in the womb refuses to come out and the veterinarian must shove his arm up the uterus to dislodge it.

Rupture, ruptured - In veterinary practice a term to describe a herniated testicle in a male pig.

Scaling - Removing plaque and tartar from teeth with an instrument designed to do so (Dental Scaler).

Scrotum - The pendulous sac between the hind legs of the male in which are two testicles (until the animal is neutered - then the sac is empty).

Seizure - A hyper excitable state. The animal may become stiff and prone or paddle furiously with its feet while drooling and champing with its jaws uncontrollably.

Shot - See injection.

Soundness - Referred to in horses. It describes a healthy state in which the horse is not lame with no evidence of locomotor disease.

Spay - Removal of the two ovaries and the uterus in order to prevent pregnancy

Spiking Fever - Seen when a fever goes high then low on a continuous basis.

Subcutaneous - Under the skin.

Tapeworm - A species if internal (in the bowel) parasites seen in many animals. Their body parts are segmented giving them a sequential tape-like appearance.

Tartar - Dried, crusty and calcified plaque and debris that builds up on teeth and below the gum line if teeth are neglected.

Taurine - An amino acid that is critically essential for the cat. Without it the cat is subject to serious heart disease.

Testicle - The male sexual organ that produces sperm.

Thrombosis - A condition in the blood especially whereby an accumulation of blood cells passes to a point where it plugs a vessel thus reducing the blood flow to the region the vessel serves.

Thyroid - Pertaining to the thyroid gland that sits at the base of the neck. This gland is responsible through thyroid hormone for maintaining body regulation and metabolism.

Tick - A small parasite, usually visible to the naked eye, sometimes the size of a kernel of corn after it has ingested the blood it has sucked out of the animal it had been adhering to. Ticks can be responsible for transmitting a number of diseases to humans and animals as a result of the fact that they bite and suck their hostsí blood, then move onto another animal.

Titer - The level of immunity to a disease measured in the blood.

Tourniquet - A device or method of stopping the flow of blood to a particular area in order to minimize loss of blood due to hemorrhage or to cause a vein to be raised so as to insert a needle into the vein.

Toxin - A material that is poisonous to the body.

Toxoplasmosis - An infection, seen in the cat, by an organism called Toxoplasma. It may be present in the cat yet causing no disease. Itís life cycle includes shedding of infective cells into the feces. Humans can contract the disease through cat feces. The organism can affect the developing fetus so that pregnant women should avoid cleaning kitty litter or use strict precaution, even disposable gloves if they do so.

Trichiasis - Especially in some dogs where we see eyelashes growing inside the eyelids causing the lashes to constantly irritate the eye. Surgical correction is needed.

Uremic - A condition whereby components of the urine are present in the blood. This can be toxic to the animal.

Uvula - In this text specifically Uvula Palatina, the fleshy mass hanging from the top of the palate at the back of the throat.

Vaccination - An injection of a vaccine which is made up of a weakened, modified or dead form of the disease for which the medicine is intended. This form of the disease cause the body to respond with immune chemicals rather than causing disease.

Vaccine - A drug made up of viral or viral-like particle, dead or alive but modified.

Virus - An organism that can only be seen under an electron microscope. Itís size allows it to invade virtually any organ of the body and any body cell.

Whipworm - A species of internal parasites that are rod shaped with a long whip like appendage at one end. They live in the bowel.